The Secret History of D

The Secret History of Democracy

Edited by

Benjamin Isakhan
Australian Research Council Discovery Early Career Research Award (DECRA) Research Fellow, Centre for Citizenship and Globalization, Deakin University, Australia

Stephen Stockwell
Professor of Journalism and Communication, School of Humanities, Griffith University, Australia

Introduction, conclusion, editorial matter and selection © Benjamin Isakhan and Stephen Stockwell 2012, 2011
All remaining chapters © respective authors 2012

All rights reserved. No reproduction, copy or transmission of this publication may be made without written permission.

No portion of this publication may be reproduced, copied or transmitted save with written permission or in accordance with the provisions of the Copyright, Designs and Patents Act 1988, or under the terms of any licence permitting limited copying issued by the Copyright Licensing Agency, Saffron House, 6–10 Kirby Street, London EC1N 8TS.

Any person who does any unauthorized act in relation to this publication may be liable to criminal prosecution and civil claims for damages.

The authors have asserted their rights to be identified as the authors of this work in accordance with the Copyright, Designs and Patents Act 1988.

First published 2011
First published in paperback 2012 by
PALGRAVE MACMILLAN

Palgrave Macmillan in the UK is an imprint of Macmillan Publishers Limited, registered in England, company number 785998, of Houndmills, Basingstoke, Hampshire RG21 6XS.

Palgrave Macmillan in the US is a division of St Martin's Press LLC, 175 Fifth Avenue, New York, NY 10010.

Palgrave Macmillan is the global academic imprint of the above companies and has companies and representatives throughout the world.

Palgrave® and Macmillan® are registered trademarks in the United States, the United Kingdom, Europe and other countries.

ISBN 978–0–230–24421–4 hardback
ISBN 978–0–230–37510–9 paperback

A catalogue record for this book is available from the British Library.

A catalog record for this book is available from the Library of Congress.

10 9 8 7 6 5 4 3 2 1
21 20 19 18 17 16 15 14 13 12

Contents

Acknowledgements	vii
Notes on Contributors	viii

Introduction: Democracy and History   1
Benjamin Isakhan and Stephen Stockwell

Part I   Pre-Athenian Democracy

1   What is so 'Primitive' about 'Primitive Democracy'?
Comparing the Ancient Middle East and Classical Athens   19
Benjamin Isakhan

2   Before Athens: Early Popular Government in Phoenicia
and Greek City-States   35
Stephen Stockwell

3   Republics and Quasi-Democratic Institutions in Ancient
India   49
Steven Muhlberger

4   Digging for Democracy in China   60
Pauline Keating

Part II   Democracy in the 'Dark Ages'

5   Behind a Veil: Islam's Democratic History   79
Mohamad Abdalla and Halim Rane

6   Ideals and Aspirations: Democracy and Law-Making in
Medieval Iceland   92
Patricia Pires Boulhosa

7   Democratic Culture in the Early Venetian Republic   105
Stephen Stockwell

Part III   Indigenous Democracy and Colonialism

8   Africa's Indigenous Democracies: The Baganda of Uganda   123
Immaculate Kizza

vi *Contents*

9 The Hunters Who Owned Themselves 136
Philippe Paine

10 Aboriginal Australia and Democracy: Old Traditions,
New Challenges 148
Larissa Behrendt

11 The Pre-History of the Post-Apartheid Settlement:
Non-Racial Democracy in South Africa's Cape Colony,
1853–1936 162
Poppy Fry

Part IV Alternative Currents in Modern Democracy

12 Birthing Democracy: The Role of Women in the
Democratic Discourse of the Middle East 177
K. Luisa Gandolfo

13 The Streets of Iraq: Protests and Democracy after Saddam 191
Benjamin Isakhan

14 Monitory Democracy? The Secret History of Democracy
since 1945 204
John Keane

Conclusion: Democratizing the History of Democracy 219
Benjamin Isakhan and Stephen Stockwell

References 225

Index 244

Acknowledgements

This book came from our long conversations about the nature and origins of democracy. Such dialogues were inspired by a wide-ranging and diverse set of recent global events. The investigations that followed led us to the works of several like-minded scholars who shared our concern and passion for the history of democracy. Thankfully, we have been able to assemble work from many of them here and we are in debt to each of our contributors for their scholarly diligence in meeting tight deadlines with quality writing. As editors, we consider ourselves fortunate to have worked with such a diverse and dedicated group of contributors, and we thank them all for their input and advice. We must make special mention of Steven Muhlberger and Phillipe Paine, for aiding our very earliest discussions and ideas about this project, and of John Keane, for his continuing support and encouragement, without which this project may never have come to fruition.

We are also indebted to the exceptional academic, editorial and administrative talents of our research associate, Anne Richards. To the staff of our publisher, Palgrave Macmillan, we owe special thanks, particularly to Alison Howson for her initial support, to Amber Stone-Galilee for her editorial work and to Liz Blackmore for her administrative assistance.

At Griffith University we would like to acknowledge specifically Kay Ferres, former Dean of the Faculty of Humanities and Social Sciences, for her support and for the resources she made available for the completion of the project. We would also like to thank our colleagues and friends at Griffith University, particularly those in the School of Humanities, the Griffith Islamic Research Unit, the Key Centre for Ethics, Law, Justice and Governance and the Griffith Centre for Cultural Research – all of whom provided the challenging and nurturing environment necessary for the completion of such a project. Benjamin would also like to thank La Trobe University's Centre for Dialogue and his colleagues at the Centre for Citizenship and Globalization, Deakin University.

Personally, Benjamin would like to thank his family and friends for their much needed words of encouragement and love. Stephen would like to thank his parents for their continuing support, and his wife Ann and his son Matthew for their patience and love.

Notes on Contributors

Mohamad Abdalla combines the role of serious scholar, imam and noted public intellectual. He has degrees in Science (with honours) and a PhD in Islamic Science, he is the founding director of the Griffith University Islamic Research Unit and he acts as co-director of the National Centre of Excellence for Islamic Studies, Australia. He is the author of the recently published book *Islamic Science: The Myth of the Decline Theory* (Verlag, 2008) and co-editor of *Islam and the Australian News Media* (Melbourne University Press, 2010).

Larissa Behrendt is a Eualeyai/Kamillaroi woman. She is the Professor of Law and Director of Research at the Jumbunna Indigenous House of Learning at the University of Technology, Sydney. Larissa is a Land Commissioner at the Land and Environment Court and the Alternate Chair of the Serious Offenders Review Board. She is the author of several books on Indigenous legal issues. She won the 2002 David Uniapon Award and a 2005 Commonwealth Writer's Prize for her novel *Home* (University of Queensland Press, 2004). Larissa is Board Member of the Museum of Contemporary Art, Director of the Bangarra Dance Theatre and Chair of the National Indigenous Television service.

Patricia Pires Boulhosa has degrees in history and law from the Pontifical University of Sao Paulo, and a PhD in medieval Icelandic history from the University of Cambridge. She has held the Snorri Sturluson Icelandic Fellowship, and in 2006 delivered the Jón Sigurðsson Memorial Lecture. Her publications include *Icelanders and the Kings of Norway: Mediaeval Sagas and Legal Texts* (Brill, 2005) and *Gamli sáttmáli: Tilurð og tilgangur* (Sögufélag, 2006), as well as articles on the historiographical use of medieval Icelandic texts. She is currently completing a translation into Portuguese of the medieval poetic text *Völuspá* and a study of Icelandic medieval fisheries and trade.

Poppy Fry is Assistant Professor of History at Saint Anselm College in Manchester, New Hampshire. She received her doctorate from Harvard University in 2007. Her dissertation explored the relationship between ethnic identification and British colonial authority in South

Africa's Eastern Cape between 1800 and 1936. She is the author of 'Siyamfenguza: Agriculture, Trade, Witchcraft and the Rise of Fingo-ness in South Africa's Eastern Cape, 1800–1835', forthcoming in the *Journal of Southern African Studies*.

K. Luisa Gandolfo is a researcher affiliated to the Centre for Middle Eastern and Mediterranean Studies at the Panteion University in Athens, Greece. She completed her doctoral studies at the University of Exeter and has published papers concerning religion, socio-economic change, and identity in the Palestinian community in Jordan. She is currently engaged in further research concerning issues of faith, identity, and culture in Jordan, Palestine and Syria.

Benjamin Isakhan is Australian Research Council Discovery Early Career Research Award (DECRA) Research Fellow at the Centre for Citizenship and Globalization at Deakin University, Australia. Previously, Ben has been Research Fellow with the Centre for Dialogue at La Trobe University and Research Fellow for the Griffith Islamic Research Unit, part of the National Centre of Excellence for Islamic Studies, Australia. Benjamin is the author of *Democracy in Iraq: History, Politics and Discourse* (Ashgate, 2012) as well as several scholarly book chapters, refereed journal articles and conference papers. Broadly, his work concerns issues such as democracy in Iraq, the history of democracy, Orientalism and the media, and Middle Eastern politics and history.

John Keane is Professor of Politics at the University of Sydney and at the Wissenschaftszentrum Berlin (WZB). In 1989 he founded the Centre for the Study of Democracy (CSD). Among his many books are *The Media and Democracy* (Polity, 1991); *Democracy and Civil Society* (University of Westminster Press, 1988); *Reflections on Violence* (Verso, 1996); *Civil Society: Old Images, New Visions* (Polity, 1998); *Global Civil Society?* (Cambridge University Press, 2003) and *Violence and Democracy* (Cambridge University Press, 2004). His latest book, *The Life and Death of Democracy* (Simon & Schuster, 2009), is the first comprehensive survey of democratic ideas and institutions for over a century.

Pauline Keating is Senior Lecturer in the History Programme at the Victoria University of Wellington (New Zealand), and has taught modern Chinese history there since 1989. Her doctoral research, undertaken at the Australian National University, is published under the title *Two Revolutions: Rural Reconstruction and the Cooperative Movement in Northern Shaanxi, 1934–1945* (Stanford University Press, 1997). She is

x *Notes on Contributors*

currently drawing a comparison between the rural cooperative movements launched during China's Republican period and the post-Mao village self-government project which, although developing in profoundly different contexts, raise interesting questions about different understandings of 'rural democracy' in China.

Immaculate Kizza is a professor of English at The University of Tennessee at Chattanooga, where she teaches courses in Transitional and Modern British Literature, African American Literature, and African Literature and cultures. She holds a PhD in English from the University of Toledo, Ohio. Among her publications are *Africa's Indigenous Institutions in Nation Building: Uganda* (Edwin Mellen, 1999) and various book chapters and journal articles in British, African American and African studies.

Steven Muhlberger is Professor of History at Nipissing University in North Bay, Ontario, Canada, where he has taught since 1989. He earned his PhD in early medieval history at the University of Toronto, and has published his first book, *The Fifth-Century Chroniclers* (Francis Cairns, 1990). He has also written two books on chivalry and the medieval laws of arms, *Jousts and Tournaments* (Chivalry Bookshelf, 2002) and *Deeds of Arms: Formal Combats in the Late Fourteenth Century* (Chivalry Bookshelf, 2005). He is co-author, with Phil Paine, of 'Democracy's Place in World History' (*Journal of World History*, 1993) and editor of the World History of Democracy website.

Philippe Paine is an independent Canadian scholar who has researched and written on the cross-cultural history of democracy for two decades. He is the author, with Steven Muhlberger, of the widely cited 'Democracy's Place in World History' (*Journal of World History*, 1993), a series of *Meditations on Democracy*, and other writings on history, anthropology, politics and culture, available on the World History of Democracy website and on a long-running blog.

Halim Rane has a Bachelor of Human Sciences degree in Sociology and Islamic Studies, a Master's degree in Media Studies, and a PhD in International Relations. He is currently Deputy Director of the Griffith University Islamic Research Unit and Lecturer at the National Centre of Excellence in Islamic Studies. Dr Rane is the author of *Reconstructing Jihad amid Competing International Norms* (Palgrave, 2009) and co-editor of *Islam and the Australian News Media* (Melbourne University Press, 2010).

Stephen Stockwell is Professor of Journalism and Communication at Griffith University, Australia. Prior to entering academia he worked as journalist for *4ZZZ*, *JJJ* and *Four Corners*, as press secretary for state and federal politicians and as media manager for the Queensland ALP. His many publications include the books *Political Campaign Strategy: Doing Democracy in the 21st Century* (Australian Scholarly Press, 2005) and, with Paul Scott, *The All Media Guide to Fair and Cross-Cultural Reporting* (AKC-CMP, 2000). He has contributed chapters in *Government Communication in Australia* (Cambridge University Press, 2007) and in *Moral Panics and the Media* (Open University Press, 2006), and articles for *Media International Australia*, *Australian Journalism Review*, *Fibreculture Journal* and *M/C: A Journal of Media and Culture*.

Introduction: Democracy and History

Benjamin Isakhan and Stephen Stockwell

The notion that democracy could have a 'secret' history might at first seem strange to many readers. Indeed, the history of democracy has become so standardized, is so familiar and appears to be so complete that it is hard to believe that it could hold any secrets whatsoever. The ancient Greek practice of *demokratia* and the functions of the Roman Republic are foundational to Western[1] understanding of politics; school textbooks introduce the Magna Carta and the rise of the English Parliament; Hollywood blockbusters recount the events surrounding the American Declaration of Independence; many best-selling novels have been written about the French Revolution; and the gradual global spread of the Western model of democracy has been a recurrent news story since the end of the Cold War. So pervasive is this traditional story of democracy that it has achieved the status of received wisdom: endlessly recycled without criticism by policy-makers, academics, in the popular media and in classrooms across the world.

The central argument of this book is that there is much more to the history of democracy than this foreshortened genealogy admits. There is a whole 'secret' history, too big, too complex and insufficiently Western in character to be included in the standard narrative. But even in this standard history of democracy there are many alternatives that open up the possibilities of what democracy might be: participatory or representative; majoritarian or minimalist; demotic or elitist; with positions filled by election or by lot; with sovereignty resting in one (the constitutional monarch) or in the many (the will of the people). So what is democracy? How do we judge the good from the bad?

This is not the place for a rigorous definition of democracy. Indeed, there are simply too many definitions of democracy and disagreements over how we measure its successes and failures to cover in this introduction. While nearly all would agree with Abraham Lincoln that '[d]emocracy is the government of the people, by the people, for the people' (Lincoln, 1863: 210), there remains no consensus on some of the most fundamental questions about democracy, such as what conditions are necessary for its development, how it ought to be measured, what institutions and practices ensure its maintenance and how it might best be conducted today. Broadly, the debates over definitions of democracy can be understood as belonging in one of two camps.

The first is circumscribed by the minimalist, 'scientific' definition of democracy, which argues that the inherent elitism of representative institutions is a small price to pay for functionality, civil rights and justice. This position has a long history, which goes back to Thomas Hobbes; but it was most compellingly justified by Joseph Schumpeter in the face of fascism and has undergone its most substantial revision in the recent work of John Rawls (Hobbes, 2002 [1651]; Rawls, 2001; Schumpeter, 1947 [1942]). The second broad category asserts that democracy should be more inclusive, with all citizens, not just the elites, playing an equal part in the decision-making process. Central to this understanding of democracy were Carole Pateman's calls for it to be conducted along participatory lines, Jurgen Habermas' understanding of the role of communicative action in creating a politics of emancipation, and Ernest Laclau's and Chantal Mouffe's advocacy of a radical democracy that embraces difference (Habermas, 1987 [1981]; Laclau and Mouffe, 1985; Pateman, 1970).

However, it would be more than a little ironic if there were no such debate over the characteristics of democracy. In democratic societies, the robust and, at times, vehement nature of disagreements over the definition of democracy can be taken as indicative of the importance of this form of governance and of its ability to absorb a variety of opinion. Indeed, attempts at a comprehensive and static definition of democracy are not only plagued by difficulties, they are also anti-democratic, striving to control and contain something that, by its very nature, must respond to the varying and complex needs of people over time. It is democracy's dynamism, its responsiveness to the will of the people, that must be central to any definition of democracy. Along these lines, Jacques Derrida celebrates the multiplicitous nature of democracy in his understanding that democracy's 'emancipatory promise' is always 'to come' (Derrida, 2006 [1993]).

It is reasonable to assert that, in order for us to move towards this emancipatory promise of democracy, three key factors must be evident: a willingness to participate; an equality of access to information, free speech and voting; and the civic virtue required to appreciate the others' arguments, to accept the rule of law and to be bound by the majority. Our contention in this book is that, if democracy can be understood in this way, then it is inconceivable that it has only occurred in the small collection of historical epochs with which it is usually associated. Indeed, as Steven Muhlberger and Phil Paine assert: 'If one insists on perfect democracy in a community before conceding its relevance to the history of democracy, then democracy has no history and never will' (Muhlberger and Paine, 1993: 26).

This book therefore documents an imperfect and largely 'secret' history of democracy. To achieve this, the volume includes a collection of historical accounts from leading scholars in their respective fields, each one dedicated to documenting the development of democratic practices in unexpected and under-explored quarters. Starting in the ancient world, this collection details the very earliest models of collective governance developed in Mesopotamia, the Indus Valley and ancient China, as well as documenting the possible transmission of these practices via the trade networks of the Phoenicians to the pre-classical city-states of Greece. Following on, our collection re-considers the politics of the so-called 'Dark Ages', unearthing the remarkably complex deliberative mechanisms and elective practices at work within the various Islamic empires, as well as in medieval Iceland and Venice. The volume also details the complex inter-relationship between colonial forces and the indigenous democratic systems found among the Baganda people of Uganda, the Métis of Western Canada, Aboriginal Australians and black South Africans. On to more recent times, it tells the other stories of democracy and of the making of the modern world – from Middle Eastern feminists through to the streets of post-Saddam Iraq – stories which have been suppressed beneath layers of patriarchy and prejudice. Finally, the collection concludes with an essay that considers recent trends and future possibilities in the practice of democracy and argues that a new epoch has begun in which power-monitoring and power-contesting mechanisms take precedence over familiar representational structures.

Some of what is referred to here as 'secret' histories will be well known to those who have studied political processes in a particular area, at a particular time or among particular people. For example, it will be familiar to many experts in Chinese history that there were proto-democratic systems at work in ancient China, just as the democratic debates amongst the Cape Colonists of the late nineteenth and early twentieth centuries will be familiar to experts in African politics of that

4 *Introduction: Democracy and History*

time. However, disciplinary isolation has meant that such remarkable findings have largely remained hidden and are rarely contextualized or incorporated into a macro-level view of global political history. Indeed, while the evidence has continued to mount concerning the use of non-hierarchical, egalitarian and inclusive models of power among peoples as diverse as the ancient Phoenicians and the Australian Aborigines, this knowledge has remained curiously absent from the broader discussion of the history of democracy. The editors of this book are not historians, anthropologists or regional experts by training. Instead, we come to historical and political studies with an interdisciplinary approach designed to scrutinize widely held assumptions and to offer alternative insights. Our mutual concerns about contemporary politics led us to ask questions about the origins of democracy, and the surprising answers we began to uncover made us increasingly critical about the pervasive view that democracy has a limited and exclusive history. Overwhelmingly, we found that political scientists or historians dealing with democracy's history had come to rely on familiar sources and widely held presuppositions about what democracy is and about its origins. Instead of confronting new truths, illuminating dark corners or following difficult directions, they seemed largely content to recycle the familiar and satisfying story with which we are all well familiar.

As democracy continues to spread and its standard history continues to be recounted, it is the right time for alternative approaches to democracy to be considered. It is time for the democratic impetus to be understood in the broader context of human history, as something that is evident, at many times and in various guises, in the political past. But, before we can begin the process of revealing these 'secret' histories of democracy, we must closely examine the standard history of democracy, subjecting it to scrutiny, screening it for inconsistencies and carefully chronicling its trajectory.

The standard history of democracy

The standard history of democracy typically begins in ancient Greece. Most scholars of democracy still maintain that it was only in Greece that a bridge was built between the will of the people and their government. For example, in his *Democracy Ancient and Modern*, Moses Finley makes the remarkable claim that '[i]t was the Greeks, after all, who discovered not only democracy but also politics, the art of reaching decisions by public discussion and then obeying those decisions as a necessary condition of civilized social existence' (Finley, 1973: 13–14). While such claims are sometimes tied to the earliest councils and assemblies found in extant Greek literary sources or to the drafting of the Spartan constitution, they are most commonly associated with ancient Athens. It was here, around 508 BCE, that Cleisthenes devised a sophisticated method of participatory governance centred on the notion of the *polis* incorporating the city and its citizens' (Aristotle, 1984 [332 BCE]: 20–2). This new political model was given the name *demokratia*, a composite of two other words, *demos* (roughly 'the people') and *kratos* ('power', 'rule'), meaning 'rule by the people'. For the Athenians, *demokratia* involved participation in the assembly of the citizen body, which debated the whole spectrum of governmental activity – from war and peace and major public works to minor domestic disputes. All adult male citizens were expected to take part in the meetings of the assembly, which were convened about forty times a year. Citizens had the right to *isegoria* – the freedom to voice their concerns in front of their fellow citizens. Furthermore, the assembly elected a few key officials and experts to positions of authority, while every citizen had a good chance of being chosen by lot for a short-term position in public office.

As significant and widely lionized as the democratic practices of ancient Greece are, it is also worth remembering that the Greek city-states of antiquity functioned as slave societies and were certainly not egalitarian, inclusive or democratic to the vast majority of their inhabitants. The model of the Athenian *polis* did, however, last for almost two centuries before Athens was conquered and subjugated by Alexander of Macedon.

A parallel, if slightly less convincing, chapter in the standard history of democracy is that of the Roman Republic. Despite the fact that the Roman Republic outlasted the Athenian *polis*, by Greek standards Rome was far from being a democracy. While in early Roman history the workings of the Senate (originally composed by the heads of clans) and the *comitia curiata* (the general assembly of all arms-bearing men) were complex but relatively egalitarian, the Republic gradually descended into the oligarchy that the Athenians had been so determined to avoid. Indeed, in the surviving fragments of Cicero's dialogue *The Republic*, the author argues that the Roman Republic was in fact the perfect form of government because it combined elements of democracy with a virtuous aristocracy, committed to avoiding moral corruption and concerned with the welfare of the broader community (Cicero, 1998). While the *plebs* ('common people') had some access to the inner workings of the government through their representative tribunes, state affairs remained the domain of the elite. Eventually the Republic was undermined by a

6 Introduction: Democracy and History

series of wars, corruption, scandals and a decline in civic spirit, and the Empire arose from its ashes.

Thus, according to the standard history of democracy, the torch of self-government which had burned so brightly among the inhabitants of the Athenian *polis* and of the Roman Republic was extinguished for more than 1,000 years. So pervasive is this view that several key scholars of democracy have adopted it without question or critique. In his impressive two-volume *Modern Democracies*, James Bryce claims:

> With the fall of the Roman republic the rule of the people came to an end in the ancient world...For nearly fifteen centuries...there was never...a serious attempt either to restore free government, or even to devise a regular constitutional method for choosing the autocratic head of the State...Despotic monarchies everywhere held the field...When a rising occurred it was because men desired good government, not self-government.
>
> (Bryce, 1921: 30–1)

More recently, renowned political scientists and historians such as John Dunn and Robert Dahl have echoed these sentiments. For his part, John Dunn has argued, in the preface to his edited volume *Democracy: The Unfinished Journey, 508 BCE to CE 1993*, that with the demise of the Greek *polis* democracy was 'eliminated not just from the history of Greece itself, but from virtually any other civilized society for by far the greater part of the two thousand and more years' (Dunn, 1992: v–vi). Similarly, Robert Dahl has claimed in *On Democracy* that, 'as everyone acquainted with European history knows, after its early centuries in Greece and Rome the rise of popular government turned into its decline' and 'it vanished from the face of the earth for nearly a thousand years' (Dahl, 1998: 7, 15).

Taking an enormous historical leap forward, the traditional story of democracy usually picks up again with the signing of the *Magna Carta* around CE 1215. In this significant document the king shared his authority with a Great Council constituted by noblemen and ecclesiastics. Eventually, this Great Council evolved into the more familiar Parliament (a noun derived from the French *parler*, 'to speak') during the reign of Edward I (1272–1307), who summoned it in order to ask it to endorse his taxation needs. In the middle of the fourteenth century, under the auspices of Edward's grandson, Edward III (1327–77), the Parliament was split into the House of Lords and the House of Commons. This relatively complex system allowed for the power of the king to be balanced by that of the Parliament – which itself was divided by the interests of the two chambers. Although the introduction of the House of Commons has clearly influenced the development of representative democracy, it must be remembered that it originally consisted of borough representatives who had been elected by a mere 10 per cent of the adult male population, whose right to vote was based on wealth and whose purpose was to legitimate the King's tax regime. It wasn't until the English Civil War (1642–51) and the Bill of Rights (1689) that the Parliament and the basic democratic rights were constitutionally entrenched.

The next chapter in the traditional story of democracy occurred not in Europe but in the newfound colonies of America. There, according to Alexis de Tocqueville's seminal study *Democracy in America*, the emigrants who arrived on the shores of New England at the beginning of the seventeenth century created a situation in which '[a] democracy more perfect than antiquity had dared to dream of started in full size and panoply from the midst of an ancient feudal society' (de Tocqueville, 1864 [1835]: 35). This process began with the American Revolution and the 1776 Declaration of Independence, in which the colony threw off the shackles of monarchical government. Then the framers of the Constitution of the United States deliberated over, and drafted, their document until it was completed in Philadelphia in 1787. Although the constitution retained slavery and had other imperfections, it was cleverly crafted so as to dispense with the authority of a monarch while it retained what the Americans saw as the merits of the English system.

In 1789, as the Americans were ratifying their new constitution, in France the representatives of the Third Estate (the middle classes and peasants) founded the National Assembly, advocating a system of popular government constituted by the entire French nation. The citizenry heeded this call, and a bloody rebellion swept across much of France. Chanting '*liberté, égalité, fraternité, ou la mort!*' ('liberty, equality, fraternity, or death!'), the insurgents went on to storm the Bastille in Paris on the 14 July 1789, and they set in motion a series of events that ended with the demise of the monarchy. Later in the same year, the French Constituent Assembly adopted 'The Declaration of the Rights of Man and of the Citizen', which, in 1791, became the preamble for the constitution and set in place a representative democracy with near-universal male suffrage. Though disrupted by Napoleon's rise, France established itself as a source of democratic models and ideas that contrasted with the Anglo-Saxon methods of Britain and the United States.

8   *Introduction: Democracy and History*

Moving forward, the standard history of democracy tends to view the last 200 years as a triumphal march for the Western liberal model. British class differences, highlighted by the Chartists, were managed by the Reform Acts of 1832, 1867 and 1884, which gradually extended the franchise to most males. Disparities in wealth contributed to a series of democratic revolutions that took place across Europe in 1848. In France, bloody protests led to the formation of the Second Republic, which placed emphasis on universal male suffrage and unemployment relief. News spread quickly of the events in Paris, and it was not long before a series of violent protests and subsequent democratic reforms occurred across the Habsburgs' Austrian Empire, Germany, Italy and Poland. In the early part of the twentieth century the franchise in Western democracies was extended to women; but totalitarian dictatorships took hold of Germany, Italy, Russia, Japan; much of Eastern Europe and Latin America; and parts of Asia. As David Held says, democracy is a 'remarkably difficult form of government to create and sustain', and the forces of 'Fascism, Nazism and Stalinism came very close to eradicating it altogether' (Held, 2006: 1).

After the defeat of fascism in the Second World War, US-sponsored democracy spread, beginning with the occupied nations of Germany and Japan, then across Europe and its colonies in the 1950s and 1960s, and in South America and Asia during the 1970s and 1980s. By the early 1990s, the Soviet bloc was crumbling, to be replaced by attempts at liberal democracies even in Russia itself. In the standard story of democracy, the end of the Cold War heralded the triumph of the West's conviction that its liberal model was 'the final form of human government' (Fukuyama, 1989: 1). Much has been made of this 'third wave' or 'global resurgence' of democracy, some arguing that the twentieth century had in fact been 'democracy's century', where more than half the world's population came to live in 'electoral democracies' by the turn of the millennium (*Democracy's Century: A Survey of Global Political Change in the 20th Century*, 1999; Diamond and Plattner, 1996; Huntington, 1991). Since 2000, democracy has continued to flourish, through the success of a series of people's movements in the former states of the USSR, including the 'Rose Revolution' (Georgia, 2003), the 'Orange Revolution' (Ukraine, 2004) and the 'Tulip Revolution' (Kyrgyzstan, 2005). In the Middle East there have been positive, if inconclusive, democratic developments in Morocco, Algeria, Qatar, Lebanon, Kuwait and Palestine, even as the 'Bush doctrine' installed manufactured democracies in Afghanistan and Iraq. At the time of writing, ongoing developments in Burma, Pakistan, Nepal, Thailand and Iran, as well as the 'Arab Spring' of late 2010 and 2011, indicate the continuing popularity of democracy, through movements opposed to autocratic power and in favour of inclusion, diversity and debate. It is fair to say that, despite all its problems and imperfections, democracy today stands as the widely preferred form of human governance.

This sequence of events – from the humble beginnings in Attica to the global spread today – constitutes the standard history of democracy. There is, however, a very serious problem with this widely accepted story. While it records many important events and inspirational moments, it is profoundly flawed. For those whose heritage does not include a direct link to Greek assemblies, the British Parliament or the American Congress, the accepted history of democracy provides a distant and exclusive narrative, which limits one's ability to embrace democracy. The Western cast of the standard history suggests that only the West knows democracy and that only the West can bring democracy to the rest of the world. Indeed, when successes have occurred in the global uptake of Western liberal democracy, they have been seen as a sign of the merits of this model and as a vindication of European hegemony, while failures are seen as a result of the inability of non-Europeans to grasp the complexity of democracy and of their preference for violence, disorder and autocracy. Our contention here is that it is neither democracy itself nor the cultural contexts in which it is practised that are the problem, but the limited and limiting narrative which underpins our very narrow understanding of what democracy is and from whence it comes. Ironically, this narrative of democracy is relatively un-democratic, persistently maintaining that democracy is not really for all the people, will not work in certain contexts and is unlikely to take root amongst those whose history falls outside of its dominant narrative.

These sentiments are far from new. In fact, it can be argued that the standard history of democracy has long been underpinned by twin discourses which contemporaneously assert the West's alleged propensity to democratization and the supposed non-European tendency to despotism. For example, influential Greek authorities such as Herodotus, Aristotle and Xenophon repeatedly sought to contrast the civic virtue and democratic spirit of the Greeks against the brutal despotism of Persia and other Asiatic peoples (Aristotle, 1981; Herodotus, 1996; Xenophon, 1986). Later, when modern representative democracy emerged and became stronger across Europe, a whole host of important intellectuals contributed to the growing orthodoxy that Europeans had a proclivity for democracy, which had differentiated them from the increasing number of 'uncivilized' peoples who benefited from the colonial project

10   *Introduction: Democracy and History*

(Hegel, 1952 [1837]; Mill, 1972 [1817]). The most stinging critique of this Euro-centric view is Edward Said's *Orientalism*, which argues that the colonial project was driven by notions of Asiatic ineptitude that were distilled down from 'essential ideas about the Orient – its sensuality, its tendency to despotism, its aberrant mentality, its habits of inaccuracy, its backwardness – into a separate and unchallenged coherence' (Said, 2003 [1978]: 205). One does not have to subscribe to all of Martin Bernal's positions to note that he makes a similar point strikingly well in his *Black Athena* trilogy, which asserts that the strength of Euro-centrism and anti-Semitism in Europe led to the development of the 'Aryan model' of historiography, in which the cultural and technological achievements of Europe came to be seen as distinct from and superior to those of Asia and Africa (Bernal, 1991 [1987], 1991, 2006).

To say that this legacy has had an impact on perceptions of democracy and its history today would be a massive understatement. So pervasive is the dialectic between Western democracy and non-European despotism that it has been cited by various 'enemies' of democracy – tyrants and fundamentalists, pejorative policy pundits and politicians, and racialist journalists and academics – who use it to argue that certain peoples, or certain regions, simply do not have the requisite historical or cultural background to practise democracy successfully. To cite one very well known example, political scientist Samuel P. Huntington has dedicated much of his work to arguing that each region of the globe has its own individual religio-cultural essence, which plays a large part in determining that region's receptivity to democratic systems (Huntington, 1984). For example he labels Islam and Confucianism 'profoundly anti-democratic', claiming that they would 'impede the spread of democratic norms in society, deny legitimacy to democratic institutions, and thus greatly complicate if not prevent the emergence and effectiveness of those institutions' (Huntington, 1991: 300, 298). Such views are not only Euro-centric and overtly racist, they are also alarming in their historical inaccuracy.

A secret history?

The foremost concern of this volume is therefore to bring to the surface some of the lesser known 'secret' histories in the story of democracy and to open up debate and discourse on the complex origins and multiple trajectories of this sophisticated form of governance. In doing so, we hope not only to move beyond the traditional narrative of democracy by broadening its history so as to include lesser known examples, but also to break down the intellectual orthodoxy that underpins this traditional story and to argue against the imposition of grand narratives on the haphazard, imperfect and incomplete history of democracy. We are not, therefore, attempting to create our own comprehensive alternative history of democracy, but to contribute to the growing body of literature that seeks to expand and explore democracy and its history.

This broader view of democracy's history arguably begins with Alan Hattersley's *A Short History of Democracy* (Hattersley, 1930). Throughout the predictable chapters on Athens, Rome and the French Revolution there are some pleasant surprises, as Hattersley develops a remarkably nuanced picture of the history of democracy. He begins with a chapter on 'Primitive Democracy', arguing that there is much evidence to suggest that something like democracy was practised even by our most remote ancestors. He also discusses democratic thought in the Middle Ages and the influence of the Reformation on the rise of democracy, finding evidence that concepts such as 'rule by consent' were being debated throughout the thirteenth, fourteenth and fifteenth centuries. However, apart from his early and brief nods to primitive societies, Hattersley's vision of the history of democracy remains particularly Euro-centric. In contrast, Muhlberger and Paine's more recent article 'Democracy's Place in World History' argues that 'most people in the world can call on some local tradition on which to build a modern democracy' (Muhlberger and Paine, 1993: 25). To demonstrate their case, the two scholars focus on examples of democratic governance in contexts as diverse as traditional Chinese village life, African tribal moots, ancient Indian republics and Native American societies. Thus they establish that democracy not only has a far richer and more complex history than is normally conceded, but also that, if we fail to acknowledge this alternative legacy of democracy, we are in effect narrowing our vision of human political history.

These themes are reiterated in a handful of articles by Nobel Prize winning economist and philosopher Amartya Sen, who argues that democracy can be thought of as a universal value with global rather than Western roots. Sen points out that to equate the European developments of the standard history with a Western only commitment to egalitarianism or collective forms of government has been a profound misreading of world history (Sen, 1999: 15). Instead, '[t]he championing of pluralism, diversity, and basic liberties can be found in the history of many societies' (Sen, 2003: 29–30). A more robust engagement with this global history of democracy undermines the notion that democracy is a Western idea, and has the potential to 'contribute substantially to

12 *Introduction: Democracy and History*

better political practice today' (Sen, 2003: 35). Similarly, in *The Theft of History* Jack Goody pays particular attention to the Europeanization of democracy, arguing as follows:

> The notion that democracy only emerged as a feature of modern, indeed western, societies is a gross simplification as is the attribution of its origin to the Greek city–states... many early political systems, including very simple ones, embodied consultative procedures designed to determine the will of the people. In a general sense the 'value' of democracy, though sometimes held in abeyance, was frequently, if not always, present in earlier societies and specifically emerged in the context of opposition to authoritarian rule.
>
> (Goody, 2006: 256)

Most recently, this theme of exploring the broader and deeper history of democracy has formed the central impetus of John Keane's magnum opus, *The Life and Death of Democracy* (Keane, 2009). In the first attempt at a comprehensive history of democracy for over a century, Keane brings to light many previously under-appreciated democratic moments and concludes:

> Its universality... stems from its active commitment to what might be called 'pluriversality', the yearning of the democratic ideal to protect the weak and to empower people everywhere, so that they can get on with living their diverse lives on earth freed from the pride and prejudice of moguls and magnates, tyrants and tycoons.
>
> (Keane, 2009: 855)

While this broader and richer perspective on democracy and its history includes too many stories to be contained in one volume, we have collected here a series of papers which address some of the glaring omissions in the standard history of democracy. However, there is an important period in the 'secret' history of democracy that pre-dates even the earliest city-states and civilizations of the ancient world. Long before the reforms of Cleisthenes, pre-historic peoples huddled together around fires or under banyan trees, to deliberate and discuss the issues facing their communities. Ronald M. Glassman's two-volume *Democracy and Despotism in Primitive Societies* identifies 'campfire democracy', at work in hunting–gathering societies, where the need for co-ordinated food collection and defensive strategies gave rise to some of the earliest forms of collective decision-making, and these, in time, took on various political and judicial functions (Glassman, 1986: 37–8, 46–53). Later, in the more sophisticated horticultural or herding tribal societies, 'kinship democracy' is said to have emerged. This consisted of a more complicated system, in which the council of the entire clan met to send off representatives to the broader tribal assembly (Glassman, 1986: 127–8). While Glassman is particularly sensitive to the (often) ageist and sexist nature of these 'primitive' democracies as well as to the reality that certain oligarchic or expedient tendencies are likely to have emerged there, his study nonetheless opens up significant questions about the origins of democracy and the possibility that it embodies a universal human proclivity. It is worth noting that Glassman concludes the first volume of his study by demonstrating that, among the Tosaday people of the Philippine rainforest, a form of pure band democracy still exists. There are no distinctions between males and females, the old or the young, and all the community members are deeply involved in every aspect of discussion, leadership and decision-making (Glassman, 1986: 224–5).

In Part I ('Pre-Athenian Democracy'), the contributors address the growing body of evidence which suggests that, as human beings created and lived in the world's first city-states across the Middle East, the Mediterranean, the Indus Valley and China, they adapted 'primitive' democratic mechanisms to deal with the complexities of city life. Benjamin Isakhan's chapter, 'What is so "Primitive" about "Primitive Democracy"?', argues that, long before Athens, many ancient Middle Eastern city-states had councils and assemblies where each citizen had the right to speak and vote on social, administrative and political matters. Exploring further the connection between the ancient Middle East and classical Greece, Stephen Stockwell ('Before Athens: Early Popular Government in Phoenicia and Greek City States') examines the evidence for a Phoenician democracy and for its possible influence on Greek political development, suggesting that popular government had a longer history than is generally acknowledged. There were also assemblies and proto-democratic practices in ancient India, and Steven Muhlberger's 'Republics and Quasi-Democratic Institutions in Ancient India' draws on a variety of historical and religious sources, to conclude that the antediluvian republics of the subcontinent are among the most significant examples of democracy in the ancient world. Pauline Keating's 'Digging for Democracy in China' illustrates that China too has a history of democratic institutions and practices in the counter-cultures that developed alongside Confucianism.

Part II ('Democracy in the "Dark Ages"') sheds light on a major gap in the standard history of democracy, between the fall of the Roman

14 *Introduction: Democracy and History*

Republic and the rise of the English Parliament – a long stretch of time, which included the so-called 'Dark Ages' in Europe. However, Islam flourished throughout this period. As Mohamad Abdalla and Halim Rane's chapter ('Behind a Veil: Islam's Democratic History') shows, Islamic doctrine and politics frequently utilize democratic mechanisms such as consultation and consensus in decision-making, as well as systems of representation and the peaceful transferral of power. Patricia Piers Boulhosa's chapter ('Ideals and Aspirations: Democracy and Law-Making in Medieval Iceland') examines Iceland's dynamic medieval legal system in order to appreciate the community's close involvement in law-making and brings a critical perspective to a significant experiment in autonomous and inclusive self-governance. Stephen Stockwell explores the democratic tendencies of medieval Venice in a second chapter in this book ('Democratic Culture in the Early Venetian Republic'), pointing out that Venice played a major role in keeping democratic tendencies alive between ancient times and the Renaissance by means of experiments with sovereign assemblies and frank exchange between citizens.

Part III ('Indigenous Democracy and Colonialism') explores a number of indigenous societies that exhibited collective governance or egalitarian politics at the time of European colonialism, indicating the potential of a far deeper, richer and largely 'secret' history of indigenous democracy. Immaculate Kizza's chapter on 'Africa's Indigenous Democracies: The Baganda of Uganda' records a very important moment in the broader history of democracy and alludes to ways in which its legacy can be used to reinvigorate democratic debate and discourse in Africa today. In a chapter entitled 'The Hunters Who Owned Themselves', Philippe Paine examines the Buffalo hunt of the Métis in Western Canada, where an assembly decided the rules of the hunt and elected guides and camp chiefs. Larissa Behrendt's contribution to this volume ('Aboriginal Australia and Democracy: Old Traditions, New Challenges') examines the democratic tendencies evident in traditional Aboriginal Australian approaches and then argues that such practices continue despite government intervention in the Australian Aborigines' own attempts at self-determination. In a chapter entitled 'The Pre-History of the Post-Apartheid Settlement: Non-Racial Democracy in South Africa's Cape Colony, 1853–1936', Poppy Fry excavates a little-known aspect of South African political history to reveal that, before apartheid, property rather than race was the basis of the franchise for the multi-racial government in the Cape Colony.

Part IV ('Alternative Currents in Modern Democracy') examines aspects of the global spread of democracy over the last century, to appreciate the contribution of peoples' movements and civil society organizations against authoritarian power and in favour of a more democratic and inclusive political order. K. Luisa Gandolfo's 'Birthing Democracy: The Role of Women in the Democratic Discourse of the Middle East' reveals the pioneering work of Islamic feminists from the late nineteenth century onwards, who transcended ascribed roles and shaped democratic practices in the Middle East. Benjamin Isakhan's 'The Streets of Iraq: Protests and Democracy after Saddam' points to the fact that, after Saddam Hussein, the Iraqi people have frequently exercised their democratic right to protest and to play an active role in their own governance, while helping to create a robust democracy. The final chapter, John Keane's 'Monitory Democracy? The Secret History of Democracy since 1945', takes a broader view of the post-1945 rise of democracy, to examine the unacknowledged shift from old-world representative institutions towards a form of what Keane calls 'monitory democracy', where the surveillance of power and the introduction of power-contesting mechanisms have had fundamental implications for how we think about, and practise, democracy today.

What these fundamental changes indicate, and indeed what the work of each of the contributors signifies, is that it is time to re-think the standard history of democracy. While the editors admit that our 'secret' history has many limitations and shortcomings, these are to do, at least in part, with the complex and divergent history of democracy itself. By moving beyond traditional narratives towards an understanding of democracy's history that celebrates the complexity of its overlapping trajectories and intersecting practices, we are inevitably going to stray into unfamiliar and uncertain territory. Indeed, to accept the imperfections revealed in the history of democracy is to acknowledge that there is no pure form of democracy to uncover, no halcyon days to lionize and no grand narrative to tell. Instead there are many imperfect democratic moments, where people have fought and sacrificed to improve their situation and that of their fellow human beings. In a very real sense, this book argues for a more democratic view of the history of democracy. One that, at the very least, pauses to consider the democratic potential found in all regions, in all cultures and in all historical epochs. We therefore hope to open up the field for future research, and we invite other scholars to challenge the existing story of democracy, to search for alternative narratives with marginalized movements and to create a rich debate on the question of democracy's history. We hope that, with this standard history brought into question and these 'secrets' revealed, people all over the world may come to have a greater sense of ownership

16 *Introduction: Democracy and History*

over democracy and take pride in practising and re-creating it for their time, for their situation and for their purposes. It is our ambition that this book not only set the tone for future discussion, but also play a part, however small, in understanding and aiding the struggle of all peoples against tyranny and oppression and towards new, historically relevant frameworks for the practice of governance by the people.

Note

1. The authors acknowledge that the uses of the terms 'West' and 'East' throughout this book are problematic given that they rely on a Euro-centric vision of the world. Unlike the terms 'North' and 'South' which have a clearly defined geographical boundary in the equator, the terms 'East' and 'West' are ideological, originating in Europe to divide the Eurasian landmass between the European or Western and the Asiatic or Eastern. Despite their Euro-centric origin and geographical inaccuracy, these terms remain in common parlance and are used throughout this monograph.

Part I
Pre-Athenian Democracy

1
What is so 'Primitive' about 'Primitive Democracy'? Comparing the Ancient Middle East and Classical Athens

Benjamin Isakhan

Among studies of the ancient world and its politics, there is an overwhelming emphasis on the significant achievements of the Greeks. This is, at least in part, because there are records of the administration of their societies and the 'Athenian Revolution' might be better understood not so much by what the Athenians did – as most of their activities have at least some precedent – as by what they wrote down. However, of the many texts produced in Greece from the fifth century BCE onwards, only fragments remain. This means we must be cautious about making general inferences based on these sources, as they may well have been written in the context of a great many other texts, which have since been lost (Davies, 1978: 13–20). This is particularly true of the Greek texts that concern democracy. In a very real sense, we don't know much about Greek democracy, about how it functioned, or the core principles on which it was founded and grew. As the renowned scholar of classical Athenian politics Josiah Ober has conceded, 'we have no surviving texts written with the explicit intention of explaining the principles on which Athenian democracy was predicated' (Ober, 1994: 151). In addition, as Ober points out elsewhere, '[m]ost ancient [Greek] texts were written by elites, specifically for an elite readership' (Ober, 1989: 43). Beyond such concerns, much of the problem with relying on the scholarship of the ancient Greeks themselves is the fact that 'All the Athenian political philosophers and publicists whose works we possess were in fact degrees oligarchic in sympathy' (Jones, 1969 [1953]: 41). Key writers such as Plato, Aristotle, Isocrates (in his later works), Thucydides, Xenophon and 'The Old Oligarch' [Pseudo-Xenophon] appear to have

20 *Pre-Athenian Democracy*

viewed democracy as a bad example of government, in which the brutish will of the masses usurps the natural position of the wealthy and well-educated elite. Further still, much of their writing reflects the fact that they saw Athenian democracy as being very far from reflecting a political ideal, as they constantly sought to move beyond it to discussions of their own utopian models.

Despite their criticisms of democracy, the Athenians were certain in their belief that the Greeks had a unique proclivity for democracy and that they alone had invented this advanced form of government. As the fifth-century historian Thucydides (460/55–400 BCE) notes in his rendering of Pericles' funeral speech, '[l]et me say that our system of government [democracy] does not copy the institutions of our neighbors. It is more the case of our being a model to others, than of our imitating anyone else' (Thucydides, 1972 [410 BCE]: II.37). Foreshadowing this view, throughout his account of the Greco-Persian Wars of 490 and 480–479 BCE, Herodotus repeatedly juxtaposes the liberty, egalitarianism and civic strength of the Greek model of democracy and the tyranny, oppression and civic weakness of foreign governments such as that of the Persian Empire (Herodotus, 1996 [460 BCE]: III.80–8; VII.211–13). Similarly, in his *Politics*, Aristotle (384–322 BCE) argues that it is because 'non-Greeks are by natural character more slavish than Greeks that they tolerate master-like rule without resentment' (Aristotle, 1981 [350 BCE]: 1285a16). As a whole, the Greeks premised much of their argument about such issues on an assumption not only about their own civility and democratic nature, but also about the backwardness and barbarity of non-Greeks and about their history of tyranny and oppression.

Regardless of all of these intractable problems – the scarcity of Greek texts about democracy, the elite framework and disdain towards democracy found in the texts we do have, and the overtly racialist assumptions embedded in the narrative – the notion that Athenian democracy was somehow unique and superior to similar experiments elsewhere has today achieved the status of intellectual orthodoxy.[1] Indeed, to challenge the idea that Greece was the home of the first democracies is to swim against the great tide of scholarly consensus. Of those innumerable classicists, historians, political scientists and political theorists who concern themselves today with democracy in ancient Athens,[2] the overwhelming majority are content to assert that something unique did happen among the Greeks, and they are reluctant to look any further, even if just to pay a passing homage (or a patronising nod) to earlier democratic developments.[3] As Flavius Josephus, a Jewish historian of the first century CE, put it:

> I cannot but greatly wonder at those men, who suppose that we must attend to none but Grecians, when we are inquiring about the most ancient facts, and must inform ourselves of the truth from them only...I mean this, if we will not be led by vain opinions, but will make inquiry after truth from facts themselves [then we must acknowledge that it was]...the Egyptians, the Chaldeans, and the Phoenicians that have preserved the memorials of the most ancient and most lasting traditions of mankind...these also have taken especial care to have nothing omitted of what was done among them; but their history was esteemed sacred, and put into public tables, as written by men of the greatest wisdom they had among them.
>
> (Josephus, 1700 [75]: I.2)

This chapter seeks to be a corrective to the problem highlighted by Josephus. It seeks to delve deeper into the ancient history of democracy than is normally permitted, back to a time preceding the developments of classical Athens, when the earliest signs of organized society and complex governmental systems emerged across the ancient Middle East. It then seeks to compare and contrast these ancient Middle Eastern examples with those of classical Athens and to offer new insights into, and questions about, the nature and history of democracy. Building on some recent work (Fleming, 2004; Isakhan, 2007a; Keane, 2009: 78–155), this chapter also hopes to move the discussion beyond the phrase usually associated with ancient Middle Eastern democracies, that of 'primitive democracy'.

The term 'primitive democracy' was first used in relation to ancient Mesopotamian governance by a renowned Assyriologist, Thorkild Jacobsen, in his detailed analysis of ancient Middle Eastern myths and epics such as *Enuma Elish* and the *Epic of Gilgamesh*, as well as of the political practices of some of the region's earliest city-states (Jacobsen, 1970 [1943], 1970 [1957], 1977a [1951a], 1977b [1951b]). Here Jacobsen found reference to assemblies which presided over judicial decisions, debated issues of core concern to their community, such as war and peace, and elected the leaders of both the divine and the earthly realms. This chapter argues that, while the Middle Eastern experiments were less rigid and formalized, they were in no measurable sense more 'primitive' than the later example offered by classical Athens. However, this essay also cautiously notes that, while not all of the elements which made ancient Athens significant occurred in the same way and at the same time in the ancient Middle East, all of them did exist at varying times and in varying guises across these earlier civilizations. To demonstrate

22 Pre-Athenian Democracy

this thesis, the remainder of the chapter utilizes several of the key criteria by which we commonly measure Athenian democracy – the functioning of its assembly, the mechanisms of justice and of the law, the varying voting and elective procedures, the rights and freedoms of the citizens, and the systematic exclusion of 'non-citizens' – and discusses precedents and parallels drawn from the extant evidence concerning the ancient Middle East.

Athenian and Middle Eastern assemblies

The story of classical Greek democracy really begins when the aristocracy of Athens issued Cleisthenes a mandate, around 508 BCE, to formulate a political system that would eschew the centralisation of power. Cleisthenes, an adept and popular politician who had long advocated a system of 'rule by the people', devised a model of governance that became known as *demokratia*. One of the central criteria by which Cleisthenes' model is measured is the Athenian assembly, an outdoor meeting which presided over issues as vast as 'war and peace, treaties, finance, legislation, public works, in short, on the whole gamut of governmental activity' (Finley, 1973: 18–19). All adult male citizens were encouraged to attend these assemblies, which convened about forty times a year and frequently attracted numbers of around 6,000.[4]

However, contrary to the popular assumption that such assemblies were lively places open to varied opinion and lengthy debate, it is much more likely that the sheer size of these gatherings prohibited a robust exchange of views. Instead, the vast majority of the audience was required only to listen and vote, and just a few (elite, wealthy and well-educated) citizens made pre-prepared speeches or proposed motions. There was little discussion and, while controversial statements may have been met with protests or laughter, mostly the communication flowed in one direction (Hansen, 1999 [1991]: 142–6). This situation was to deteriorate substantially after two brief oligarchic coups, the first one in 411/10 BCE, under the pressure of the Peloponnesian War (431–404 BCE) and the second one in 404/3 BCE, following the victory of the Spartans at the end of that same war. The re-assertion of democracy in Athens (403/2 BCE) saw the power of the assembly severely weakened and restricted. Not even the most privileged citizen could table a motion according to his whim. Instead, the assembly could only discuss and decide matters placed on the agenda by the council (*boule*), and even then the People's Court could overturn the will of the people (Hansen,

1999 [1991]: 151–2). This raises a question as to whether Athenian politics was really so much determined by the debates and deliberations of 'the people', or was a highly formalized mechanism designed to sanction state activity rather than create it (Laix, 1973; Larsen, 1954; Perlman, 1963, 1967). The council set the issues that needed to be ratified, the elite citizens delivered them in well-crafted and populist speeches, and the citizens, for their part, served as a rubber-stamp that could be erased by the court.

The Athenian assembly, with all its merits and drawbacks, did not stand alone in the ancient world. There is evidence of ancient Middle Eastern assemblies dating back some 2,000 years before the reforms of Cleisthenes, which are remarkably similar in their democratic impetus. They convened to make decisions regarding matters as diverse as irrigation projects, trade missions, land surveying, administrative issues and to judge the serious offences of citizens, or cases where the security of the city-state was under threat (Jacobsen, 1970 [1957]: 138; Saggs, 2004: 131). They formed the nucleus of the city-state's municipal administration and allowed the collective resources of the community to be pooled in order to reach consensus for concerted action. As the assemblies of the Greek world, they functioned alongside a sophisticated matrix of other councils and courts, and were divided between 'an upper house of "elders" and a lower house of "men"' (Kramer, 1963: 74). In the city-state of Shuruppak, which had its political and economic zenith from 2600 to 2350 BCE, for example, power was divided between the temple priests and a second chamber of magistrates, with more mundane and common concerns, who formed a plural executive and had limited powers and a revolving tenure (Bailkey, 1967: 1218). Such procedures were extended in later city-states such as Sippar, which, from 1890 to 1590 BCE, appears to have been governed by a twin-chamber assembly: an upper house of nobility and a lower house of commoners (Oppenheim, 1969: 9–10). Here, as was often the case in Attica, the upper house consisted of the more senior, qualified and wealthy members of the society, who rotated leadership of the various magisterial and administrative positions on an annual basis, while the lower house consisted of the free adult male population (Leick, 2001: 176).

At times, assemblies were also in evidence in the great empires of the ancient Middle East. For example, the population of the Assyrian capital, Ashur, was able to congregate in an assembly which reached agreement under the guidance of the more senior, wealthy and influential members of the community. Such assemblies were often summoned when differences of opinion between the palace and the elders reached

24 *Pre-Athenian Democracy*

a stalemate. Here 'historical documents describe assemblies of citizens deliberating for days...[where] majority votes were often sought and reached...[and] it was always possible that minority views would raise the problem again if its legal solution was a failure' (Schemeil, 2000: 104). As in Athens, the power of the state was balanced by a thriving private sector, as the Assyrian merchants grew in wealth, and subsequently in influence. The great merchant families appear to have convened in a building commonly known as the 'city house', where they 'made decisions on commercial policy, fixed the rates of export tax...acted as a diplomatic body...and controlled relations with Anatolian rulers on whose cooperation and protection the caravans and resident merchants relied' (Leick, 2001: 203).

Examples of sophisticated assemblies can also be found amongst the ancient Israelites. Here, using methods that parallel earlier Sumerian developments, the book of 'Exodus' reveals that Israelite leaders such as Moses were nominated via a mandate coming directly from God, which was confirmed by the assembly of elders (Mullen, 1980). Later, as C. Umhau Wolf demonstrates, various councils and bodies of elders are evident throughout several of the key books of the Old Testament,[5] in an era which witnessed the Israelites pass through a turbulent time in their political history. In introducing his study, Wolf notes:

> In the Old Testament certain terms and relationships appear which suggest that democracy, in the broadest definition of the term...was prevalent in the earliest times and that vestiges of democratic procedures may be discerned in both political and religious concepts throughout the later periods of Israelite history.
>
> (Wolf, 1947: 98)

These councils appear to have been convened for both religious and political purposes and held at the city gate or at the door of the tabernacle. As in Athens, the more elderly, experienced or gifted rhetoricians amongst them tended to be widely respected, and in consequence they dominated much of the proceedings. When deliberations came to a close, a proclamation was made that reiterated the key decisions and announced the people's consent. Later, during times of monarchy, such assemblies continued to wield 'at least strong advisory powers, if not full veto power, over the king' (Wolf, 1947: 104). Indeed the potential for despotism was kept in check by the people's assembly, and the actions of the king required the approval of a complex bureaucratic hierarchy of temple officials, prophets, priests, courtiers and, in some cases, the entire body of citizens (Martin and Snell, 2005: 399–400; Schultz, 1981: 146; Wolf, 1947: 100–8). In fact ascension to the throne itself required neither blood lineage nor divine right, but the consent of the majority, which 'had the power to reject any candidate for the kingship, even the heir apparent' (Wolf, 1947: 105).

Justice and the law

Returning to Athens, it is worth noting that another core element of its democracy was the notion of justice and equality before the law. To cite an example, the great orator Aeschines (397–322 BCE) stated that 'democratic cities are governed by the established laws' and all citizens have the obligation 'to obey the laws we have established and to punish those who do not obey them' (Aeschines, 2001 [347 BCE]: 1.4–6). Perhaps more succinctly, in Thucydides rendering of Pericles' funeral speech, Pericles states that 'everyone is equal before the law' (Thucydides, 1972 [410 BCE]: II.37). To ensure such equality and to mete out justice, the Athenians used the popular assembly which, for the fifth and the first half of the fourth century, also functioned as a court of law where complex cases were presided over, witnesses were brought to testify, criminals were tried and heavy sentences were dealt out. Indeed, when it came to serious offenses that might require the death penalty, all citizens had the right to trial in the assembly before they could be executed. However, during the first half of the fourth century, the Athenians had devised a separate judicial system, which tried most cases away from the assembly: after 362 BCE, the latter no longer functioned as a court of law (Hansen, 1999 [1991]: 76, 158–9).

In terms of the rule of law in the ancient Middle East, it is instructive to turn to the extensive legal codes developed across the region in order to ensure that justice was served in cases as diverse as crime, slavery, agriculture, debts and loans, marriage, property rights, sexual offenses, theft and, of course, the important matter of goring oxen. In one such law code, that of Lipit-Ishtar, who ruled the city of Isin from 1934 to 1924 BCE, the king demonstrated his concern for social justice by claiming at the beginning of the prologue that his laws are designed 'to establish justice in the land, to eliminate cries for justice, to eradicate enmity and armed violence, to bring well-being to the lands of Sumer and Akkad' (cited in Roth, 1997 [1995]: Epilogue I). Similarly, Hammurabi, the 'King of Justice', ruled the Babylonian empire from 1792 to 1750 BCE and developed a set of 275–300 legal prescriptions, commonly referred to as 'the Code of Hammurabi'. What is particularly

26 Pre-Athenian Democracy

interesting about these laws is that they frequently make reference to an assembly of judges who preside over complicated legal issues, interpreting the law and applying it to difficult situations. Indicating the importance of the judges and of the judicial assembly, the first four laws concern the penalty for giving false testimony before the assembly, which in many cases was death. The fifth law states that,

> [i]f a judge renders a judgement, gives a verdict, or deposits a sealed opinion, after which he reverses his judgement, they shall charge and convict the judge of having reversed the judgement which he rendered and he shall give twelve-fold the claim of that judgement; moreover, they shall unseat him from his judgeship in the assembly, and he shall never again sit in judgement with the judges.
>
> (cited in Roth, 1997 [1995]: Law 5.6–30)[6]

However, comparisons between classical Greece and ancient Babylon in terms of legal codes and equality before them do not end with Hammurabi. In addition to delegating judicial duty to mayors, elders and judges, later Babylonian kings also advocated a system in which an assembly would be summoned to try the more important and complex civil and criminal cases. Such assemblies, like those of Athens, had the power to issue the death sentence. As Jacobsen points out, this judicial system is democratic in nature, the major decisions over right and wrong, or life and death, being vested in the assembly, a forum open to the entire community of citizens (Jacobsen, 1970 [1943]: 159–63).

Ancient Egypt, too, was at times governed by a series of overlapping assemblies and councils, with a central government that included several different departments, such as the Treasury and the Ministry for Agriculture. At the head of this extensive bureaucracy was the Vizier, who 'presided over important civil cases referred to him from lower courts; he dealt with questions of land tenure and the witnessing of wills; and he considered criminal cases requiring heavy sentences' (Aldred, 1998: 196). However, even he was unable to bring new laws into effect without them being duly debated and deliberated upon across a variety of separate councils and assemblies. Beyond this, the various separate councils appear to have wielded considerable power over the day-to-day agricultural affairs of their individual regions. Interestingly, an individual citizen could appeal directly to the Vizier regarding decisions made by a council on rural affairs. The Vizier would then consult with the relevant officials and usually suspend the verdict, so that it could be reconsidered for a designated period of time, before the final decision was put into action (Van den Boorn, 1988: 168–71). Although this was not democracy in the pure sense of the term, at the very least it indicates an egalitarian bureaucracy concerned with the citizens' rights, their equality before the law and the provision of avenues for due process and appeal.

Voting and elections

Another way by which we commonly judge classical Athens to be democratic is through the various voting and elective mechanisms it employed in order to reach a final decision or to designate particular citizens to positions of power. When it came to issues concerning domestic or foreign policy, the Athenian assembly of the fifth century voted by a show of hands, but an exact count of the votes was never apparently undertaken. This changed in the fourth century, when the assembly was required to mimic the procedure of the People's Court and to vote by placing small discs of bronze in urns (Hansen, 1999 [1991]: 130, 147). Furthermore, the assembly elected a few key citizens to positions of power; the 500 or so Jurists and Legislators were selected by lot in the assembly, as were the few key magistrates who put themselves forward for important governmental posts. Finally, every citizen had more than a good chance of being chosen by lot for short-term positions, such as that of chairman, which was of great prominence, or that of a low-ranking support staff (Easton, 1970: 192–95). No matter what their state, elected representatives had limited powers, were under intense public scrutiny and would remain in office for no longer than a year.

As has already been established, from the very earliest days of Mesopotamian civilization we have evidence that the citizens of the first city-states convened in assemblies. Emergency assemblies were often summoned when the security of the city-state was under threat, and they needed to elect a king. At times, they used remarkably complex voting mechanisms, such as kneeling or walking to the speaker to indicate approval, or sitting to indicate disapproval (Schemeil, 2000: 104). When a king was elected, he became the supreme leader of the people and was able to 'promulgate and carry into effect new law' (Jacobsen, 1970 [1943]: 158). However, the appointment was to be held for a limited term by each incumbent and expired when the pending emergency had been resolved. Later, in the extended kingdom of Ebla, around 2500 BCE, we find that the king was elected by popular vote 'for a seven-year term and shared power with a council of elders' (Manglapus, 2004).

28 Pre-Athenian Democracy

Then, after serving the first term, the incumbent was entitled to run for a second one or to retire on a state pension.

In terms of complex voting procedures, the example of the Assyrian merchant colony of Kanesh is particularly interesting. Rising to economic prominence from around 2000 to 1800 BCE, Kanesh was governed by assemblies that were remarkably sophisticated and egalitarian, which suggests a 'liberal and democratic spirit among this small group of local dignitaries' (Evans, 1958: 114). Although they remained the subjects of the king and therefore subscribed to his law, the elders presided over many domestic issues, including political and judicial decision-making. In these assemblies advanced forms of voting were practised whereby the congregation would divide into three groups and each group would deliberate and vote independently before reconvening in a plenary where the final votes were counted (Larsen, 1976: 319–23; Schemeil, 2000: 104). However, when the elders failed to agree, matters were brought before the full assembly – all the adult males – which also voted on the final decision.

Rights and freedoms

Returning again to classical Athens, we find that a further cornerstone of its democracy was the personal freedom and unquestioned equality of all its citizens. For Aristotle, this was not only crucial for a democracy to flourish, but also implicitly related to the principles of justice and of the rule of law, on which Athenian democracy was predicated. Even though Aristotle clearly detests such equality, he is forced to concede that it provides the necessary conditions for the fulfilment of personal liberty (Aristotle, 1981 [350 BCE]: 1291^b30; 1317^a40). For the Athenians, then, equality and liberty are two of the key defining features of a democracy, whereby citizens had an equal share in the political world and simultaneously retained the right to conduct their personal affairs according to their own interests and desires, so long as they did not contravene the law or infringe upon the liberty of others. One of the key aspects in which Athenian citizens were seen as free and equal was in their basic right to *isegoria*, 'freedom of speech' – the freedom to voice their concerns in front of their fellow citizens. While, as has already been argued, in an assembly of 6,000 it is quite unlikely that each citizen had the opportunity to practise this right regularly, the notion of *isegoria* also extended beyond the assembly and permitted the citizen freedom of speech in his everyday life.[7] However, the assembly could punish what it considered as dangerous ideas and it is worth pointing out that the

Athenians went against the very principles of *isegoria* in their trial and execution of the philosopher Socrates, who was found guilty of atheism and corrupting the minds of the young and sentenced to die by ingesting hemlock.[8]

On the issue of freedom and equality across ancient Mesopotamia, there are several pertinent examples. The first is an event which occurred during the first dynasty of Lagash, around 2500–2300 BCE, when the people became embroiled in an early struggle against despotism. It appears as if the power of the throne had seduced the authorities of Lagash, who denied their citizens the basic political, social and economic freedoms and rights one generally expects from a free state. Corrupt judges had sided with the rulings of the elite and turned much private and temple land into state property. This created a 'bitter struggle for power between the temple and the palace – the "church" and the "state" – with the citizens of Lagash taking the side of the temple' (Kramer, 1963: 79). In Early Dynastic states such as Lagash, the temple community wielded enormous political power and 'showed a strongly democratic character' (Frankfort, 1978 [1948]: 221). In this instance, the temple generated collective political action against state-imposed corruption and oppressive systems of power, which led to the first recorded use of the word 'freedom'. In the wake of such a struggle, Urukagina (king of Lagash around 2300 BCE) established liberty as one of the main tenets of society, 'meaning the removal of abuses of the oppressed and the restoration and safeguarding of their rights' (Bailkey, 1967: 1221). He sought to establish the basic equality of all citizens by freeing the poor of their debts, by re-installing the collective and egalitarian policies of the temple, by renegotiating the rights of the citizen, by working to eradicate hunger and oppression and by returning the commandeered land to the people, all of which made Urukagina 'the first known social reformer in history' (p. 1221).

Ideals of liberty and equality were not limited to Lagash, however, and there is considerable evidence that the basic freedoms and rights of the citizen were held in high esteem across the ancient Middle East (Martin and Snell, 2005; Snell, 2001). In addition to this, the ancient Middle Easterners also valued freedom of speech. Throughout the Babylonian, Assyrian and Israelite assemblies, for example, each citizen had the right to express his opinion, while the participants openly pointed out the contradictions and inconsistencies in their opponents' arguments. When each of the willing participants had been given a chance to state his case at least once, the proceedings ended before the debate became cyclical, emotional or counter-productive (Schemeil, 2000; Wolf, 1947).

30 Pre-Athenian Democracy

In the later Assyrian colony of Kanesh, we know that such freedom of speech extended outwards, from the assembly to the private lives of the citizens where further discussion and debates concerning important social and political issues continued and loose alliances and pacts were made (Larsen, 1976: 161–70).

A later example, which is particularly demonstrative of ancient Middle Eastern concerns about the freedom and equality of citizens, can be seen during the foundation of the Persian Empire of the Achaemenids by Cyrus the Great. At that time an allegedly incompetent, cruel and unholy king known as Nabonidus ran the Neo-Babylonian Empire. 'He continually did evil against his city' by turning many of the free citizens of Babylon into slaves and forcing them to work against their will: 'Daily, [without interruption], he [imposed] the corvée upon its inhabitants unrelentingly, ruining them all' (cited in Cogan, 2003: II.124). However, when Cyrus conquered the city in 539 BCE, perhaps without fighting a single battle, he was determined to re-establish the basic rights of the individual and to encourage both religious tolerance and personal freedom. Because of their former oppression, '[a]ll the people of Babylon, all the land of Sumer and Akkad . . . rejoiced at his kingship and their faces shone . . . amidst rejoicing and happiness' (cited in Cogan, 2003: II.124). Indeed Cyrus was careful not to 'permit anyone to frighten (the people of) [Sumer] and Akkad'; instead he set about returning the social justice and 'welfare of the city of Babylon and all its sacred centres' (cited in Cogan, 2003: II.124). As for the citizens of Babylon 'upon whom he [Nabonidus] imposed a corvée which was not the god's will and not befitting them', Cyrus 'relieved their weariness and freed them from their service' (cited in Cogan, 2003: II.124).

Inclusion/Exclusion

While we have thus far focused on the positive aspects of the Athenian democracy – such as its assemblies, its juridical system, its sophisticated elective practices and its fundamental beliefs in the ideas of freedom and equality – it is worth turning now to one of the more negative aspects: the exclusion of the majority of the people of Attica from the democratic process. Indeed citizenship itself was limited by five defining characteristics: age (adult), gender (male), ancestry (Athenian), military service (completed military training) and birth (free-born people only, not slaves or children of slaves). While it is true that, as Plato (429–347 BCE) tells us, within this very restricted definition of citizenship anyone could attend the Assembly, 'be he carpenter, smith or cobbler, merchant or ship-owner, rich or poor, noble or low-born' (Plato, 1976 [380 BCE]: 319d), any study of Athenian democracy must make reference to the fact that the majority of the population was excluded from the rights and privileges that came with citizenship. Apart from slaves, women and foreigners, others too would have been excluded, for instance people with a mental or physical disability that prevented them from completing military training. In addition, those with low levels of education or socio-economic status would have been excluded from citizenship either tacitly or directly; their opinions and arguments would have been easily dismissed by the well-educated and well-practised elite and, perhaps more to the point, until payment for attendance was introduced, they would not have had the luxury of leaving the fields or their trade in order to attend the courts or the public assemblies.

By contrast, the less formalized democratic practices of the ancient Middle East meant that very different ideas of citizenship and participation from those held later on in classical Athens were in place there. As in the Greek world, 'ordinary people' were permitted to attend the assembly, and one account stipulates that the participants could include manual laborers and common people, for instance a bird catcher, a potter, and an orchardist (Jacobsen, 1939). Beyond this, while the elder men or 'fathers' dominated much of the proceedings in ways analogous to those of practices at Athens, they were also much more open to suggestions from a wider range of participants, and in some instances 'women as well as men took part in decision-making' (Saggs, 2004: 30). For example, when the assemblies of the Babylonian or Assyrian Empires found it difficult to garner consensus, they extended rather than restricted the circle of participants, often involving commoners, teenagers and women (Schemeil, 2000: 104). In terms of defining citizenship, the Hammurabi Code, for example, distinguishes between people not on the basis of age, gender, ancestry or military service, but also on the basis of class. In this way, all individuals – young and old, women and men, foreigners and locals – fall into one of three classes: the free person, who is accorded the full rights and freedoms that come with citizenship and who plays an important role in the functioning of the state and its government; the commoner, who is not granted the same privileges but is encouraged to attend the assembly and whose opinion and vote are instrumental in determining questions of administration, governance and law; and the slave, who has virtually no rights and belongs to the free person, the commoner or the palace. Therefore, in ancient Babylon, perhaps it was only the slave who remained marginalized by the state.

Conclusion

The assertion that the classical Greeks were the sole democrats of the ancient world has achieved the status of received wisdom because it is premised on several overlapping and apparently mutually confirming factors. Firstly, we have a handful of surviving texts from Greece which discuss democracy. It must be remembered, however, that none of these texts explicitly detail the procedures and principles of Athenian democracy, that most of them are decidedly anti-democratic in tone, and that they are written by concerned elitists, who in fact propose alternative models of governance. We also tend to believe that the Greeks invented democracy because that is what they themselves believed. However, we must be cautious about such assertions, particularly given that they are underpinned by racial stereotypes about non-Greeks and by an understandable lack of knowledge, on the part of ancient Greeks, about the complex political history of the Orient. Perhaps more disconcerting is the fact that we have also, and for too long, held faith in the 'Athenian Revolution' – because, at the time when democracy was being born anew in Europe and the United States in the late eighteenth century, Westerners had no knowledge of the Epic of Gilgamesh, the Laws of Hammurabi, or the Declaration of Cyrus. Indeed it is quite conceivable that our entire perspective on the origins of democracy has been shaped in part by Euro-centrism and in part by the fact that certain Greek sources were readily available in Europe at a time when the Middle Eastern ones were obscured as a result of the extinction of languages and under the hardened dirt of time. One is left to wonder how different the history and the discourse of democracy would be today if texts relating to the political landscape of ancient Middle Eastern city-states and empires had arrived to modern Europe before those concerned with classical Athens.[9]

The above comparison between the democracy of classical Athens and the regimes of the ancient Middle East serves as a corrective to the notion that only the Greeks invented and practised democracy. In the interest of scrutinizing the traditional history of democracy, the examples of the ancient Middle East can be seen as something of a 'secret' history, one that has been mostly marginalized, if not completely excluded from standard accounts. This alternative history reveals that examples from the ancient Middle East rival classical Athens in terms of its lively and egalitarian assemblies, its legal framework premised on notions of justice, its complex voting mechanisms, its ideals of personal freedom and its nuanced definitions of citizenship and participation. The point here is not to dismiss the achievements of ancient Athens, nor to 'prove' once and for all that the ancient Middle Easterners 'invented' democracy, or that they were more democratic in nature or in practice than the Athenians. Indeed such assertions would directly contradict the impetus of this volume, which is concerned with discussing alternative histories and stories and with asking probing questions about the complex origins of democracy. Instead, this chapter asserts that, by conducting genuine comparisons between the ancient Middle East and classical Athens, we might move beyond frameworks of 'primitive democracy', to view instead ancient Middle Eastern democracies as powerful precursors to the important legacy left behind by the Greeks. The intention is to stimulate discussion by moving beyond linear and restrictive histories, towards a more kaleidoscopic picture of democracy, its history and its relevance today.

Notes

1. It should be pointed out here that there have also been several scholarly attempts to deny that democracy existed in Athens at all. For example, Lionel Pearson argued that until the death of Pericles in 429 BCE, the *demos* controlled only domestic policy, while more important issues concerning foreign policy were dealt with by the board of ten generals. Following the death of Pericles, the Athenians attempted to deal with foreign policy but this saw the state descend into anarchy (Pearson, 1937). Others have simply argued, as will be discussed later in this chapter, that Athens was governed by a ruling elite who only occasionally sought the approval of the masses (Laix, 1973; Larsen, 1954; Perlman, 1963, 1967).
2. For a discussion of the broad array of intersecting disciplines that are dedicated to Grecian democracy see the recent work of Josiah Ober (Ober, 2008).
3. Take for example a recent article by an otherwise fine scholar of ancient Greece, David Pritchard, who not only insists that the Greeks invented democracy but argues that any attempt to attribute similar governmental models to the Levant or Mesopotamia founder for lack of evidence, evidence which Pritchard neglects to engage with, even to refute (Pritchard, 2007).
4. The best description of the Assembly of Classical Athens is found in Aristotle's *The Athenian Constitution* (Aristotle, 1984 [332 BCE]: 43.3–6, p. 90).
5. Including *Joshua, Judges, Samuel I* and *II*, and *Kings I* and *II*.
6. There are in fact many laws within the Code of Hammurabi that concern the role of the judges in trying cases of civil law (cited in Roth, 1997 [1995]: law 9, pp. 82–3; 13, 84; 168, 113; 172, 114–15; 177, 116).
7. On the issue of private freedom and its impact on relations between Athenians, Pericles remarked 'And, just as our political life is free and open,

34 *Pre-Athenian Democracy*

so is our day-to-day life in our relations with each other' (Pericles cited in Thucydides, 1972 [410 BCE]: 2.37, p. 145).

8. We have several surviving accounts of the trial of Socrates, perhaps the best of which is found in the writing of Plato and Xenophon (Plato, 1892 [387]; Xenophon, 1897 [380]).

9. One is also left to wonder how much more of the ancient Middle Eastern story of democracy remains buried under the ground or, more devastatingly, has been destroyed or smuggled out of the Middle East in recent years, particularly since the invasion of Iraq in 2003.

2
Before Athens: Early Popular Government in Phoenicia and Greek City-States

Stephen Stockwell

Most accounts of the origins of democracy assume that the idea and its institutions sprung into life, fully formed, in Athens, after the reforms of Cleisthenes, at the end of the sixth century BCE (Dunn, 1992). This chapter explores the political and cultural environment in eastern Mediterranean cities immediately before the Athenian reforms. It responds to concerns expressed by Simon Hornblower: 'The Phoenicians...had something comparable to the self-regulating city-state or *polis* [and there is] the possibility of Phoenician origins for some of the Greek political arrangements we most admire. Scientific study in this area has, however, hardly begun' (Hornblower, 1992: 2). While some previous work in this area has been less than conclusive (Bernal, 2001 [1990]), the present chapter seeks to test the available evidence about the deeper origins of democratic ideas and institutions. It examines whether Phoenician cities had their own form of democratic government before Athens, and whether Phoenician trade into the Greek sphere of influence contributed to the intellectual milieu that gave rise to the Athenian model, particularly via earlier city-states identified by Eric Robinson as 'first democracies' (Robinson, 1997).

Unfortunately, the Phoenicians were ill-served by their stationery. The papyrus on which they used their phonetic alphabet to record their business and their diplomatic and political history has mostly rotted; 'the archives of the Phoenicians' described by Flavius Josephus are long gone (Josephus, 1700 [75]: I). The sciences – genetic, forensic, archaeological and linguistic – still have a long way to go before there is anything near a definite, authoritative view of Phoenician political culture; but new work, and old, deserves rigorous consideration. It is time to draw together the threads of available evidence about the constitutions of

35

36 *Pre-Athenian Democracy*

the Phoenician states and about the Phoenician contribution to the Greek experiments with democratic forms before the word *demokratia* was coined and before democratic practice was institutionalized in Athens.

The perennial question of how to judge what is and what is not a democracy is bound to arise in this discussion. While Athenian practices remain definitive of democracy, it is difficult for any earlier set of arrangements to establish a claim to democratic status, merely because such arrangements are different from the Athenian ones. To accommodate this distinction, some authors classify pre-Athenian models as primitive democracy or proto-democracy, while Robinson distinguishes between democracy with a 'rigorously defined system' of participation and equality, and popular government 'with "the people" having at least some say in the direction of public affairs' (Robinson, 1997: 11–12). But then Athens is hardly a model of ideal democracy from our vantage point, two and a half millennia on: it excluded women and slaves, while the latter's excess labour gave male citizens time to participate; it was militaristic, prone to violence against other city-states and imperial in its outlook; it was peremptory in its decision-making, quick to revert to tyranny and able to execute critics even when, like Socrates, they had served the city well. But for all its faults, the Athenian system was government by the people: it was based on the sovereignty of citizens, gathered in an assembly of equals, speaking and voting freely, making enforceable laws. This chapter seeks to identify a continuum of practices that move from Phoenician to Greek city-states by reviewing the available evidence of democratic mechanisms employed by the Phoenicians and by analysing the impact they had on particular city-states of archaic Greece that made early contributions to the development of democracy.

Phoenicia – Developing democracy

Phoenician civilization was based on city-states such as Sidon, Tyre, Arwad, Byblos, Beirut and Ugarit on the eastern edge of the Mediterranean, around present-day Lebanon. From 1550 to around 300 BCE, the Phoenicians created an adventurous maritime and mercantile culture, which may have reached the British Isles and even the Baltic, and which probably circumnavigated Africa more than two thousand years before Vasco da Gama (Herodotus, 1996 [460 BCE]: IV.42). The Phoenicians certainly did build a trading network from the Far East to the Atlantic, and along the way they founded Carthage, which went on to challenge the power of Rome. Their trade was based on timber, wine, olive oil, iron, glass and purple dye that they produced themselves, as well as on goods from Damascus and other places along the caravan routes further east and from Egypt and the west, across the Mediterranean (Ezekiel 27, Gore, 2004: 34–6; Markoe, 2005: 109–20).

The Phoenicians were present in the Levant from the third millennium BCE. They shared the genetic and linguistic history of the Canaanites and much of the cultural history of ancient Israel (Gore, 2004: 48). The alphabet that the Phoenicians popularized along their trading routes came from the Sinai via Israel, with which the Phoenicians were close trading partners, providing Solomon with the timber and craftsmen to build the Temple in return for grain (Logan, 2004: 36–42; I Kings, 5–7). Most significantly, the Phoenicians were exposed to the shift that Israel first brought to politics: the state depended not on the king's relationship with God, but on the people's participation in the covenant. As discussed in the previous chapter, Mosaic law created a leader constrained by the law of God just as much as the people were. The law ordained a limited monarchy and a social structure tending towards egalitarianism, with a citizenry that could itself choose judges able to lead the people in times of turmoil (Buber, 1967; Finer, 1997: 238–44; Wolf, 1947). Thus, while the Phoenicians were clearly innovators in manufacture, trade and literacy, the issue here is the impact of Mosaic ideas on innovation in the Pheonicians' own political institutions.

The Phoenician contribution to the development of democracy has been a vexed issue over the last twenty years. Their city-states were predominantly monarchic, and their kings had civic and commercial functions as well as ritual and religious responsibilities. The Phoenicians' success can be measured by the way in which their cities expanded to become significant cultural and political forces across the Mediterranean. The wealth and power of the Phoenician kings can be appreciated in the sarcophagi from Sidon, now in the Istanbul Archaeological Museum. The rise of the Phoenician cities depended to a large degree on the kings' coordination of independent sailors, who in turn required autonomy to trade all around the known world, far from the influence of their kings. These traders were the biblical 'merchant princes', and it will be seen below that they formed councils to assist the kings in the management of complexities of their cities, and consequently they gained some power (Isaiah 23.8). The interesting question is whether that power spread further than the councils of the oligarchic few, to assemblies of citizens engaged in robust debate that

38   *Pre-Athenian Democracy*

would allow some Phoenician cities to make the claim for recognition as democracies.

Debate about the Phoenician contribution to democracy was stirred by Martin Bernal's *Black Athena* series, which utilized a speculative linguistic approach to point out possible 'Afroasiatic' roots to classic Greek society (Bernal, 1991 [1987], 1991, 2006). His thesis, which was seeking to establish the contribution of Phoenician politics to the development the Greek city-state, depends to a large extent on some finer points of Marxist theory: Bernal attempted to place Phoenicia at the centre of the shift from the 'Asiatic mode of production' managed by the monarch, to a slave society where the excess production of slaves gave their owner–citizens time to participate in democracy (Bernal, 2001 [1990]). But the evidence cited by Bernal from primary sources is slight, so he makes a far from compelling case. Nevertheless, his work set off a mini-industry of academics connecting early Greece with the East, and particularly Phoenicia (Aubert, 2001; Burkert, 1992; Goody, 1996; Morris, 1992; West, 1997). This work has drawn attention to further primary sources about the constitutions of Phoenician cities and reveals that, while Phoenician cities were mostly in the hands of strong monarchs, there were moments of alternative, non-monarchical constitutional arrangements that deserve close inspection.

The earliest available material concerning Phoenician politics can be found among the Amarna Letters – Egyptian clay tablets containing many diplomatic reports from the mid-fourteenth century BCE (Moran, 1992). The tablets were found at the site of the Egyptian capital built by Akhenaten, the heretic pharaoh who insisted on monotheism and sought to abolish the Egyptian pantheon. The Egyptian state was powerful in the Levant at that time, though its power was contested. The Amarna Letters tell of the travails of various Egyptian vassals confronted with the task of holding together Phoenician cities in the face of Hittite attack and Hittite-inspired insurrection (Cohen and Westbrook, 2000).

The Amarna Letters contain references to councils of elders, or magnates, with whom local kings consulted on important matters of the state and who could even frustrate a king's will (Moran, 1992: 243). Further, these councils acted on their own behalf – as when 'Irqata and its elders' write to the pharaoh to profess their allegiance, making no reference to the local ruler (172). There are also examples of broader assemblies, where 'the citizens of Tunip' and 'people from Gubla (Byblos)' directly address Egyptian officials – which suggests a level of 'republican' organization with deliberative institutions that can represent the will of the people (130–1, 332). The most pronounced democratic moment is revealed when 'the men of Arwad' exchange oaths of rebellion with Zimredda of Sidon against the pharaoh (236). Bernal points to this material, with some justification, as evidence for 'the people, as opposed to the monarch, as sovereign' (Bernal, 2001 [1990]: 356–7). Further, one Egyptian official reveals a high level of deliberation within and among towns when he expresses his concerns about concerted opposition to his position: 'my towns are threatening me (and) they have all agreed among themselves against me' (Moran, 1992: 138). The weight of evidence in the Amarna Letters is convincing, as Flinders Petrie claimed more than a century ago, that municipalities existed in Phoenicia in the fourteenth century BCE (Petrie, 1898: 139). On the balance of evidence from the Amarna Letters, it can be concluded that some Phoenician municipalities were ruled, from time to time, by sovereign assemblies with deliberative functions; and the participation of citizens, and thus democratic activity, is evident in the earliest period of the Phoenician city-states.

The next significant primary source relating to constitutional arrangements in a Phoenician city is the Report of Wenamun (Goedicke, 1975). This report dates from the early part of the eleventh century BCE, about 250 years after the Amarna Letters, and it confirms that deliberative municipal forums were still flourishing in the Phoenician city of Byblos. The report follows the journey of an Egyptian priest to Byblos in his attempt to acquire timber to build a sacred barge. Egyptian influence in the Phoenician cities has clearly waned since the Amarna Letters, leaving strong local monarchies. Wenamun meets Zakarbaal, the king of Byblos, who manages all aspects of the trade with the Egyptian and who is central to the religious life of the city. Zakarbaal is advised by 'his assembly' with regard to state matters – in this case, the extradition of Wenamun to another jurisdiction, to answer charges of theft (Goedicke, 1975: 123). This assembly is probably something more than the council referred to by Ezekiel as 'the ancients of Gebal (Byblos) and the wise men thereof' (Ezekiel 27.9). Initially Wenamun's hieroglyphic for assembly resisted translation, but it has now been transcribed as *mw'd*, which is close to the Hebrew word *mo'ed*, which is typically translated as 'assembly' (Wilson, 1945: 245). For example, the *mo'ed* is the assembly or council that sends forth 250 'men of renown' to confront Moses and his brother, Aaron, after they order the stoning of a man who gathered sticks on the Sabbath (Numbers 16.2–3). The Report of Wenamun establishes that the Phoenicians did have a word for 'assembly', even if it was borrowed from the Hebrew. With or without the philological

40 Pre-Athenian Democracy

connection, there is a clear inference that Zakarbaal's assembly is something more than an elitist oligarchic council, and the possibility is raised that Byblos was bicameral at the time.

As trade increased, the power of the king became constrained by the wealth of a merchant middle class keen to influence public affairs: 'after Hiram in the tenth century [the kings of Tyre] are not imposing figures' (Drews, 1979: 47; see also Markoe, 2005: 105). Throughout their long history, the Phoenician cities fell under the sway of the Egyptians, Assyrians, Babylonians and, later on, Persians and Macedonians. Invasion and internal dissension saw the kings' power decline while the people's power grew. During these periods of invasion and upheaval, the councils of elders exerted their authority. Most significantly for the discussion of Greek developments in the second half of this chapter, it is in the seventh-century BCE treaty between Asarhadon of Assyria and Baal of Tyre that the council of Tyre's elders is seen to govern alongside the monarch. It was agreed that the Assyrian governor would work 'in conjunction with you (Baal), in conjunction with the elders of your country' (Aubert, 2001: 146; Markoe, 2005: 101).

In the following century, it is clear that power was not simply vested in the king and merchant princes. Josephus notes, from the vantage of the first century CE, that, after Nebuchadnezzar II's siege of Tyre (585–572 BCE), that city was without the monarchy for seven years and was administered for short terms by suffetes (or judges):

> after [Ithobal] were judges appointed, who judged the people: Ecnibalus, the son of Baslacus, two months; Chelbes, the son of Abdeus, ten months; Abbar, the high priest, three months; Mitgonus and Gerastratus, the sons of Abdelemus, were judges six years.
>
> (Josephus, 1700 [75]: I.21)

It is most likely that the judges were elected by the assembly, and even Sandro Bondi, who is otherwise resistant to suggestions of democratic rather than dynastic interpretations of Phoenician constitutions, admits that Tyre was 'a republic headed by elective magistrates' at this period (Bondi, 2001: 153).

Suffetes also governed the Tyrian colony of Carthage, with the support of the senate and of the people's assembly (Markoe, 2005: 103–4). Carthage flourished from before 800 BCE to 146 BCE, when it finally fell to Rome after three wars (the Punic Wars). As Carthage reached the height of its power during the classical Greek period and then figured so importantly in Roman foreign policy, much more survives about Carthaginian constitutional arrangements than about those of the original Phoenician cities (see for example Aristotle, 1981 [350 BCE]; Herodotus, 1996 [460 BCE]; or Polybius, 1889 [150 BCE]). The Carthaginian constitution required two suffetes, who were elected annually to govern on the advice of the senate of elders. Where there was a lack of unanimous agreement between the suffetes and the senate, the popular assembly was called upon to decide the issue. While Aristotle led the way in describing the Carthaginian system as an 'oligarchy', he accepted that formal and informal checks and balances ensured the constitution's effectiveness and longevity (Aristotle, 1981 [350 BCE]: 1272b–1273b). Central to those checks and balances were elections, trade guilds, town meetings and an attitude of deference to the citizenry as the final arbiter of political decision, all of which suggests equality and participation close to democratic standards. The Greek historian Polybius (200–118 BCE) indicates that democracy in Carthage explains Rome's dominance over it:

> In Carthage therefore the influence of the people in the policy of the state had already risen to be supreme, while at Rome the Senate was at the height of its power: and so, as in the one measures were deliberated upon by the many, in the other by the best men.
> (Polybius, 1889: *Histories*, VI.51)

Towards the end of the Phoenician period there is clear evidence that the people eclipsed the monarchy. Later Roman sources – for instance Arrian (CE 86–160) – go so far as to suggest that the 'inhabitants' of Sidon, or 'the people of Sidon', were the ones who made peace with Alexander the Great (Arrian, 1893 [145]: II.15, 1970 [145]: 81). Quintus Curtius Rufus (first or early second century CE) tells how Strato, king of Sidon, surrendered to Alexander in 333 BCE, 'prompted by his citizens' wishes rather than his own' (Rufus, 2001 [40]: IV.1.16). When the Greeks sought to replace the king, the nominated citizens disdained the opportunity to become the monarch and instead nominated a member of the royal family who had been reduced to meagre circumstances by his honesty. This speaks of people confident about their democratic rights to speak and to participate in the political life of the city. As Alexander's army approached Tyre, it was met by 'representatives' sent by 'the commonwealth' or the 'community' (Arrian, 1893 [145]: II.15, 1970 [145]: 81; Bondi, 2001: 154). Alexander wished to offer sacrifice at the temple of the Tyrian Heracles, but when this message was relayed by the ambassadors, it was 'the people' that passed a decree to refuse him entry – which resulted in an extensive campaign before Tyre was laid waste (Arrian, 1893 [145]: II.15).

42 *Pre-Athenian Democracy*

It is clear from this historic arc that the Phoenician cities commenced with strong leadership and ended with relatively weak kings or no kings at all. It is also clear that all along the way, from the fifteenth century BCE to the fourth, the leaders were advised by councils and assemblies which gradually allowed the people to take greater power. There is a lack of evidence as to how broadly these institutions represented the populace and how free and unconstrained their deliberations were, but on balance it may be concluded, from the few occasions when the people are visible, that Byblos, Sidon and Tyre, at least, had something more than an autocracy or oligarchy and much closer to democracy.

Phoenician influence on emerging Greek city-states

In Homer's *Iliad*, Phoenician craftsmanship is the byword for excellence: when instructed by Hector to give her best gown in sacrifice to the goddess Minerva, Hecuba chooses one embroidered by Sidonian women (Homer, 1950 [700 BCE]: 338–51); when Achilles offers a prize for the fastest man at the funeral of Patroclus, it is a Sidonian bowl imported by the Phoenicians (Homer, 1950 [700 BCE]: 823–31). It can be concluded from these references that the Phoenicians were already influential in the Greek sphere in the eighth century BCE, when Homer is supposed to have created the *Illiad*, if not in the twelfth century BCE, when the Trojan War most likely occurred.

There is certainly clear archaeological evidence of Phoenician influence in Rhodes from 800 BCE (Lipinski, 2004: 145–146). As they spread through the Aegean, the Phoenicians brought not only trading goods but also ideas, myths and knowledge from the Egyptian, Assyrian, Babylonian and Israeli worlds. The Phoenicians typically established 'enclaves of craftsmen in communities where native technical skills were less developed' (Drews, 1979: 46). It is most likely that the transmission of these new technical skills depended on the recently developed Phoenician alphabet, which Herodotus sees as stimulating the creation of the Greek alphabet (Herodotus, 1996 [460 BCE]: V.60). It is also likely that it was from the workshops in these enclaves that the nascent scientific method emerged, to be crystallized and refined into philosophy by Greeks with Phoenician heritage, such as Thales of Miletus (Herodotus, 1996 [460 BCE]: I.170, II.81).

The transmission of these ideas did not happen over night; rather, Greece emerged from its 'Dark Ages' over the generations, in gradual increments, prompted by a range of ideas from a range of sources, but particularly from the Phoenicians. As those ideas coalesced, they sparked cultural enlightenment in Greece, which led to the classical age and hence to the birth of 'western civilisation' (Gore, 2004: 37; Solmsen, 1975). Greece benefited from a number of developments coinciding in the period from 800 to 500 BCE. The overthrow of tribal kings, long-distance sea trade, intensive agriculture, mining and manufacture, the introduction of new techniques and technologies, the scientific approach, improved mathematics and coinage 'created a stratum of newly rich agrarian proprietors (with wealth) not matched by any equivalent power in the city' (Anderson, 1974). The rise of this emerging class prompted various city-states to experiment with new political forms. One idea central to the Greek enlightenment is that of democratic governance.

While democracy has come to be regarded as quintessentially Greek (and therefore Western), consideration of democratic experiments in the Phoenician city-states raises the question whether these experiments too were transferred to the Greek sphere of influence, to be developed, systematized and eventually named. Phoenician influence might be found by looking for indications of its occurrence among the Greek cities that were the early adopters of democracy. While there are centres of Phoenician influence where democracy did not flourish (Miletus was a tyranny when Thales was active there), nevertheless consideration of the sixteen sites suggested by Eric Robinson in his work on early popular governments before Athens reveals repeated examples of Phoenician influence (Robinson, 1997).

Chios is a case in point. The island is considered an early adopter of democracy on the strength of the inscription on a stone recovered in 1907 from a road wall near the village of Tholopotami in southern Chios, now in the Istanbul Archaeological Museum (Meiggs and Lewis, 1988: 14). The inscription is dated to the mid-sixth century BCE, between 570 and 550, after the reforms of Solon but well before those of Cleisthenes in Athens (Jeffery, 1956: 160). The inscription is not complete, but it does set out laws on the accountability of magistrates: judicial decisions must follow the 'ordinances of the people', judges will be punished if they accept a bribe and their decisions may be tested in regular, monthly meetings of the people's council (Jeffery, 1956: 162; Robinson, 1997: 90–1). The people's council (*boule demosie*) was composed of fifty elected representatives from each tribe, and three tribes at least are known: 'Chalazoi, Totteidai, Klytides' (Archontidou-Argyri and Kyriakopoulou, 2000: 196). Thus the people's council was composed of at least 150 citizens. The inscription suggests there could also have been an assembly of all the people with even broader powers, but the partial

44 Pre-Athenian Democracy

inscription means that the assembly's purpose is unclear. There is little further textual or archaeological confirmation of Chian democracy at such an early date. Aristotle records the overthrow of authoritarian oligarchs in Chios, but provides no date and no sketch of its subsequent constitution (Aristotle, 1981 [350 BCE]: 1306b3–5).

Given the sparsity of the evidence, it is not surprising that the so-called constitution stone of Chios has caused so much controversy about its dating, the order of its sides and the quality of its democracy (Jeffery, 1956: 160). There is also a question as to whether or not the stone really comes from Chios. Russell Meiggs and David Lewis (1988: 17) mention that the red trachyte stone on which the constitution is inscribed is not common on the island of Chios, but that it is plentiful in nearby Erythrae. Similarly, Ove Hansen points out that the two mentions of the goddess Hestia are out of place if the inscription is from Chios, because there is no evidence of a cult worshipping this goddess there, while there is plenty of evidence that she was worshipped at Erythrae (Hansen, 1985: 276). But there is textual evidence that the people of Erythrae also overthrew their autocratic oligarch (Aristotle, 1981 [350 BCE]: 1305b18–23); so, if the stone did come from there, then the arguments about democracy in Chios could be simply transferred to Erythrae.

The important question for this research is whether there is any evidence of Phoenician influence in either city, and investigation finds that both cities bear the imprint of Phoenicia in their foundational institutions and imagery. From the eighth century BCE, the symbol of the Chian city-state was the sphinx, in the distinctive form of a winged female figure with the body of a lion, which originated in Phoenicia (Archontidou-Argyri and Kyriakopoulou, 2000: 18). Distinctive Chian amphorae, marked with the sphinx, were used for shipping wine to the ports of the Aegean and of the Black Sea from at least 640 BCE (Archontidou-Argyri and Kyriakopoulou, 2000: 156–8, 218). Phoenician influence is similarly evident in Erythrae. While the site is presently unknown, in the second century CE Pausanias (floruit CE 150) reports that one of the two temples in Erythrae was 'the sanctuary of Heracles', which was notable for its age, and that the statue of the god was from Tyre in Phoenicia (Pausanias, 1918 [100]: VII.5.5). In the case of either Chios or Erythrae, there is clear evidence of Phoenician influence ahead of their experiments with democracy.

Further work on Robinson's list of sixteen sites of early democracy reveals both archaeological and textual evidence of Phoenician influence at many of them (Robinson, 1997). Phoenician trading routes were well established from the archaic period on, extending all around the Greek sphere of influence, from Thasos in the northern Aegean to Sicily in the west. From the mid-eighth century BCE there is archaeological evidence of a Phoenician influence in city-states that were early adopters of democratic governance in the eastern Aegean, such as Kos and Samos (Lipinski, 2004: 155). There is also evidence of a Phoenician presence further west in the Aegean, on the island of Euboea, where Chalcis, its capital, was an early democracy, and in Naxos, which was a democracy in the second half of the sixth century BCE (Lipinski, 2004: 147; Robinson, 1997: 91, 117–18). There is textual evidence of Phoenician traders on the Greek mainland in the archaic period at Argos, a city also on Robinson's list:

> According to the Persians best informed in history, the Phoenicians... having migrated to the Mediterranean and settled in the parts which they now inhabit, began at once, they say, to adventure on long voyages, freighting their vessels with the wares of Egypt and Assyria. They landed at many places on the coast, and among the rest at Argos, which was then preeminent above all the states included now under the common name of Hellas. Here they exposed their merchandise, and traded with the natives for five or six days...
> (Herodotus, 1996 [460 BCE]: I.1)

There is further textual evidence of Phoenician influence at Elis, on the west coast of the Peloponnese, which was another early adopter of democracy; its territory included Olympia. Pausanias gives us the following account:

> Thasians, who are Phoenicians by descent, and sailed from Tyre, and from Phoenicia generally... in search of Europa, dedicated at Olympia a Heracles, the pedestal as well as the image being of bronze. The height of the image is ten cubits, and he holds a club in his right hand and a bow in his left.
> (Pausanias, 1918 [100]: V.25.12)

To sail to the cities mentioned above, the Phoenicians would have had to sail past Cnidus and Megara, and then not far past Elis, to reach Achaea and Ambracia, all early adopters of democracy. From the west coast of Greece it is not far to two colonies of Achaea with democratic heritages: Metapontum and Crotone in southern Italy. From there it is an easy sail to Sicily and on to Carthage to meet the Phoenician trade

46   *Pre-Athenian Democracy*

route along the north of Africa. The African route passes Cyrene, another of Robinson's early adopters.

The Phoenicians originally had a number of trading posts around Sicily, but they consolidated the north–west of the island, when various Greek cities began to colonize the fertile river valleys of the south–east (Markoe, 2005: 232–4). At least until the battle of Himera in 480 BCE, the Phoenicians, and then the Carthaginians, continued to seek good relations with the Greek portion of the island, including cities like Syracuse and Acragas, which adopted democracy early. From the above, it is apparent that many of the city-states listed by Robinson as early democracies had a strong Phoenician connection. It is therefore reasonable to conclude that the Phoenicians brought much more than trading items, religious statuary and the alphabet; it is very likely that with the Phoenicians came ideas of non-monarchic forms of government and the practices of collective decision-making.

Beyond Robinson's list, there is the interesting case of Sparta, where Phoenician influence on the formation of democratic institutions is discernible. While an Athenocentric view of democracy relegates Athens' traditional enemy to the fields of autocracy and oligarchy, a number of recent authors see early Sparta as governed by a constitution that 'stipulates that a Spartan popular assembly should meet at regular intervals ... about 600 BCE ... well ahead of Athens' (Hornblower, 1992: 1). It also seems likely that the 'Spartan systems, like the Carthaginian, followed Phoenician prototypes' (Drews, 1979: 47). The Spartan constitution is often attributed to a mythical figure, Lycurgus, who is credited with institutionalizing *eunomia*, good order through effective laws (Forrest, 1980: 64). With or without Lycurgus, W. G. Forrest dates the Spartan constitution to the first half of the seventh century BCE, when the Spartan system of dual kingship was moderated through the expansion of the *gerousia*, a council of the elders, and through the election of new members by a popular assembly (Forrest, 1980: 59). Early Phoenician trade with Sparta is apparent at this time from the processing of mollusc dye by Phoenician methods at the Spartan port Gytheum and from the Phoenician ivory carvings and terra cotta masks found at the sanctuary of Artemis Orthyia in Sparta (Culican, 1975: 55–64; Fitzhardinge, 1980). Over the following century, the assembly established broader powers, to overrule the elders and to appoint annually its own officials, the ephors, who presided over civil cases, conducted foreign policy and came to exercise executive power (Forrest, 1980: 77). Aristotle was an early commentator who pointed out the similarities between the Spartan and Carthaginian constitutions (*Politics*, 1273ᵃ). It is unlikely that the Spartans copied the Carthaginians, whose development had just begun in the seventh century BCE; it is much more plausible that they were both influenced by the earlier Phoenician experience. It is most likely that the Phoenicians brought ideas of popular government and diffused political power into the Spartan sphere of influence, where they found fertile soil in a period of change.

Finally, there is the question of Athens itself. While Phoenician influence is attested in Athens by trade and taxations agreements, by coins and by various artistic motifs, there remains little evidence of any direct Phoenician influence on Athenian political institutions (Markoe, 2005: 52, 124, 219–20). Indirectly, however, the Athenians of the fifth century BCE were surrounded by city-states influenced by the Phoenicians that were experimenting with a new form of government. The Athenians cannot have avoided being influenced by such developments in their decision to devise a system of governance that they came to name *demokratia*.

Conclusion

The preceding discussion establishes significant democratic experimentation in Phoenician cities throughout their history from 1500 to 300 BCE, most significantly Tyre in the seventh and sixth century BCE. Further clear evidence has been established of significant and sometimes foundational Phoenician involvement in the Greek city-states that adopted democracy early in comparison to Athens. The Phoenicians brought more than just trade into the Greek sphere; they also brought the experience of people governing themselves and, clearly in the case of Sparta and on the balance of probabilities in other cities, the Phoenicians had a formative influence on the rise of democratic political institutions. Cleisthenes' reforms in 508 BCE were vital in formalizing democracy in the equality of citizens participating in a set of interlocking institutions with regular meetings and a sovereign assembly, but these ideas and institutional forms had already been tried and tested in Phoenicia and in a range of the Greek city-states. One point that emerges clearly from the discussion above is that, before democracy was an idea, let alone an ideology, it was a practical exertion of political will by the people. This chapter does not claim the Phoenicians 'invented' democracy, nor does it seek to lessen Athens' contribution to the development of democracy. The Athenian contribution to the development of democracy cannot be underestimated, but this chapter establishes that the Athenian contribution was based on powerful ideas that were already circulating among those Greeks who had contact with the Phoenicians. Thus the argument is established for a longer and deeper history of popular government by an active citizenry than is generally conceded.

3
Republics and Quasi-Democratic Institutions in Ancient India

Steven Muhlberger

Over the last century it has been established that ancient India, once visualized as ruled entirely by absolute monarchs and age-old hierarchical religious institutions such as the 'caste system', was for long periods home to republics comparable to the Greek *poleis* (city-states) of archaic and classical times, republics that have as good a claim to be called democracies as the communities in the West that gave us the term (Sharma, 1968; Sharma, 1991 [1959]). One might expect this discovery to have some effect on how ancient history, the history of democracy, and even world history are visualized. Yet to this day, outside of India, even professional historians know next to nothing about those ancient republics and other Indian examples of government by discussion. This chapter will briefly describe these republics, try to place them in historical context, and argue that they should be part of the world view of every student of democracy.

Commentary on democracy's nature and prospects all too often falls back on stereotypes and prejudices, repeated over many decades, that freedom or liberty is the special heritage of the ill-defined West, and that the equally ill-defined 'East' can benefit from the blessings of Western culture in general and from modern democracy specifically only if they are introduced from the West, by imitation or direct intervention. This complex set of prejudices and generalizations is anchored in the conviction of the uniqueness of Greek democracy and political thought. One of the most important aspects of the ancient Indian experience is that it shows that the Greeks were not the only ones who experimented with popular rule in antiquity.

Democracy in the republics of Ancient India

It is perhaps understandable that the Indian republics are almost unknown. The sources of ancient Indian history present considerable difficulties. All the indigenous ancient literature from the subcontinent has been preserved as part of a religious tradition, Brahmanical, Buddhist or Jaina. The largest and most influential Indian literary tradition, the Brahmanical, is distinctly hostile to anything resembling democracy. Brahmanical literature gives kingship a central place in political life and seldom hints that anything else is possible. For moral philosophers and legislators such as Manu, kingship guaranteed a social order based on caste (*varna*), which divided society into functional classes; in particular, a king was charged with upholding the privileges of the priestly Brahmans. The earliest European readers of the *Manu-Smrti* (Manu, 1886 [100 BCE]), Kautilya's *Arthasastra* (Kautilya, 1951 [300 BCE]) or other Brahmanical treatises found it very easy to visualize Indian society as a politically static one in which, ever since antiquity, 'monarchy was the normal form of the state' (Altekar, 1958 [1949]: 1). After all, monarchy was the norm in Europe, and early modern India was without question dominated by emperors and kings and would-be kings.

Greek and Roman accounts of India indicated that this might not always have been the case (Altekar, 1958 [1949]: 110–1; Jayaswal, 1943 [1911–13]: 58). These works, whose veracity was sometimes doubted, spoke of numerous oligarchies and democracies. During the nineteenth century, research into the Pali Canon, the earliest version of the Buddhist scriptures, confirmed this picture of widespread republicanism (Majumdar, 1951: 396–411). Thomas William Rhys Davids, the leading Pali scholar, pointed out in his *Buddhist India* that this early literature showed clans making their public decisions in assemblies, moots, or parliaments (Rhys Davids, 1903).

Rhys Davids' observation was not made in a vacuum. Throughout the nineteenth century, students of local government in India (many of them British bureaucrats) had been fascinated by popular elements in its village life (Maine, 1974 [1889]). The analysis of village government was part of a continuous debate on the goals and methods of imperial policy and of the future of India as a self-governing country. Rhys Davids made the ancient institutions of India relevant to this debate. His reconstruction of a republican past was taken up by nationalistic Indian scholars of the 1910s (Jayaswal, 1943 [1911–13]; Majumdar, 1969 [1918]). Later scholars were sometimes embarrassed by the pioneers' enthusiasm, but those pioneers made possible a much different view of ancient political life in India (Altekar, 1958 [1949]; Sharma, 1968; Sharma, 1991 [1959]). They established that in ancient India monarchical thinking was constantly battling with another vision, of self-rule by members of a guild, a village, or an extended kin-group – in other words, any group of equals with a common set of interests.

Though evidence for non-monarchical government goes back to the Vedas, republican polities were most common and vigorous in the Buddhist period, 600 BCE–CE 200 (Sharma, 1968: 15–62, 237). Non-monarchical forms of government were omnipresent. There was a complex vocabulary to describe the different types of groups that ran their own affairs (Agrawala, 1963 [1953]: 426–44). *Gana* and *sangha*, the most important of these terms, originally meant 'multitude'. By the sixth century BCE, these words referred both to a self-governing multitude, in which decisions were made by the members working in common, and to the style of government characteristic of such groups. In the case of the strongest of such groups, which acted as sovereign governments, the words are best translated as 'republic'.

Some of the best sources are Greek, which have the advantage of speaking in a familiar political language. Arrian's *Anabasis of Alexander*, derived from the eyewitness accounts of Alexander's companions, portrays that conqueror as meeting 'free and independent' Indian communities at every turn (Arrian, 1893 [145]). The prevalence of republicanism and its democratic form is explicitly stated by Diodorus Siculus (first century BCE). After describing the mythical monarchs who succeeded the god Dionysus as rulers of India, he says: 'At last, however, after many years had gone, most of the cities adopted the democratic form of government, though some retained the kingly until the invasion of the country by Alexander' (quoted in Majumdar, 1960: 236, compare with p. 223). This statement seems to derive from a first-hand description of India by Megasthenes, a Greek ambassador to the Indian emperor Chandragupta Maurya around 300 BCE (Stein, 1893: 1.232–3). The context suggests that republics dominated the entire northern half of the subcontinent.

If we turn to the Indian sources, we find that there is nothing far-fetched about this idea. The Pali Canon, the grammar of Panini, and Kautilya's *Arthasastra*, all rich sources, allow us to map north India in this era and to identify numerous *sanghas* and *ganas* (Agrawala, 1963 [1953]: 445–57; Altekar, 1958 [1949]: 118–22; Kautilya, 1951 [300 BCE]: 407; Schwartzenberg, 1978: 16 [Plate III.B.2]). According to Panini (fifth century BCE), all the states and regions (*janapadas*) of northern India were ruled by an identifiable warrior people, some subject to a king of

52 Pre-Athenian Democracy

their own blood (in Agrawala, 1963 [1953]: 426–8; Sen, 1974: 157–9), others governing themselves in a republican manner. In all of them, the government was dominated by people classified as *ksatriyas* – or, as later ages would put it, members of the warrior caste. In many states, political participation was further restricted to a specific royal clan, the *rajanya* (Agrawala, 1963 [1953]: 430–2). It seems likely that political power was restricted to a number of 'royal families' whose heads were consecrated as kings, *rajas*, and thereafter took part in deliberations of state (Altekar, 1958 [1949]: 135; Sharma, 1968: 12–3, 99–109, 112, 175–6).

Our Indian republics are beginning to sound extremely undemocratic. No doubt most republics thought of their *gana* as a closed club – as did the citizens of Athens, a slave-holding polity that made it nearly impossible for immigrants or their descendants to become citizens. But, as in ancient Athens, there are other factors which modify the picture and make it an interesting one for students of democracy.

First, the closed nature of the ruling class is easy to exaggerate. In some republics power was shared by all *ksatriya* families (Altekar, 1958 [1949]: 114). This may not sound like much of a difference, since the restriction to the warrior caste seems to remain. But the *varnas* of pre-Christian-era India were not the rigid castes of later periods (Wagle, 1966: 132–3, 156–8). Such a classification was useful for debating purposes, but it was not a fact of daily existence. Those republics that threw open the political process to all *ksatriyas* were not extending the franchise from one clearly defined group to another, albeit a larger one, but to all those who could claim, and justify the claim, to be capable of ruling and fighting. Other evidence suggests that in some states the enfranchised group was even wider, especially when wealth derived from peaceful economic activity gave access to the political process (Agrawala, 1963 [1953]: 436–9).[1] This interpretation is supported by the fact that *sreni* or guilds based on an economic interest were often part of the armed force of a state and were recognized as having jurisdiction over their own members (Drekmeier, 1962: 275–7; Majumdar, 1969 [1918]: 18–29, 60–3).

In the Indian republics, as in the Greek *poleis* or in the European cities of the High Middle Ages, economic expansion enabled new groups to take up, and eventually demand a share in, sovereignty.[2] If it was not granted, one could always form one's own mini-state. As Panini's most thorough modern scholar has put it, there was 'a craze for constituting new republics' which 'had reached its climax in the *Vahika* country and north-west India where clans constituting of as many as one hundred families only organized themselves as *Ganas*' (Agrawala, 1963 [1953]: 432; compare with Hyde, 1973: 56–7).

Furthermore, power in some republics was vested in a large number of individuals. A well-known *Jataka* tells us that in the Licchavi capital of Vesali there were many thousands of political participants (see Cowell, 1895 [380 BCE]: 1.316). Other sources confirm this, usually in the form of criticism.[3] Thus the *Lalitavistara*, in an obvious satirical jab, depicts Vesali as being full of Licchavi *rajans*, each one thinking, 'I am king, I am king' – and thus as a place where piety, age and rank were ignored (Agrawala, 1963 [1953]: 430; Majumdar, 1980: 140; Sharma, 1968: 101).

The numerous members of a sovereign *gana* or *sangha* interacted with each other as members of an assembly. Details of the working of such assemblies can be found both in Brahmanical and Buddhist literature. Panini included in his grammar the terminology for the process of corporate decision-making (Agrawala, 1963 [1953]: 433–5). The Buddhist 'Pali Canon' gives a much fuller, if somewhat indirect, depiction of democratic institutions in India. This is found in three of the earliest and most revered parts of the canon: the *Maha–Parinibbana–Suttanta*, the *Mahavagga*, and the *Kullavagga* ('Maha–Parinibbana–Suttanta', 1881 [480 BCE]; 'Kullavagga', 1882 [480 BCE]; 'Mahavagga', 1881 [480 BCE]). These works, taken together, preserve the Buddha's instructions for the proper running of the Buddhist monastic brotherhood – the *sangha* – *after* his death. They are the best source for voting procedures in a corporate body in the earliest part of the Buddhist period. They also give some insight into the development of democratic ideology.

The rules for conducting the Buddhist *sangha* were, according to the first chapter of the *Maha–Parinibbana–Suttanta*, based in principle on those commonly found in political *sanghas* or *ganas*. Business could only be transacted legitimately in a full assembly, by a vote of all the members. If, for example, a candidate wanted the *upasampada* ordination, the question (*ñatti*) was put to the *sangha* by a learned and competent member, and the other members were asked three times to indicate dissent. If there was none, the *sangha* was taken to be in agreement with the *ñatti*. The decision was finalized by the proclamation of the decision of the *sangha* ('Mahavagga', 1881 [480 BCE]: 1.28).

Of course, unanimity was not always possible. The *Kullavagga* provides other techniques used in disputes that were dangerous to the unity of the *sangha*, those which concerned the interpretation of the monastic rule itself. If such a dispute degenerated into a bitter and confused debate, it could be decided by majority vote or referred to a jury or committee specially elected by the *sangha* to treat the matter at hand ('Pattimokkha', 1885 [480 BCE]: 4.9–14). Here we see a combination of well-developed democratic procedure and fear of simple majority rule.

54   Pre-Athenian Democracy

The rules for taking votes sanctioned the disallowance by the vote-taker of results that threatened the essential law of the *sangha* or its unity ('Pattimokkha', 1885 [480 BCE]: 4.1, 4.10). Yet the idea that only a free vote could decide contentious issues was strong. No decision could be made until some semblance of agreement had been reached.[4] Limitations on voting were introduced because Buddhist elders shared the great fear of all Indian republics and corporations: disunity (Altekar, 1958 [1949]: 129–30; Majumdar, 1980: 140).

The rules of the Buddhist *sangha* are by far the best known ones from the period we have been discussing, but neither the Buddha nor his earliest followers invented their complex and carefully formulated parliamentary procedures out of whole cloth. R. C. Majumdar's conclusion, first formulated in 1918, still seems valid: the techniques seen in the Buddhist *sangha* reflect a sophisticated and widespread political culture based on the popular assembly (Majumdar, 1980: 137, 1969 [1918]: 233–4).

The clear connection between ideal monastic governance and contemporary republicanism is evident in the *Maha–Parinibbana–Suttanta*. The king of Maghada sends a minister to the Buddha, to ask how he can destroy the Vajjian confederacy. Rather than answer directly, the Buddha speaks to Ananda, his closest disciple, outlining the civic virtues necessary for Vajjian's prosperity and security, adherence to which will prevent Maghadan success. The account includes the following 'political' advices:

> 'Have you heard, Ananda, that the Vajjians hold full and frequent public assemblies?'
>
> 'Lord, so I have heard,' replied he.
>
> 'So long, Ananda,' rejoined the Blessed One, 'as the Vajjians hold these full and frequent public assemblies; so long may they be expected not to decline, but to prosper ... So long, Ananda, as the Vajjians meet together in concord, and rise in concord, and carry out their undertakings in concord ... so long as they enact nothing not already established, abrogate nothing that has been already enacted, and act in accordance with the ancient institutions of the Vajjians as established in former days ... so long as they honor and esteem and revere and support the Vajjian elders, and hold it a point of duty to hearken to their words ... so long may they be expected not to decline, but to prosper.'
>
> (Sharma, 1968: 81–4, 93–7)

Significantly, the scripture writers have the Buddha stating that he had previously taught the Vajjians 'these conditions of welfare', and the immediately following passages show him establishing a number of conditions for a successful monastic communal life that are consciously parallel to the list of 'republican virtues' given to the Vajjians and include full and frequent assemblies, concord, preserving and not abrogating established institutions, honoring elders and others ('Maha-Parinibbana-Suttanta', 1881 [480 BCE]: 1.1). These precepts, and others that follow, were the main point for the monks who have transmitted the *Maha–Parinibbana–Suttanta* to us. We, however, may wish to emphasize another point: the Buddha saw the virtues necessary for a righteous and prosperous community as being much the same, no matter whether that community was secular or monastic. Foremost among those virtues was the holding of 'full and frequent assemblies'.[5]

Modern India and its democratic past

The Pali Canon gives us our earliest, and perhaps our best, detailed look at Indian republicanism, its workings, and its political philosophy. About no other republics do we know as much as we do about the Buddhist *sangha* and the Licchavis in the time of Buddha – even though we do know that republics survived and were a significant factor until perhaps the fourth century CE, for a period of over 800 years. Scattered inscriptions, a great number of coins, and the occasional notice in Greek sources, the *Jatakas* or other Indian literature give us a few facts. Any history of Indian republicanism is necessarily a rather schematic one. No one who has looked closely at the sources, however, doubts the existence of these republics. Their significance for Indian history and for the broader history of democracy is a different matter. The question has hardly been raised in non-Indian scholarship, while Indian scholars have taken different views over the course of the last century or so.

What have modern historians made of what we might call the golden age of Indian republicanism? We have already distinguished above between two eras of scholarship on the topic. In the first, patriotic enthusiasm and the simple thrill of discovery of unsuspected material characterized scholars' reactions. The former attitude was especially seen in K. P. Jayaswal's *Hindu Polity*. Jayaswal's work was avowedly aimed to show that his countrymen were worthy of independence from Britain.

56 *Pre-Athenian Democracy*

The history of 'Hindu' institutions demonstrated an ancient talent for politics:

> The test of a polity is its capacity to live and develop, and its Contribution to the culture and happiness of humanity. Hindu polity judged by this test will come out very successfully... The Golden Age of [the Hindu's] polity lies not in the Past but in the Future... Constitutional or social advancement is not a monopoly of any particular race.
>
> (Jayaswal, 1943 [1911–13]: 366–7)

In Jayaswal's book, scholarship was sometimes subordinated to this argument. In his discussion of ancient republics (which was not his only subject), the evidence was pushed at least as far as it would go to portray the republics as inspiring examples of early democracy. A similar, though quieter satisfaction can be seen in the contemporary discussions of R. C. Majumdar (1969 [1918]) and D. R. Bhandarkar (1919).

Later, following the independence of the modern Republic of India, a more restrained attitude was adopted by younger scholars, who felt that earlier claims about ancient republicanism and democracy were overstated. The general tendency was to emphasize that the republics were not modern democracies. The clan basis and the exclusiveness of the ruling class were much discussed. Sometimes writers bent over backwards, to divorce the Indian republican experience from the history of democracy (Drekmeier, 1962: 279; Ghoshal, 1966: 185–7; Majumdar, 1980: 139–44; Stein, 1985: 62).

The theme that most attracted the attention of scholars was the ultimate failure of republicanism and the creation of monarchical, bureaucratic states based on the principle of *varna*. This was the result not so much of conquest, but of the slow abandonment of republican ideals by republicans themselves. By the third and fourth centuries CE, states known to be republics in earlier times were subject to hereditary executives. Eventually such republics became monarchies (Altekar, 1958 [1949]: 137–8; Majumdar, 1980: 144). This movement, away from any degree of egalitarianism, was aided by literary champions of hierarchy. Such Brahmanical classics as the *Mahabharata*, the writings of Kautilya and the *Manu-Smrti* are manifestations of this trend (300–200 BCE). Kautilya, who is traditionally identified with the chief minister of the conqueror Chandragupta Maurya (after 300 BCE), is known for his advice to monarchs on the best way to tame or destroy *ganas* through subterfuge. Perhaps a more important part of his achievement was to formulate a political science in which monarchy was normal, even though his own text shows that *ganas* were very important actors in the politics of his time (Kautilya, 1951 [300 BCE]: 410). Similarly, the accomplishment of the *Manu-Smrti* was to formulate a view of society where human equality was non-existent and unthinkable.

Kings and ideologues were not the only enemies of the *ganas*. *Ganas* that claimed sovereignty over certain territories or populations were always faced by the competing claims of other corporate groups (Altekar, 1958 [1949]: 124; compare with the Italian situation presented in Hyde, 1973: 104). How were these problems to be resolved, other than by force? The king had an answer: if he were acknowledged as 'the only monarch [i.e. *raja*, chief executive] of all the corporations', he would commit himself to preserving the legitimate privileges of each of them and protect the lesser members of each *gana* from abuses of power by their leaders (Kautilya, 1951 [300 BCE]: 410). It was a tempting offer, and the result was the acceptance of a social order in which many *ganas* and *sanghas* existed, but none was sovereign and none was committed to any general egalitarian view of society. They were committed instead to a hierarchy in which they were promised a secure place. Such a notional hierarchy seems to have been constructed in north India by the fifth century CE (Majumdar, 1969 [1918]: 42–59). Even the Buddhist *sangha* accommodated itself to it – which may have contributed to its own disappearance from India.

Conclusion

That republicanism eventually came to an end in India and was entirely forgotten might seem to justify a somewhat dismissive attitude towards these ancient democracies. Yet no one casually dismisses Greek democracy, despite its similar failure and despite the fact that there is no continuity between ancient and more modern experiments in democracy. Ancient Athens has influenced modern thinkers and political reforms only through the indirect means of literary inspiration. If the literary material and other sources are less rich for ancient India, they were sufficient, a century ago, to infuse a generation of nationalist scholars with a wider view of the political possibilities available to modern India; while the existence of ancient republics still excites citizens of today's democratic India. Further, the parallel development of republics in Greece and on the subcontinent has interesting implications for our understanding of world history. One cannot help wondering in how

58 *Pre-Athenian Democracy*

many other parts of Eurasia republican, quasi-democratic states may have co-existed alongside the royal dynasties.

Another important feature of the historiography of Indian republicanism is the way it grew out of, and has contributed to, the investigation of grassroots and local institutions, which has revealed the importance of quasi-democratic practices both before and after the heyday of the sovereign republics. It was such a focus that allowed scholars to cut through inappropriate, clichéd characterizations of India (represented at various times by such phrases as 'Oriental despotism', 'hydraulic civilization'). Such a focus is necessary to compensate for the usual overemphasis on monarchs and the texts and monuments that are produced for them, if one is going to get a balanced view of human political development (Muhlberger and Paine, 1993: 25–8). The quasi-democratic institutions of the subcontinent constitute a compelling case to examine more closely the record of other parts of the 'East' such as Egypt and Iran (Cole, 1999; Kurzman, 2008). The significance of India is not that the history of the republics, or the later history of autonomous corporations and guilds in India, means that India is inherently a demo-cratic culture. Nor did the mere existence of ancient democracies in India make the current republic more likely to succeed as a modern democracy than other parts of the world, where quasi-democratic devel-opments cannot be documented in any detail at all. Rather, this material shows, as Jayaswal argued long ago, that no culture can be safely and decisively dismissed as providing sterile soil for democracy now or in the future, simply because it has experienced long periods of aristo-cratic, monarchical, or autocratic rule. A little over a century ago, no one knew about the republican past of India, and only a tiny minority really believed, one suspects, in India's democratic future. Ancient and modern India have since 1900 provided material to show that there is more room in any culture for democratic development than pessimists would allow.

Notes

1. Ghoshal rejects Agrawala's interpretation of the evidence in Panini and Kautilya, and insists on a strict (but anachronistic) division between politi-cal, military, and social and economic groups (Ghoshal, 1966: 195, n. 5). A fair reading of Kautilya shows that 'corporations' of whatever sort could be impor-tant political and military factors, whether they were sovereign or not, and whether they 'lived by the name of raja' or not (Kautilya, 1951 [300 BCE]: 407).
2. There are several works which document relevant European examples (Forrest, 1966: 67–97; Hyde, 1973: 48–60; Mundy, 1954).

3. *Jataka* 301 also mentions 7707 kings, 'all of them given to argument and disputation' (Cowell, 1895 [380 BCE]: III.1). The precision of 7077 is deceptive; it is a commonly-used ideal number. Similarly imprecise if suggestive numbers can be found in *Jataka* 465 (Cowell, 1895 [380 BCE]: IV.94); in the *Mahavastu*, 'twice 84,000 Licchavi rajas residing within the city of Vesali' (Sharma, 1968: 99); and in *Jataka* 547 (Cowell, 1895 [380 BCE]: VI.26) 60,000 *ksatriyas* in the Ceta state, all *rajano* (Agrawala, 1963 [1953]: 432).
4. The 'Pattimokkha' shows how the vote-taker was permitted to prevent the will of the majority from succeeding even in a secret vote, by throwing out the results if the winners' opinion went against the law, or his interpretation of it. In other sections, the emphasis is on reconciling monks to a decision which they were opposed to. Voting is one method of doing so; manipulation of votes preserves the religious law without splitting the *sangha* ('Pattimokkha', 1885 [480 BCE]: IV.14, 25–6).
5. In this sense Majumdar was right in calling the Buddha 'an apostle of democracy' (Majumdar, 1969 [1918]: 219). For an opposing view, see Drekmeier's *Kingship and Community in Early India* (Drekmeier, 1962: 113).

4
Digging for Democracy in China

Pauline Keating

Histories of democracy in China usually begin with the late nineteenth-century reform movement. Non-government reformers, dismayed by China's manifest weakness in the face of Western aggression, embarked on a search for ways to make China wealthy and powerful. They became convinced that Western 'wealth and power' were rooted in democratic political systems: governments based on elected representative institutions seemed able to mobilize all of their citizens behind development goals. By the 1890s we see a concerted push among China's mainstream scholar–activists for political reform along Western lines. Radicals in the 1900s formed a revolutionary party and promised a democratic republic once the Manchu monarchy was removed. Revolution in late 1911 destroyed the monarchy, and the Republic of China was founded in February 1912.

No Chinese government since 1912, neither the Republican governments in the 1912–49 period nor the People's Republic since 1949, have been Western-style democracies. Throughout the twentieth century and up to the present, therefore, successive generations of reformers lamented the failure of democracy in modern China. They typically call for an end to one-party rule, for the establishment of the rule of law, for the convening of national elections and for the replacement of China's rubber-stamp national assemblies with people's congresses that wield real power. The pro-democracy elites have driven what is called a 'Chinese democracy movement'. This movement has occasionally made breakthroughs, and it is now much bigger than it once was. It remains, however, a failed movement. China today is judged, both by Chinese democrats and by foreign observers, to be far from democratic.

In their debates about the kind of democracy China should have, China's twentieth-century democrats typically selected from a range of

Western democratic theories, and they often said that modifications to Western models were needed in order to achieve a better fit with Chinese political traditions, temperaments and behaviours. The sinifications of Western democracy, however, are usually judged by Western analysts to result in a more authoritarian, less liberal type of democracy. Examples of illiberal democrats usually include Liang Qichao (regarded by some as 'China's first democrat'), Sun Yatsen (the 'father of the nation'), and the 'third-way' democrats of the 1930s. A common assumption is that, because China lacks a democratic tradition, any sinification of the Western model must result in something less than 'democracy'.

That kind of narrative is open to challenge. A narrative that begins in the late nineteenth century, focuses on China's failed 'struggles for democracy' and documents compromises, repression and futile strivings is a narrative that bypasses a rich, vibrant history of Chinese democracies, which have deep historical roots and owe nothing to Western models. Such democracies are to be found in ancient Chinese philosophies, which helped to shape both elite and folk political cultures; in education theory and practice in Confucian China, including the 'tradition of remonstrance'; and in the arena of local self-government – both the elitist discourse on the subject and the communitarian institutions premised on self-government. These democracies were invariably immobilized or driven underground by despotism, particularly when despotism was exercised violently. But they survive today as living traditions and are becoming increasingly visible in the spheres of citizen action that constitute an expanding civil society in twenty-first-century China. The aim of this chapter is to dig up some of China's old democracies and to consider their contemporary relevance.

Democracies in Ancient China

China's imperial governments were autocracies that, in H. G. Creel's words, 'misused Confucianism to justify despotism' (Creel, 1960: 4). From the time when Emperor Wu (156–86 BCE) adopted Confucianism as the Han state ideology until the fall of the last Confucian monarchy in 1911, a state-defined Confucian orthodoxy was wielded as a weapon to enforce compliance and subservience (in the name of political order and social harmony) and to concentrate power in the hands of the emperor.

Confucius was born in the mid-500s BCE. Confucian philosophy was the product of the 'one hundred schools of thought' of the Warring States era, an ideological ferment characterized by a search

62   Pre-Athenian Democracy

for 'peace and order in a time of political confusion and change' (Schrecker, 2004: 10). The political changes that occurred roughly from 500 to 200 BCE represent a revolution: the transition from the *fengjian* (feudal) system to the *junxian* system of centralized rule by non-hereditary bureaucrats. Much of Confucianism's richness and profundity derives from its incorporation and subtle blending of ideas, often contending ideas, from the different schools of thought that emerged during the Warring States period. It was also enriched by the contributions of early Confucianists such as Mencius (372–289 BCE) and Xun Zi (300–237 BCE). Like all the world's great systems of thought, Confucianism is read differently by different people. Since the age of Confucius, Chinese critics, dissidents and rebels have used Confucian ideas to justify reform and to legitimate protest; this applies in the twentieth and twenty-first centuries as much as in the imperial period.

The 'mandate of heaven' concept (*tianming*) is probably the most important example of an ancient idea with democratic content and strong contemporary relevance. Historians locate its origin thirty-one centuries ago when, in 1122 BCE, it was used by Zhou rebels to justify their overthrow of the Shang state (Schrecker, 2004: 5). Mencius elaborated the idea eight or nine centuries later and gave it an essentially democratic meaning. From the ancient 'Heaven sees as the people see. Heaven hears as the people hear', Mencius went on to argue: 'The people are the foundation of the country; the country is tranquil only when the foundation is firmly laid' (cited in Chen, 1997: 30). Rulership, therefore, is conditional. In Confucius' view, only a moral man had the right to rule, and governments were to be 'for the people'. Mencius went even further, to suggest 'government by the people' and to claim the 'righteousness' of rebellion when Heaven withdrew the monarch's mandate to rule.[1] He went as far as to say: 'The people are the most important in a country, the spirits of the land and grain (guardians of territory) are next, the sovereign is of slight importance' (cited in Chen, 1997: 30).

Joseph Levenson warned against reading too much democracy into the idea of a heavenly mandate. The Son of Heaven (*tianzi*) held the heavenly mandate (*tianming*) as long as he enacted heaven's will (*tianyi*).

> Heaven's son, mandate and will were unequivocally the classical fount of supremacy, and the people's will...was purely symbolic,

not effective, in establishing legitimacy. Heaven's hand could not be forced.

(Levenson, 1968: 12)

Jerome Grieder expands Levenson's point, arguing that the rise of the Confucian ruler was a moral imperative before it was a social choice because the position arose from something more than a contract with the people (Grieder, 1981). Levenson and Grieder make here true readings of Confucian *orthodoxy*; but we need to remember that a Mencian populism was never far below the surface of mainstream Confucianism – a populism that was expressed strongly in counter-cultural traditions, which legitimized rebellions. Chinese history is full of popular rebellions, and a few of them did topple dynasties. Throughout China's imperial and post-imperial history, governments have needed to demonstrate a concern for the people's welfare in order to justify their claims to heaven's mandate.

Datong, variously translated as 'great unity', 'one world' or 'great harmony', is another ancient idea that has been repeatedly revived and revised during at least three millennia of Chinese history. By no means exclusive to Confucianism,[2] this idea was most fully elaborated in the Book of Rites, compiled in the Han dynasty. For Confucius, *datong* was the golden age of antiquity, the good society characterized by egalitarianism and a cooperative communitarianism. Schrecker is particularly interested in the way in which, in the hands of subsequent Confucian writers, *datong* came to represent 'a good society uniting the strengths of *fengjian* and *junxian*, a society that joined the security and spirituality of the former with the justice and humanism of the latter' (Schrecker, 2004: 25–6). This good society was largely a *democratic* one; it was characterized by 'economic levelling, access for all to education and culture, and responsibility to all for the governance and welfare of society' (Schrecker, 2004: 26). Mencius' famous 'well-field' or 'equal-field' system points up the good society's economic democracy.[3] The sage's instructions were that, in every nine equal plots of land, one was to be reserved as communal property and farmed cooperatively. Reformers (including the reforming emperors) and revolutionaries alike have, at various times through the centuries, revived the well-field system in order to make land ownership more equitable and to promote mutual aid.

Confucianists developed a habit of pointing to the golden *datong* age of the past in order to expose social decay and moral decline in the present. This is said to have cultivated a pessimistic conservatism among the elites, a pessimism that left them rooted in the past,

64 *Pre-Athenian Democracy*

blinded them to historical progress and discouraged entrepreneurial risk-taking. That kind of argument, however, apart from obscuring innovation and development in Chinese history, ignores the way in which the *datong* ideal has inspired both popular rebels and elite reformers through millennia in China. The 'heavenly kingdom of great peace' (*taiping tianguo*) promised by the anti-Confucian Taiping rebels in the 1850s was based, in large part, on Confucianism's *datong* (Ono, 1989: 5; Schrecker, 2004: 124). Kang Youwei's utopian *Da Tong Shu* (*The Book of Great Harmony*), completed in 1902, is a striking example of the modern application of the *datong* ideal through visionary reform (Kang, 1956). So too is the use made of it by neo-Confucian Liang Shuming in his rural reconstruction project of the 1930s (Alitto, 1979; Ip, 1991: 479; Schrecker, 2004: 185).

Education and democracy

The centrality of education and scholarship in pre-modern China is rooted in Confucius' belief in the essential goodness of human nature; another root is the idea that education (self-cultivation) is both the route to human perfection and the means by which humane government will be realized. The Confucian conviction, says Grieder, 'is that the state is a moral community, that government is a moral enterprise' (Grieder, 1981: 10, 24). A moral ruler required virtuous – that is, educated – people to advise him. A critical development during the *fengjian-junxian* transition, therefore, was the gradual replacement of a hereditary aristocracy with an officialdom selected on the basis of educational achievement.

European visitors to China in the seventeenth and eighteenth centuries admired the civil service examination system as a 'meritocracy'. Their translations of Confucian texts and letters home stimulated a close study of Chinese government and Confucian philosophy by European Enlightenment scholars, including, most famously, Liebnitz and Voltaire.[4] Reflecting on the significance of the cult of China in eighteenth-century Europe, Creel goes as far as to suggest the following:

> The philosophy of Confucius played a role of some importance in the development of democratic ideas in Europe and in the background of the French revolution. Through French thought, it indirectly influenced the development of democracy in America.
>
> (Creel, 1960: 5)

Voltaire and Liebnitz tended to look for what they wanted to find in China, and their big claims about the Confucian system were soon challenged both by their philosopher colleagues and by navy men who had fallen foul of Chinese bureaucrats in Canton (Spence, 1999: 120–1, 133–4). China's examination system was certainly a remarkable institution, but it was always flawed, and it became more cumbersome and decrepit as it aged. It never produced the good society imagined by Confucians – a society in which all men are educated, and therefore wise and morally upright. At any time in the system's 1,300-year history, the 'cultivated talents' which graduated were never more than a tiny proportion of China's population.[5] Even so, aspects of China's civil service bureaucracy, manned by examination graduates, did merit some of the praise lavished on it by the Europeans who observed it.

Roger Des Forges lists features of the examination system that he judges to be 'democratic'. He notes the efforts made to guarantee fairness – the regulations against contact between examiners and students, for example. He also notes the distribution of degrees according to regional quotas, so that all areas of the country were represented within the bureaucracy. The sale of degrees, usually deplored as a corrupt practice, opened some positions to those with little formal education but practical capabilities. In Des Forges view, even the much maligned *baguwen* (eight-legged essay) improved the quality of democracy by allowing enthusiastic, if less well educated students to succeed in the examinations, so that they could participate in governing the country.[6] The system also had inbuilt mechanisms for checking nepotism and abuses of power; the 'law of avoidance', for example, prevented officials from serving in their home provinces, and the regular rotation of office-bearers prevented imperial officials from becoming 'local lords' (Des Forges, 1993: 28–9).

Arguably more important than any of the features that Des Forges identifies, however, is the Confucian 'tradition of remonstrance'. The civil service examination system produced scholar–officials (*shi*). These highly educated men governed society on behalf of the emperor and mediated between state and society. The scholar–official was meant to be the voice of the people and to ensure that the emperor's rulership was *for* the people; this required that he alert the emperor to the failures of his government to 'nurture the people' (*yangmin*), and even to criticize the emperor himself. Confucius' basic reason for wanting intellectual elites to man the corridors of power was that these could act towards restraining imperial despotism – or so he thought. Criticism of despotism, therefore, was not only sanctioned by Confucius; it was required.

66 *Pre-Athenian Democracy*

Merle Goldman puts it well: 'Confucianism did not legally guarantee a loyal opposition, but it justified one ideologically. To criticize government misdeeds was not the literati's right, as in the West, but their responsibility' (Goldman, 1981: 3).

The tradition of remonstrance was well established as early as the Han Dynasty (205 BCE–CE 220), and the duty of the scholars to 'act as moral judges of their sovereigns' was strongly reiterated by Neo-Confucianists from the Song period (960–1279) onwards (de Bary, 1983: 57). Frederic Wakeman, in his study of intellectual politics in the late imperial period, offers a typology of five 'intellectual species' (Wakeman, 1972: 35). He puts the mainstream and generally dutiful civil statesman at one end of his spectrum, and the aesthete and the hermit (dropouts) at the other end. Between those three categories are the 'statecraft' practitioners, who 'established a tradition of intellectual engagement in governance', and the 'literatus whose unbending moral integrity and idealism came the closest to intellectual dissent' (Wakeman, 1972: 35). The latter expressed a form of 'moral opposition to state authority ... that had deep roots in the Confucian canon' – an opposition that became a 'habitual commitment' in the Song dynasty and was most often a stand taken by scholars outside the bureaucracy or by retired civil servants (Wakeman, 1972: 35).

Wakeman examined the Ming state's attempts to control 'a great surge of education' in the mid-sixteenth century. The surge was the consequence, and then the renewed cause, of a significant rise in literacy levels, intensified competition for official posts and rapid growth of private academies, many based in urban centres. Unemployed scholars gravitated towards the academies, where, not surprisingly, critiques of the examination system and of its curriculum began to flourish. Government concern about the 'boastfulness' of 'private scholars' and about the way in which the academies 'summoned local ne'er-do-wells to chat emptily and neglect their occupations' led to the closure of academies by imperial edict in 1575 (Wakeman, 1972: 44–5). The ban was soon lifted, and the newly opened academies became actively engaged in high-level politics, much more than their predecessors were.

Scholars associated with the Donglin Academy, founded in 1604, launched passionate attacks on corrupt officials and self-consciously assumed the role of 'superior men' (*junzi*), which was 'to do good, and do away with evil' (Gu Xuancheng, cited in Wakeman, 1972: 45). As J. K. Fairbank has noted, the Donglin men gave little attention to the practical problems of government: it was 'a preoccupation with morality that lent animus to their attacks on officials high and low' (in

Fairbank and Goldman, 2006: 141). A campaign of terror from 1624 to 1627 closed down the Academy, effectively ending the Donglin reform movement. But the vicious persecution of the Donglin scholars also severely damaged the prestige of the Ming state; it was overthrown by a peasant rebellion and by a Manchu invasion in 1644 (Spence, 1999: 18).

The Donglin academicians are striking examples of 'loyal critics' in the Confucian tradition. So too are the 'Ming loyalists' of the early Qing dynasty, men who had earned their examination degrees under the Ming and found it impossible to give their loyalty to the new Qing government after 1644. The fact that the new rulers were not Han Chinese but 'barbarian' Manchus probably explains the vehemence and sharpness of the dissidents' attacks on despotism, on the evils of the imperial bureaucracy and on what they judged to be the 'empty talk' characterizing contemporary Confucian scholarship – especially the metaphysics and abstractions deriving from the ideas of Ming scholar Wang Yangming (1472–1529). More stridently than most 'orthodox critics', the early Qing critics called for political decentralization and constraints on imperial power, for far-reaching local government reforms and for a return to original Confucianism, to be achieved by stripping the layers of misinterpretation that had accumulated over the centuries around the classics (Grieder, 1981: 38).

As critics of despotism and advocates of a return to a 'pure' Confucianism, the seventeenth-century dissidents draw attention to the democratic content of 'onte Confucianism'. Historians, however, are want to point out that a 'pure' Confucian philosophy did not ever, in the imperial period, serve as a blueprint for government. From the 200s BCE onwards, it was Legalism (another of the '100 Schools' of the Warring States period) that actually underpinned the administrative structure of China's imperial states. There is no democracy in Legalism; neither the Legalists' laws nor their dynastic laws (designed to serve a dynasty) were in any way consensual or contractual. For such historians, it is pointless to look for democracy in 'Confucian China', because Confucian governments were, in fact, Legalist governments.

W. Theodore de Bary disagrees, however. In his insightful analysis of Confucian and Legalist attitudes to law, and of the Neo-Confucian critiques of dynastic law, he challenges the representation of Confucian government as 'Legalist'. He notes that, after the fall of the totalitarian Qin dynasty (221–205 BCE), there was a 'rejection of Legalist totalitarianism, its punitive deterrent methods, and its assertion of state power for its own sake' (de Bary, 1998: 94). Although the Legalist apparatus for

68 *Pre-Athenian Democracy*

central administration was retained, the Han and later dynasties were willing to allow 'a looser, more autonomous customary practice on the local level, where the Confucian ethos was generally thought to pre-vail'. So the rural localities, in de Bary's argument, remained a realm of 'Confucian communitarianism' throughout the imperial period (de Bary, 1998: 94). Furthermore, Neo-Confucianists from the Song period onwards issued significant challenges to the 'laws and systems of the dynastic states' and reasserted a Confucian insistence on the priority of 'self-cultivation (or self-discipline) for the governance of men' (de Bary, 1998: 100). Of particular relevance to the topic under discussion is the 'constitutional program' proposed by early-Qing dissident Huang Zongxi (1610–95) in his 1662 work *Mingyi daifang lu*.[7]

Huang described dynastic laws as 'unlawful' because they served the private interests of the imperial family rather than the interests of the people (de Bary, 1998: 100). Because history had proven that it was futile to depend on the ruler's capacity for 'self-restraint', the ruler himself had to be constrained by law. Huang wrote in 1662:

> In ancient times all-under-Heaven were considered the master, and the prince was the tenant. Now the prince is master, and all-under-heaven are tenants. That no one can find peace and happiness anywhere is all on account of the prince... Now men hate their prince, look on him as their 'mortal foe', call him 'just another guy'.
> (Huang, cited in de Bary, 1993: 92)

As well as putting legal constraints on the monarch, Huang augmented the role of the scholar-officials (*shi*), calling for an expansion of both their number and function and for the reestablishment of the prime-ministership (disestablished in the late fourteenth century). Huang, however, did not have the Neo-Confucians' trust in the heroism and commitment of the *junzi*; there was need for, in de Bary's words, 'a supporting infrastructure such as that later identified by Montesquieu in *L'Ésprit des Lois* (1784) with the "corps intermediaries" between state and society at large' (de Bary, 1998: 101). In de Bary's argument, Huang's plan is Confucian because it depends 'on the personal vocation of the Noble Man [*junzi*] and the esprit de corps of the *shi*', but is 'nonetheless a constitution in the systemic sense insofar as Huang will no longer rely on the good intentions and exemplary character of the ruler, but insists on institutional limits to the exercise of the ruler's power' (de Bary, 1998: 104–5).

Historians who search for the seeds of a modern democracy movement in late Imperial China tend to lament the unwillingness of intellectual reformers and critics to be more *disloyal* than the tradition of 'loyal criticism' allowed. Even the more radical dissidents remained attached to the idea of a 'sage–king' with authoritarian prerogatives, and at no point did they come close to building organized movements for political change by establishing networks of reform societies, much less political parties. As Wakeman shows, the academies established in the late Ming period were, in important respects, politically autonomous. But the Donglin Academy, which, at first glance, looks like a political party in the making, explicitly restricted membership to a 'coterie of superior men', because, says Wakeman, 'virtue, not issues, was at stake' (Wakeman, 1972: 52). In his judgement, a 'reforming mission' that depended on 'so small and so particular an association...was bound to be politically impotent' (Wakeman, 1972: 52).

The same judgement is made of the early Qing dissidents. Grieder allows that scholars such as Gu Yanwu and Huang Zongxi expressed a 'liberality of spirit'. Nevertheless, they did not, he says, 'extend beyond this to encompass in any sense a formal liberalism, no matter how rudimentary...Rousseau would have remained entirely an enigma to these Confucian thinkers' (Grieder, 1981: 46). Gu and Huang may well have 'prepared men's minds to consider the monarchy and ideology as divisible entities', but they did not question 'the adequacy of imperial government as a political enterprise' (such questioning did not begin until the late nineteenth century). Because of this, and because they remained politically disengaged, their political criticism 'existed in a vacuum, unrelated to any movement for political reform, much less revolutionary change' (Grieder, 1981: 47).

That judgement needs qualification, however. Any assessment of the means and modes of political opposition in imperial China must take account of the brutal efficiency with which imperial states, and the Ming and Qing states in particular, stamped on anything that looked even slightly like organized opposition among the elites. As Frederick Mote points out, 'the concept of "party" (*dang*) had been resoundingly rejected by the throne in the eleventh century. Rulers then and thereafter always distrusted associations of officials pressing for their group goals' (Mote, 1999: 737). Any 'horizontal peer-group collaborations' were assumed to be motivated by personal profit and influence (Elman, 1989: 390),[8] a prejudice that the Donglin movement had to confront and that it really failed to surmount. The new Qing government made a particular point of strictly monitoring the existing

70 Pre-Athenian Democracy

academies and, in 1652, banned the establishment of new private ones. The ban was lifted in 1733, but by then both old and new academies were firmly under state control. As Elman points out, 'the imperial government's large-scale intervention in academics after 1644 aimed to depoliticize Chinese literati and mobilize them in support of Manchu rule', and it was largely successful in achieving its aim (Elman, 1989: 403).

Not until the mid-nineteenth century, when the dynasty was losing its grip, do we see the re-emergence of semi-independent associations of scholars, especially in the Jiangnan area, where reconstruction after the Taiping rebellion was particularly urgent and where scholar-class resistance to the Manchus in the seventeenth century had been particularly strong. A more radical development occurred in the 1890s. In reaction to China's defeat by Japan in 1894, a group of literati outside government formed a 'study society' (*shehui*) with a political agenda – the 'study of national strength'. It was quickly shut down, and the government reinforced its strict ban on independent societies and 'parties' (*dang*). Increasingly, however, the government was incapable of suppressing the new organizations, and in the last decade of Manchu rule we see a burgeoning of study societies that were, as Philip Kuhn notes, 'window-dressing for dissent movements' (Kuhn, 2008: 2).

A conclusion we can draw from the Chinese states' attitude to independent organizations of literati, from their determined stymieing and suppression of any and all clubs or societies that concerned themselves with politics, is that even small groupings of reform-minded scholars had the potential to form a strong, or at least a troublesome opposition to authoritarian and hegemonizing states. Given the ferocity of state suppressions, elite-class dissidents invariably cloaked their dissent in the language of Confucian orthodoxy. The small minority which tried to organize itself politically devised a range of strategies to disguise the political aims of its associations. As we have seen, the Confucian academies and study societies that were fronts for political activity tended to gain traction only in periods of dynastic decline, when the state was too weak to obliterate them. Strong Chinese states have effectively stamped on all opposition groups. Violence has always been democracy's greatest enemy (see Keane, 2004: 1).

Local self-government

Prasenjit Duara points to the way in which the narrative of the European Enlightenment and 'the indigenous narrative of Chinese feudalism (*fengjian*)' briefly came together in the late nineteenth century in the writings of reform nationalists (Duara, 1995: 152). Chinese scholars at century's end were absorbing and debating a significant range of European political theories. Interest in the *fengjian* system had resurfaced earlier, in the 1860s. This time saw the return of age-old debates about reducing the role of the central state in the localities and about developing grassroots 'self-government' (*zizhu*) capabilities, so that a significant degree of societal autonomy could pertain at grassroots level. By the 1890s, reformers such as Liang Qichao and Huang Zunxian were working at combining ancient principles of *fengjian* with Western law (Duara, 1995: 155), very much like what Huang Zongxi had been doing back in 1662 (but without any reference then to Western systems).

As noted earlier, de Bary insists that imperial states, after the brutal but brief Qin reign, were more willing to leave the localities to their own devices. Nevertheless, Confucian governments believed that they were obliged to 'nurture the people' both materially and spiritually. Because, for most of imperial history, the community schools below the county level were privately run, not state-sponsored, the state needed to devise other ways of moulding the people's minds. De Bary gives close attention to the role played by the 'community compact' (*xiangyue*), a 'local, autonomous community-aid collective' that, as well as serving the state's goal of moral indoctrination and uplift, was promoted by reformers for achieving communitarian outcomes such as 'mutuality, reciprocity and cooperation among community members'. In other words, reformers sought to counter the state's imposition of 'superior power or punitive law' and to achieve, instead, a 'well-ordered, self-sustaining, and relative autonomous local community' (Alitto, 1979: 206; de Bary, 1998: 59, 63).

From the time of the Song dynasty, when Lü Dazhun and afterwards Zhu Xi revived the *xiangyue* idea and infused it with communitarian ideals, the community compact has been periodically resurrected by local government reformers committed to a restoration of some *fengjian* institutions. As hard as reformers pushed their communitarian goals, the imperial state strove even harder to co-opt the *xiangyue* for statist purposes. *Xiangyue*, claims de Bary, has a very 'checkered and conflicted history ... that illustrates better than does any other local institution the persistent tension between Neo-Confucian communitarian ideas and Chinese imperial rule' (de Bary, 1998: 58).

Reformers of the last decade of the nineteenth century resuscitated the old communitarian tradition of local self-government and attempted to build it into their vision of a new China, ruled constitutionally by a

72 Pre-Athenian Democracy

strong state that left space for self-sustaining and relatively autonomous local communities. By the end of the 1890s, there were two movements: the local self-government movement, which aimed to build a democratic China from the bottom up and was largely rooted in China's own democratic traditions, and a top-down constitutional movement, which pressed for a constitutional monarchy and drew heavily on foreign models of constitutionalism. By the early 1900s the Manchu government was willing to take notice of both movements.

After a constitutional study mission submitted its report in 1906, the imperial court announced a nine-year programme that would have resulted in elections for a national parliament in 1915. Elite-class impatience with what was judged to be Manchu foot-dragging and dissembling in relation to constitutional reform was one of the triggers of the 1911 revolution.

The Manchu government's interest in a reform of local (sub-county) government was driven by its need to get access to local resources and mobilize local energies behind modernization projects. Its goals were purely statist, and had nothing to do with grassroots democracy. Some provincial officials, however, experimented with local self-government reform strategies that had at least some *fengjian* characteristics. Most well-known is Governor Zhao Erxun's 1902 experiment in Shanxi province. He overhauled community associations, known locally as *xiangshe*, so that they were purged of corrupt officials and more closely expressed the communitarianism of the Neo-Confucian self-government ideal. This required planning based on careful investigation of local conditions, keeping *xiangshe* membership small (no more than ten villages, ideally) and appointing leaders who were respected locals; each *xiangshe* leader was to be selected by the county magistrate from a list of nominees drawn up by people who owned about two acres or more of land (Thompson, 1988: 194).

Zhao Erxun's Shanxi experiment attracted some high-level interest in Beijing and in the provincial centres. But Zhao was transferred to the governorship of Hunan in 1903, and his reform model was relegated to the dustbin in 1909, when new local self-government regulations were formally announced; the state-sanctioned programme made no pretence of reaching down to the villages or effecting a balance of power between the county magistrate and grassroots leaders (Thompson, 1988: 211). The collapse of the monarchy in 1911 made no difference. The republican governments of the 1912–49 period were as intent on state-strengthening as the late Qing state had been. Only the non-government rural reconstruction experiments of the 1930s attempted to enact local government reforms premised on local empowerment, community rehabilitation and cooperativism. The outstanding example in this respect is Liang Shuming's experiment based in Shandong province's Zouping county. Liang found in the Song dynasty's community compact an institution that, he judged, 'Westerners were incapable of even imagining' (Alitto, 1979: 206). With its central focus on morality, it was to be an organization 'aimed at making [*junzi*] of the masses'. More than that, it was to be a ' "positive, activist" organization of enthusiastic mass participation' that would ' "build up the power of the peasantry", so essential to the rest of Liang's program' (Alitto, 1979: 207).

Conclusion: The role of old democracies in 'new China'

This chapter has pointed out traditions of democracy that, with a bit of digging, can be found in ancient and imperial China; they are discernible both in orthodox Confucianism and in the counter-cultures that frequently challenged imperial orthodoxy. Can these traditions be renovated and gain traction in twenty-first-century China? The Beijing government continues to keep firm clamps on Chinese democrats who champion Western-style democracy and human rights, but we can anticipate better chances for a democratization rooted in indigenous traditions. Two examples are instructive here, namely the post-Mao village self-government movement and the environmental movement. Both hold the promise of a renegotiated state–society relationship that resonates with traditional ideals and tensions and in which at least some power has shifted to the people.

   A prerequisite for any renegotiated relationship is that Chinese society recovers the ground it lost over the last two centuries. The processes of societal breakdown and state-strengthening that began in the nineteenth century and accelerated in the Maoist era significantly reduced the Chinese people's ability to organize itself and function autonomously. Sylvia Chan observed in 1998: 'Chinese society is [now] so penetrated by the state and so fragmented that it is not a united force *vis-à-vis* the state' (Chan, 1998: 250). There are good grounds, however, for anticipating a societal recovery in the twenty-first century. Since the early 1980s, the post-Mao state has been calling on society to take responsibility for public services that it judges can be safely left in the hands of local people. The partial 'retreat' of the state from local spheres has made room for the formation of new grassroots solidarities, and this gives some Chinese democrats cause to hope that a

74 *Pre-Athenian Democracy*

strengthening of society *vis-à-vis* the state is in train. Many pin their hopes on the village self-government project that took off in the 1980s. In some significant respects, this project can be represented as a revival of Confucian China's local self-government tradition, based on some *fengjian* ideals.

The contemporary programme, for example, has made considerable use of the *xiangyue*. Often referred to now as 'village constitutions', the *xiangyue* are, says Allen Choate, 'the result of prolonged discussions in village meetings, often taking more than a year to achieve consensus' (Choate, 1997: 12). They list the villagers' duties and obligations, but also their rights. Choate concedes that 'duties' probably have precedence over 'rights'. He believes, however, that, where they did exist in the mid-1990s, the charters reflected 'community values and a collective approach to democratic practices' (Choate, 1997: 12). And even among sceptical observers who find no evidence of democratic aspirations among the policy-makers who authorised the programme, there are some who hope that village self-government might end up being a 'Trojan horse' of democracy (Schubert, 2002). Wang Xu, in his 2003 study, suggests that democratization is going on behind the government's back. As well as 'seeping' upwards, the democratic system being built in the grassroots villages will, he hopes, end up lending more legitimacy to the central government, thus 'empowering it' (Wang, 2003).

These insights can be usefully applied to our second example, China's contemporary environment movement. The first organized action for environmental repair and protection began in the private sector in the mid-1990s. Like its Confucian predecessors, the Chinese Communist Party state regarded the non-government organizations (NGOs) with deep suspicion and, in 1998, took measures to limit both their growth and their autonomy. Increasingly, however, the Beijing government is facing up the need for both assertive state-led initiatives and concerted social action to address an environmental crisis that is threatening economic growth. In this context, a dramatic change is occurring. Despite the regulations that constrain them, the number of environmental NGOs has grown substantially since 1994. There is now a striking degree of cooperation between the green groups and governments at all levels. Guobin Yang finds here the growth of a state–society partnership that the modern democracy movement, with its strategies of confrontation and conflict, has never been able to achieve. Because the green movement focuses heavily on popular education, and because it emphasizes cooperation, participation and dialogue with authorities, it is seen to be cooperating with the party state in building a 'harmonious society'. Because it is meeting an urgent need, the green movement is being given the space and license to develop a sturdy organizational base, something that democracy activists in the past century have failed to gain (Yang, 2005: 7).

The societal mobilization we are seeing in twenty-first-century China is shaping a state–society partnership in which the state does not completely dominate, but provides the space and support that village self-government and green organizations need in a country where developers have become 'laws unto themselves'. This partnership can be regarded as a developing democracy, a democracy that draws sustenance from a repertoire of cultural values, political behaviours and social ideals to be found in China's own democratic history.

Notes

1. The injunction 'it is right to rebel' (*zaofan youli*) is often attributed to Mencius but is, in fact, Mao Zedong's idea. Nevertheless, Elizabeth Perry points out, 'two affinities between Mencius and Mao: the importance of popular – in particular *peasant – support* in establishing political legitimacy and the natural propensity of those who are hard-pressed economically to rebel against rapacious officials' (Perry, 2008: 40).
2. *Datong* is, of course, central to Daoism. It also features strongly in Mohism, especially in the Mohist advocacy of 'universal love' (Des Forges, 1993: 24).
3. The Chinese character for 'well' (*jing*) depicts nine equal squares. Mencius asked that the middle square be reserved as communal land.
4. Other enlightenment scholars who wrote about China include Montaigne, Malebrancht, Bayle, Wolf, Montesquieu, Diderot, Helvetius, Quesnay and Adam Smith (Clark, 1997: 42).
5. In the mid-eighteenth century, degree-holders constituted about 1.1 million in a population of about 180 million (Hsü, 1975: 109). When literati without degrees and literate commoners are added, the proportion of 'educated' people might have reached between 5 and 10 per cent of the population in the eighteenth century.
6. Introduced in the Ming dynasty, the *baguwen* was divided into eight sections ('legs'). Its critics have always deplored the essay's emphasis on form over content.
7. de Bary translates the title as 'Waiting for the dawn: A plan for the prince' (de Bary, 1993).
8. This is because, as Elman explains, the 'classical ideal was one of impartiality, whereby government officials followed prescribed avenues of loyal behavior based on hierarchical ties between ruler and subject' (Elman, 1989: 390).

Part II
Democracy in the 'Dark Ages'

5
Behind a Veil: Islam's Democratic History

Mohamad Abdalla and Halim Rane

For all the impressive contributions Islamic civilisation has made to humanity, particularly in terms of science and knowledge, democracy is almost never associated with Islam. From the Western perspective, at the heart of the alleged divergence between Islam and the West is a predominant view that Islam is antithetical to democracy. This has been promulgated by the writings of a whole collection of scholars who portray Islam as a radical and fundamentally undemocratic movement, which poses a threat to the future of Western civilization. Judith Miller, for instance, writes that, 'despite their rhetorical commitment to democracy and pluralism, virtually all militant Islamists oppose both' (Miller, 1993: 45). Similarly, Martin Kramer offers that Muslim appeals to democratic principles 'bear no resemblance to the ideals of Europe's democracy movements' (Kramer, 1993: 40). For his part, Bernard Lewis gives a more nuanced account, stating that there are prospects for the compatibility of Islam and democracy due to Islam's proximity to the Judeo-Christian and Greco-Roman heritage, but that, as Islam manifests itself politically, it 'seems to offer the worst prospects for liberal democracy' (Lewis, 1993: 89). For Lewis, as for many other Western scholars of the region, there has always been an absence of democracy in the Muslim world, and Islam is responsible. He writes that democracy is 'a product of the West – shaped by a thousand years of European history, and beyond that by Europe's double heritage: Judeo-Christian religion and ethics; Greco-Roman statecraft and law. No such system originated in any other cultural tradition' (Lewis, 1993: 93–4). Put bluntly by Lewis, 'the history of Islamic states is one of almost unrelieved autocracy' (Lewis, 1993: 94).

The writings of these scholars of Middle Eastern history and political Islam only explain part of the story of why Western knowledge of

80 *Democracy in the 'Dark Ages'*

the history of democracy is almost exclusively devoid of reference to Islam. Indeed, a review of the major works on the history of democracy reveals that Islam is rarely considered, and the Middle East all but ignored. For example, John Dunn's edited volume *Democracy: The Unfinished Journey, 508* BCE *to* CE *1993* and his later book, *Democracy: A History*, both contain not so much as a single reference to Islam's democratic past (Dunn, 2006, 1992). This legacy of ignoring Islam and the Middle East altogether can be found in recent works which have examined the global spread of democracy. For example, works such as the four-volume *Democracy in Developing Countries* include studies on Latin American, Asian and African democracies, but eschew the Islamic world and certainly all of the Arab states, on the premise that they 'generally lack much previous democratic experience, and most appear to have little prospect of transition even to semi-democracy' (Diamond et al., 1989: xx). Indeed, one of only a handful of scholarly works on the history of democracy to acknowledge the contribution made by Islam is Harold Rogers' *The History of Democracy from the Middle East to Western Civilisation*, which contains a chapter on democracy in Muslim countries but makes little reference to the deep historical roots of Islamic democracy (Rogers, 2007). Such roots are acknowledged in John Keane's rich engagement with the democratic legacy of Islam, in which he pays homage 'to the vital contributions of Islam to enlivening, and geographically expanding, the old principle that human beings are capable of gathering in assemblies and governing themselves as equals' (Keane, 2009: 128).

While it is true that not every aspect of 'Western democracy' is consistent with Islam, there are fundamental principles of what may constitute good governance that are shared by both. As Richard Bulliet points out:

> Some of the people who say that democracy has no place in Islam, what they really express is a sense that the word 'democracy' as presented in international discourse appears to be wholly owned by the West . . . The word itself has, for some, a connotation of cultural imperialism. If you talk about representative government without the baggage of these institutions in the US, but on more idealistic grounds, then it makes perfectly good sense to a lot of Muslims. The idea of citizenry participating in government is, particularly within Sunni Islam, sort of a bedrock theory.
>
> (Bulliet, cited in Handwerk, 2003)

Building on this sentiment, earlier work by the authors of the present chapter has effectively argued that the higher objectives (*maqasid*) of Sharia law are certainly consistent with those of democracy (Abdalla and Rane, 2009). This chapter provides greatly needed textual and historical evidence to support this claim and some of the underlying principles of democracy as found in Islam. It begins by noting that in the seventh century, while Europe was experiencing its 'Dark Ages', Arabia had been liberated from tribalism by Islam, which asserted a new social and political order, based on social justice, equality and the rule of law, as well as on a range of other principles that served to form the basis for some of the first democratic systems of governance in the region. Using specific examples from the era of the Prophet Muhammad's[1] rule (622–32), from that of his companions and immediate successors, the Rashidun period (632–61) and from the succeeding Umayyad dynasty (661–750), this chapter will document how Islamic principles were utilized in the governance of the *ummah* (Islamic community). Drawing on the core principles of the Quran and the prophetic model, including *shura* (consultation), *ijma* (consensus), *bay'ah* (electoral endorsement) and *ijtihad* (independent reasoning), the early days of Islam brought with them societies modelled on the principles of equality, freedom of expression and political participation and form the basis of an Islamic democracy.

Equality

One of the fundamental principles of democracy that is articulated within Islamic doctrine is that of equality, which has manifested itself historically in four main dimensions (Kamali, 2002). First, there is legal equality, by which all human beings are afforded basic rights and protections, including their life and property, irrespective of race, colour or religion. Second, there is a judicial equality, which grants all human beings access to courts for a fair hearing and treatment, again regardless of race, colour or religion. Third, there is equality in terms of opportunity; and, fourth, there is equality in the domain of religious rights and obligations. These principles of equality are deeply ingrained in the practices of Islam, which has no priestly class or hierarchy of the clergy. Islam also requires all of its followers – men and women equally – to perform religious duties such as the five times daily prayers (*salat*), fasting during the month of Ramadan (*sawm*), payment of the welfare tax (*zakat*) and performing the pilgrimage to Mecca (*hajj*).

82 Democracy in the 'Dark Ages'

These principles are also embedded into the doctrine of Islam, where the Quran recognizes equality and condemns discrimination and prejudices based on tribalism, racism and religion (Quran, 49.13). It clearly states that there is no compulsion in religion and that all children of Adam are honourable, regardless of faith, colour, gender or race (Quran, 2.256, 17.70). The same can be found in Islam's second source of legislation, the Hadith, where maxims of the Prophet Muhammad underpin principles of equality, as does for instance the statement: 'All people are the children of Adam, and Adam was from dust' (Hadith 4900, cited in Barabankawi, 1997: 383). The practical example of Prophet Muhammad established a precedent for equality in Muslim society, making it normative within the Islamic tradition. Among other practices that created an environment of equality was his physical participation in battles and the manual work he did with common people, digging a trench during the battle of al-Khandaq and helping in the construction of the first mosque. Commenting on the personal involvement of the Prophet, one of the most prolific contemporary Arab Muslim scholars, Sa'id Ramadan al-Buti, says:

> The scene in which the Messenger of God is at work with his companions digging the trench contains a lesson of major importance for us, in that it points clearly to the equality which is established by Islamic society among all of its members ... The Islamic law grants no special privileges to any class or group of people, nor does it single out this or that group by giving it immunity [from the consequences of the law] for any cause whatsoever, since the quality of being a servant of the One Creator does away with all such distinctions.
>
> (Al-Buti, 2001: 434–5)

The practice of equality was also extended to people from humble, disadvantaged and even enslaved classes, many of whom rose to prominent positions within the Islamic state. Such examples include a former Abyssinian slave named Bilal, who became a close companion of the Prophet Muhammad and was appointed the first caller to prayer or *mu'adthin* of the Prophet's mosque in Medina. There was also Salman Al-Farisi ('the Persian'), a slave of non-Arab origin who was loved by the Prophet so much that the latter declared him a member of his noble household. Salman's opinion was highly regarded by the Prophet, and his military and strategic advice greatly helped the Arabs. Another slave who rose to prominence was Suhaib Ar-Rumi ('the Byzantine'). The authoritative classical exegete of the Quran, Ibn Kathir, states that a special verse (Quran, 2:207) was revealed in Suhaib's praise: 'And there is a type of man who gives his life to earn the pleasure of God. And God is full of kindness to His servants' (Kathir, 2000: 580).

It is also true that non-Muslims, particularly the Jews of Medina, the Christians of Najran and the Zoroastrians of Hajar, became citizens of the Islamic state without having to change their own beliefs. This prophetic model set a standard for equitable relations with non-Muslim subjects. At the official level, and to institutionalize practices of equality, in 622 the Prophet drafted the Constitution of Medina, a formal agreement with all of the significant tribes and families of Medina, including Muslims, Jews, Christians and pagans (Al-Buti, 2001: 300–2). The constitution guaranteed the civil and religious rights of these minority communities and allowed them equal participation in the daily affairs of the state. This constitution is an important historical precedent of two theoretical premises that have influenced contemporary political theory: the ideas of a social contract and of a constitution. Equally important, it established the value of consent and cooperation for governance.

The caliphs continued the prophetic example of equality. In the year 637, Umar bin Al-Khatab (634–44), the second Rashidun Caliph and close companion of the Prophet, conducted a peace treaty with the Christian Patriarch of Jerusalem, which stated:

> Their churches are not to be taken, nor are they to be destroyed, nor are they to be degraded or belittled, neither are their crosses or their money, and they are not to be forced to change their religion, nor is any one of them to be harmed.
>
> (Arnold, 2001: 55)

Principles of equality enriched policies and continued to be practised under subsequent Muslim leaders. There are examples of Islamic states that were 'home to non-Muslims who participated in government and public life, sometimes in important positions'; a figure of this sort was the Jewish politician–poet–philosopher known in Hebrew as 'Samuel the Prince', who became vizier in medieval Granada (Feldman, 2003: 67). Throughout Islamic history 'Christians continued to hold high offices in the administration' (Houtsma et al., 1993: 849). For example Mu'awiya (602–80), the first Umayyad Caliph and the first ruler after the Rashidun Caliphs, had a Christian secretary named Sardjun, who was succeeded by his son. 'Umar b. Abd al-Aziz (well known for his justice), elected ruler of the Umayyad caliphate from 717 to 720, appointed as his

84 *Democracy in the 'Dark Ages'*

treasurer a wealthy Christian named Athanasius. Additionally, 'there were Christians in the Muslim armies, and some gave military service instead of a tribute' (Houtsma et al., 1993: 849). Although the gracious treatment accorded to the Christians (and Jews) somewhat deteriorated after this period, equal participation was still evident in Muslim lands. Hence Christians were 'promoted to highest official positions' during the rulership of the Buyids and the Fatimids. In fact, 'in the finance departments they possessed a quasi-monopoly, which lasted in Egypt down to the nineteenth century' (Houtsma et al., 1993: 850).

Equality did not extend just to former slaves and people of the book, but to women as well. As early as in the days of the Prophet, women participated in military expeditions, nursed the wounded and injured, challenged existing chauvinist cultural practices, questioned the Prophet and acted as religious scholars, by whom many a male companion was taught. They equalled and at times excelled men in the sciences of the Quran (*'ulum al-Qur'an*) and Hadith transmission (*'ulum al-Hadith*) and became renowned authorities in their fields. As Islamic civilisation unfolded after the Rashidun period, this precedent fostered an acceptance of women in various social realms. 'Amra bin 'Abd al-Rahman, key female traditionalist of the period of the Successors (early eighth century), was considered a great authority on traditions related by A'isha. Abu Bakr ibn Hazm, the celebrated judge of Medina, was among her students and was ordered by Caliph 'Umar ibn Abd al-Aziz to write down all the traditions known on her authority (Siddiqi, 1961). Furthermore, it is acknowledged that one of the most renowned scholars of the seminal Hadith text *Sahih al-Bukhari* was a woman named Karima al-Marwaziyya. In her book *Muslim Women: A Biographical Dictionary*, Aisha Bewley lists the contributions of hundreds of women throughout Islamic history, women who were represented in 'all areas of life, from scholars to rulers, whether regents or women who ruled in their own right, or women who wielded substantial political influence' (Bewley, 2004: v).

Freedom of expression

There is a general view, particularly among some Western scholars of Islam, that Islamic law places almost exclusive emphasis on duties and that the concepts of rights and freedom are alien to Islam. In the Western context, rights developed out of constitutionalism, as part of an ongoing struggle between the power of the state and individual rights and liberties. However, the relationship between the state and individual rights is fundamentally different in Islam, as rights precede state formation. Such rights as the safety and sanctity of life and property, or human dignity, were enshrined in the Quran from the outset. Moreover, those in authority were made responsible for ensuring the promotion of public benefits and the prevention of harm done to people. This entails such fundamental rights, such as the right to life, justice, equality before the law; protection of property; privacy; freedom of movement; and protection of dignity. Another important point in this context is that, in the West, by way of constitutions or bills of rights, fundamental rights are presented in a single document, whereas in the Islamic world such rights are scattered across various writings of scholars and jurists. However, there are certain broad categories in these writings under which the fundamental rights can be found.

Quoting from Islamic sources, Mohammad Hashim Kamali defines freedom as 'the ability of the individual to say or do what he or she wishes, or to avoid doing so, without violating the rights of others, or the limits that are set by the law' (Kamali, 2002: 7). This definition appears to be consistent with what is universally understood as freedom. Freedom of expression, he explains, is 'the absence of restraints upon the ability of individuals or groups to communicate their ideas to others, subject to the understanding that they do not in turn coerce others into paying attention or that they do not invade other rights essential to the dignity of the individual' (p. 7). He adds that the two basic objectives of freedom of speech are the discovery of truth and the upholding of human dignity.

Islamic law affirms the freedom of expression through its endorsement of such concepts as *hisbah* (enjoining what is right and forbidding what is wrong, or public vigilance), *nasihah* (sincere advice), *shura* (consultation), *ijtihad* (personal reasoning), and *hurriyyat al-mu'aradah* (the legitimate criticism of authority). *Shura* (consultation) is potentially a central democratic principle in Islam, as it requires political leaders to conduct the administration of the state through consultation with the community. It is established in the Quran that the Prophet Muhammad was instructed to consult his followers in community affairs (Quran 3.159, 42.38). Consultation with people was a hallmark of the Prophet's good governance. The books of Hadith and the Seerah (the biography of the Prophet) are replete with cases of consultation with members of the *umma* in matters pertaining to all aspects of life: civil, military, religious and administrative (An-Nawawi, 1999).

During the time of the Prophet it was not uncommon for the Bedouin Arabs to enter the Prophet's gatherings openly and freely and

86   Democracy in the 'Dark Ages'

to question him on various matters of faith. Not only did the Prophet welcome such a practice, but he also encouraged it despite the harshness of their approach. On other occasions the Prophet accepted being stopped and questioned whilst he was on the pulpit, delivering a sermon (Hadith 1965, cited in Barabankawi, 1997). Likewise, the Prophet also allowed the companions to give their views freely before commencement of war, as in the case of the battle of Badr, despite the seriousness of the situation. The battle of Badr would decide the fate of Islam and the community. As an astute military strategist, the Prophet initially contemplated the idea of withstanding a siege within the walls of Medina and not moving out to fight. Although this idea received the support of senior companions, it was immediately opposed by the younger companions, whose view was to march out against the enemy (Lings, 1983: 174). Not only was this view accepted by the Prophet, but it also proved the wiser option.

After the Prophet's death, the Muslim community, which was at once a religious and a political community, was left with the questions of who should rule and on what legal basis. In approaching the Rashidun caliphs, the Prophet's companions were given the freedom to express their views on who should lead the *umma*, and there is unanimous agreement among scholars that the first rulers of the community, including Abu Bakr, 'Umar, Uthman and Ali, were expected to engage in consultation with the community they governed and to encourage free expression (Feldman, 2003). This is a principle that was understood and documented by Muslim scholars, including the renowned Quranic exegete al-Qurtubi (1214–73), who stated:

> It is the obligation of the ruler to consult with the scholar on matters unknown to them and in religious matters not clear to them ... [They should] consult the leaders of the army in matters having to do with war, and leaders of the people in administrative issues, as well as teachers, ministers and governors in matters to do with the welfare of the country and its development.
>
> (al-Qurtubi cited in Afsaruddin, 2006: 160)

Women also enjoyed the right to express their views, despite prevailing contrary cultural norms and practices. Hence it was common for women to come to the Prophet's gatherings and freely to ask him questions on diverse matters. The Prophet's model set a precedent which continued after his demise, as in the case of the woman who openly and freely stood in the mosque and objected to the second Caliph 'Umar over the issue of the amount of bridal money paid to the bride. This story was narrated by an authoritative exegete of the Quran, Ibn Kathir. The second Caliph 'Umar stood on the pulpit of the Mosque of the Prophet in Medina and expressed his view, which was designed to limit the amount of dowry a man can give to his wife. After 'Umar finished and descended from the pulpit, one of the women stood up in the mosque and challenged his verdict. In support of her argument she cited the Quran (Quran, 4.20), which convinced 'Umar and made him withdraw his verdict (Kathir, 2000: 411). Notwithstanding the fact that women were allowed to pray in mosques, they were also given the liberty to challenge rulers openly.

Political participation

The majority view among Muslims regarding leadership and succession ever since the demise of the Prophet Muhammad has been based on egalitarian principles. The majority view has always maintained that any Muslims of religious and temporal merit may lead the Muslim community if they were elected by the majority of the people. The fact that monarchies actually reigned across the Muslim world for much of Islamic history does not detract from the fact that this view was espoused by the religious scholars and by the Muslim populace. The central point here is that the process of electing a leader according to the dominant Islamic perspective relied upon the collective participation of the people, treated as equal citizens of the Islamic state.

During the period of the Prophet Muhammad as well as during the Rashidun period, a system of electoral endorsement was implemented, which was known as *bay'ah*. Basically, all members of the community were given the opportunity to convey their acceptance of a particular leader through an oath of allegiance. The process of taking an oath of allegiance was not confined to men. Women also participated, since the time of the Prophet himself. In fact, Quranic endorsement was given even for the political participation of women. In the Quran, the Prophet Muhammad is instructed to accept the pledge of allegiance from women when it is offered (Quran, 60.12). Commenting on this verse, Aminah Nasir stated:

> The oath of allegiance that the Prophet took from the women after the conquest of Mecca in the year 7 AH is a document attesting to

88 *Democracy in the 'Dark Ages'*

political rights of women in Islam. It is the best testimony to the woman's role in Muslim society in the Prophetic Era and to her practice of her political rights which are enshrined in the *Quran*.

(Nasir, cited in Muhsin, 2008)

Women also participated in the second pledge of Aqaba, taken in 621, which granted the Prophet and the Muslims permission to immigrate to Medina. Women's participation is also witnessed in the realm of political decision-making. For example, when the peace treaty of al-Hudaibiyah was concluded, six years after migration to Medina, the Prophet Muhammad did not hesitate to seek the advice of his wife, Umm Salamah, regarding the conduct of his companions.

As stated above, the election process, particularly in the case of the first and last of the Rashidun Caliphs, demonstrates an insistence on the principles of consultation and popular support among the early Muslims. Though the caliphs were subject to God's law, they were selected by people (Feldman, 2003). Abu Bakr, for example, was elected by a group of people to become caliph after the Prophet. This election was supported and endorsed by the masses in the mosque of the Prophet. Before his death, Abu Bakr selected 'Umar as his successor, and this choice was subsequently ratified by the community. When 'Umar was dying, he nominated an electoral body composed of six of the most prominent companions and entrusted them with choosing his successor from among themselves. Their choice fell on Uthman, who was recognized by the community as the successor. After Uthman's death, Ali was proclaimed caliph by a congregation in the Prophet's Mosque, and most of the community thereupon pledged loyalty to him. Clearly, under each of these four right-guided reigns the constitution of the state differed on a most important point: the election of the head of state. Regardless of the method utilized, the community was required to ratify the choice of the next leader. Central to such a choice were the Quranic ordinance '[t]heir communal business is to be [transacted in] consultation among themselves' (Quran, 42.38) and the understanding that the community is entitled to participate in the most important political event of Islamic society, the election of the caliph. It is through this process that legitimacy was conferred on a leader. Particularly in the case of the first Rashidun caliph, Abu Bakr, and in that of the last, Ali, the *bay'ah* process was particularly critical to their legitimacy. Ali is quoted to have said at the time that his acceptance of the post of caliph would be conditional on the endorsement of the majority of the people.

The question of sovereignty

Having addressed the practice of equality, freedom of expression and participation of the masses in governance in the early history of Islam, one may still be left with a central point of contention in the debate about Islam and democracy: the question of sovereignty. Democracy is a system of government characterized by a sovereign people with the rights and responsibilities to participate in government and elect representatives. For scholars such as Lewis, this is the central issue: 'in principle the state was God's state, ruling over God's people; the law was God's law; the army was God's army; and the enemy, of course, was God's enemy' (Lewis, 1993: 95). According to this conception, a very limited role was left for the people beyond elaborating upon and interpreting the holy book. In the Islamic context 'there is no state, but a ruler; no court, but only a judge' (Lewis, 1993: 95). Ira Lapidus explains, in fact, that 'religious and political life developed distinct spheres of experience, with independent values, leaders, and organizations' (Lapidus, 1975: 364). Clearly, from the time of the Umayyads on, a separation between the political administration and religious institutions was apparent. The relationship between these spheres was mutually reinforcing, however. The learned people of religion known as *ulema* offered the ruler legitimacy in exchange for his commitment to ruling according to the *shariah*.

Monarchy has remained closely associated with the Muslim world. It is commonly cited as evidence of Islam being the antithesis of democracy. However, the system of monarchy has no foundation even in pre-Islamic Arabia, for the pre-Islamic Arabic tribes adhered to more egalitarian principles in terms of selecting leaders of tribes. Tribal leaders were generally selected on the basis of such criteria as elderly status, wisdom, courage and generosity – essentially qualities pertaining to abilities to enhance the tribe's survival and prosperity.

In addition, rule by a monarch has no endorsement from the Quran or the traditions of the Prophet Muhammad. To the contrary, in a Hadith that prophesizes future leadership, the Prophet classifies the rule after the caliphate as a trying monarchy (*mulkan 'āddan*) and a tyrannical monarchy (*mulkan jabriyyatan*). In a Hadith by Imam Ahmad, Hudhayfa narrated the following story from the Prophet:

> The reign of Prophecy shall remain amongst you so long as God wills. Then God shall remove it if He so wills. Then shall come the reign of Caliphate, based on the Prophetic Model, which shall remain so long

as God wills. Then He shall remove it if He so wills. Then shall come the rule of a trying monarchy (*mulkan 'āddan*). It shall last so long as God wills. Then He shall remove it when He so wills. Then shall come the rule of a tyrannical monarchy (*mulkan jabriyyatan*), which shall last as long as God wills. Then shall return a *Caliphate* based on the Prophetic model.

(*Hadith* 17680, cited in Barabankawi, 1997)

In this Hadith the Prophet warns against two types of monarchies: *mulkan 'āddan* and *mulkan jabriyyatan* (loosely translated as 'trying monarchy' and 'tyrannical monarchy' respectively). In this warning of the Prophet, monarchy is not as good as the caliphate, but it is better than tyranny. Unlike governance based on the prophetic model and on the caliphate model, monarchy is a system deprived of two fundamental aspects: *shura* (consultation) and *bay'ah* (electoral endorsement). Muslim historians and scholars generally agree that monarchy started with Mu'awiya (602–80), who was the first of the Muslim rulers to declare himself king: 'I am the first of the kings' (Al-Dhahabi, 2001: 157). Nevertheless, being closest in time to the Rashidun era, Mu'awiya was the most 'modern' of the monarchs of Islam. He 'allowed' (or at least tolerated) *hurriyyat al-mu'aradah* (legitimate criticism of authority), and he did not 'disdain public opinion'. Apparently he was convinced that 'the world is more surely led by the tongue than by the sword'. In fact, Mu'awiya

adopted several institutions of Beduin democracy – such as the Wufud, deputations from provinces and the principal tribes – to consult the views of such assemblies on as many occasions as possible, to associate them openly with public business by recognising their right to remonstrate.

(Houtsma et al., 1993: 620)

Mu'awiya allowed free speech and was 'not perturbed by their criticism and by the satires of the poets' (Houtsma et al., 1993: 620). Nevertheless, as dynastic rule became the norm after Mu'awiya, tyrannical monarchy (*mulkan jabriyyatan*) spread, leading to the 'invocation of *shura* as a desirable and even mandated social and political practice became a way to register disapproval of a political culture that had progressively grown more authoritarian by the Abbasid period (750–1258)' (Afsaruddin, 2006: 160).

Conclusion

Undoubtedly democracy, as we know it today, is a construct of Western political thought, famous for certain principles and institutions that are meant to establish good governance, equality and the rule of law. Regrettably, these principles and institutions are often declared to be the exclusive product of a Judeo-Christian and Greco-Roman heritage. A closer and objective examination of Islam, both textually and historically, disproves such a hypothesis. The discussion above highlights that Islam, both as a religion and as a civilization, has inherent foundational principles compatible with 'democracy'. The epochs considered – especially the time of the Prophet and the Rashidun – *are* the most widely lionized by Muslims today. They are seen not just as the halcyon days of the purity of Islam and its teachings, but also as the time in which the *ummah* and their government functioned most democratically. Whether in terms of equality, freedom of expression, political participation or sovereignty, it can be safely argued that Islam has been able to offer theories and practices consistent with democracy. It is our contention, therefore, that a new reading of the history of democracy is needed, one that recognizes 'democracy' as a form of participatory and representative government, but without the baggage of Western connotations. Such a concept of democracy is consistent with Islam and makes perfectly good sense to a lot of Muslims.

Note

1. Peace be upon him.

6
Ideals and Aspirations: Democracy and Law-Making in Medieval Iceland

Patricia Pires Boulhosa

When it was rumoured in 2009 that Iceland would join the European Union, in an effort to overcome its financial collapse, the European commissioner, Olli Rehn, welcomed the possibility of a membership bid by 'one of the oldest democracies in the world' (Traynor, 2009). Commissioner Rehn was only following the official line. Addressing a conference on 'Women and Democracy', the Icelandic Minister for the Environment and Nordic Cooperation, Sigríður Anna Þórðardóttir, explained that Iceland had once seen 'the first democratic parliament in Europe, and even in the world, founded in the year 930' (Þórðardóttir, 2005). This idea of a medieval Icelandic 'democracy' is perhaps unwittingly suggested by academics when they use terms such as 'Commonwealth' or 'Republic' in reference to the system of government in existence in Iceland from the time of its settlement, in the second half of the ninth century, until the time when it became a part of the Norwegian kingdom, in the thirteenth century.

Iceland's kingless state – for Icelanders had no king before they submitted to the Norwegian one – led English-speaking scholars to use the term 'commonwealth', with its very specific seventeenth-century English historical associations and anti-monarchical connotations. Icelandic scholars prefer *þjóðveldi*, literally 'people's power', a term specifically used to describe the Icelandic system of government before the submission (dated to 1262–4). In the seventeenth century the influential Icelandic scholar Arngrímur Jónsson described the Icelandic polity as a *res publica* or *civitas* with an aristocratic constitution. This seems to be in accordance with the classical tradition, which classified *res publica* as one among three types of government recognized as legitimate (Jónsson, 1985: 151–5; Svavarsson, 2003: 557–8; Wooton,

2006: 272–4). No republican or democratic classical tradition corresponds to today's understanding of 'republic' or 'democracy', but the concept of a *res publica* ruled by an aristocracy (*optimatii*), as described in Cicero's *Republic*, is perhaps closer to the Icelandic political system than the idea of 'commonwealth' professed by English republicanism (Black, 1997; Cicero, 1998 [54 BCE]; Scott, 2004; Wooton, 2006).

This essay will investigate a specific aspect of the medieval Icelandic legal system, namely the law-making process as recorded in a thirteenth-century legal manuscript. Law-making and the participation of society in the legislative process are important aspects in our contemporary discussions of democracy (Habermas, 1996). Iceland was in a unique position at that time, as in most of Europe law-making was by then a royal prerogative (Wormald, 1977). In Iceland, law-making operated within courts held at assemblies – including the *Alþingi*, the General Assembly which met every summer for two weeks at *Þingvǫllr*, in the south–west of the country, and which is often called the 'first democratic parliament'. It would not be possible to discuss all relevant aspects of the Icelandic legal system, but Icelandic scholarship is furnished with studies focussing on the government, legislature, administrative authority, and law-courts (Byock, 1982; Karlsson, 1972, 1977, 2002; Kjartansson, 1989; Miller, 1990; Sigurðsson, 1995, 1999, 2007; Sigurðsson et al., 2008). Finally, this essay will also outline the main aspects of a saga tradition which has inspired scholars to write about early medieval Iceland as a 'democracy' or a 'commonwealth'.

Law-Making

When the Icelanders submitted to the king of Norway, they were given new codified laws: a law-book known as *Járnsíða* in 1271, which was revoked by the introduction of *Jónsbók* in 1280–1. Before the submission, Icelanders did not have law-books, but they had laws which nowadays are known collectively as *Grágás*. These laws are extant in a number of manuscripts, mostly in a fragmentary state but for two fairly comprehensive manuscripts, *Codex Regius* or *Konungsbók* of 1250 (*Grágás-K*, 1850–2 [1250]) and *Staðarhólsbók* of 1260–70 (*Laws I*, 1980 [1260–70]). *Konungsbók* is the only manuscript that records whole sections usually referred to as 'constitutional matters': *Þingskapaþáttr*, known as 'Assembly Procedures Section'; *Lǫgsǫgumannsþáttr*, 'The Lawspeaker's Section'; and *Lǫgrétta þáttr*, known as 'The Law Council Section'.[1] The Lawspeaker (*lǫgsǫgumaðr*) was 'required to tell men the law' by reciting the laws at assemblies or upon request (*Laws I*, 1980 [1260–70]: 187, 193).

94   *Democracy in the 'Dark Ages'*

The *Lǫgrétta* was a special court whose members were 'to frame their laws...and make new laws' (*Laws I*, 1980 [1260–70]: 190). Although commonly described as the legislative body of medieval Iceland, the *Lǫgrétta* did not resemble modern legislative parliaments but, as will be seen below, it functioned through a special type of court system.

The special circumstances of the recording of the *Konungsbók* and *Staðarhólsbók* are particularly important to our understanding of the character and content of these writings. The manuscripts were written down in the thirteenth century, around the years of the Icelandic submission to the Norwegian king. As Icelanders prepared for the changes that the submission would bring, they were keen not only to consolidate their own rights, but also to record their legal history, in the form of current and new laws as well as laws no longer effective. The term 'law' is used here to cover a number of statements of law: the manuscripts are collections of laws (that is, abstract legal rules) and jurisprudential material (court judgements, experts' opinions, case reports and customs) dating from different periods of history, and the result of customary, legislative and jurisdictional practices (Maurer, 1874: 470–1; McGlynn, 2009: 528). They do not contain a prescriptive, fixed and codified body of legal provisions encompassing all the laws of Iceland of the pre-submission period. Konrad Maurer argues that the *Grágás* manuscripts were intended for legislative purposes, as a scholarly reference to the laws in use up to the period of their recording, and had no legal authority (Maurer, 1878: 80–1). On the other hand, Vilhjálmur Finsen and Andreas Heusler maintain that the *Grágás* manuscripts were official documents which had legal authority (Finsen, 1873: 109; Heusler, 1911: 2). However, a sharp division between jurisprudential material and laws is not useful in the context of the Icelandic legal system, especially if it is presupposed that the former would not have normative force (compare with Sigurðsson et al., 2008: 43). Before the king became the law-giver, Icelanders had a hybrid legislative system, based on a relatively fixed body of laws and customary law (that is, an embryonic form of case law), the development of which presumably began during the period of oral transmission. This can be seen in the provisions of the *Lǫgréttu þáttr*, which deals with the *Lǫgrétta*.

This provision speaks of several legal texts, written on parchments (*skrár*, 'scrolls'; but the term appears as 'books' in the translation below) kept in different parts of the country:

> It is also prescribed that in this country what is found in books is to be law. And if books differ, then what is found in the books which

the bishops own is to be accepted. If their books also differ, then that one is to prevail which says it at greater length in words that affect the case at issue. But if they say it at the same length but each in its own version, then the one which is in Skála[holt][2] is to prevail. Everything in the book which Hafliði had made is to be accepted unless it has since been modified, but only those things in the accounts given by other legal experts which do not contradict it, though anything in them which supplies what is left out there or is clearer is to be accepted.

(Laws I, 1980 [1260–70]: 190–1)

This provision has been discussed by many scholars whose insights cannot, for lack of space, be reviewed here, but especially relevant is Peter Foote's discussion of its similarities with the Valentinian Laws of Citations (ca 426–438), which selected the works of five jurists and made them the primary legal authority. Foote argues that, like the Laws of Citations, the *Grágás* provision was produced during 'a period of relative decline or debility in Icelandic legislation'; political turmoil and the impending submission to the king of Norway were partly responsible for the supposed decline (Foote, 1977: 201–2). Foote understands the *Grágás* provision as an effort for unity and synthesis designed to improve confidence in the law; it bears witness to 'the legal confusion ... caused by the number of written sources with competing claims to authority' (Foote, 1977: 203). These competing sources, he argues, were the independent and variant recordings of what was law in the view of experts (*lǫgmenn*, 'lawmen').

It has been argued here that the production of the *Grágás* manuscripts was part of the Icelanders' effort to create a body of law that consolidated their rights during negotiations with the king of Norway. The Icelanders were also keen to record their legal history and, as a result, *Grágás* contains several chronological layers. It is possible to see the provision as part of that effort, as a move to produce a unified and coherent body of laws. However, an analysis of the 'Law Council Section' may show that this was not the case. The provision quoted above shows that divergence among legal texts was not only acknowledged, but thought to be unavoidable: contradictions were part of the legal system. Although the provision establishes a textual hierarchy among the written sources, it does not do so in recognition of a state of confusion but, as will be seen, precisely because the legal system acknowledged the legal authority of all those written records (Foote, 1977: 200; compare with Líndal, 1993: 72).[3]

96   *Democracy in the 'Dark Ages'*

The structure of the Icelandic legal system itself contributed to the development of conflicting laws. For the purpose of legislative, assembly and court matters, Iceland was divided into four quarters: South, North, West and East. Each quarter held local assemblies, which took place during the spring (*várþing*, 'spring assemblies'), and law-courts (*Grágás-K*, 1850–2 [1250]: 38, 56).[4] These law-courts were able to decide on lawsuits and thus create case law. *Grágás* also mentions a local autumn assembly in which new laws could be announced, but it seems that it did not create case law, as it did not hold law-courts (*Grágás-K*, 1850–2 [1250]: 19; Miller, 1990: 19). Law-courts were also held at the *Alþingi*: four courts called Quarter Courts (*Fjórðungsdómar*), a Fifth Court (*Fimtadómr*), which judged special cases and doubled as a court of appeal, and the *Lǫgrétta*, the last instance of appeal and also a special court of legislation. In all these *Alþingi* courts lawsuits were heard and decided. Since both the local and the *Alþingi* courts were held only once a year, at particular times and places, it would have been difficult to maintain a strict uniformity within them, either in oral or written form. The *Lǫgrétta,* as the last instance of appeal and judgement, was the appropriate court to decide what was the law in cases of conflict, but even its decisions admitted of contradictions. Moreover, there was no fixed body of judges; these were selected among assembly attendees who met certain conditions.

Indeed, conflicting or contradictory judgements were admitted in decisions issued by the *Lǫgrétta*, which comprised *goðar* (chieftains with legal expertise), the bishops and the Lawspeaker, who presided over it. In this case there were procedures to be followed when the 'scrolls' could not decide what was to be law: a decision was to be reached by a majority vote by all members of the *Lǫgrétta*, who would hear the arguments of the two disputing parties and declare what was 'accepted as law in the case' (*Laws I*, 1980 [1260–70]: 191). Under particular circumstances, however, depending on the number of men who composed the majority or minority and on whether the Lawspeaker sided with the majority or minority, the conflicting groups would need to swear a 'divided judgement oath' (*Laws I*, 1980 [1260–70]: 191). The provision does not give further explanation of this particular kind of 'divided judgement', but such judgements were admitted in other courts, according to various procedures, when a unanimous judgement or a majority could not decide the case. It is worth quoting a section of the law concerning 'divided judgement' in the Fifth Court:

> In every case where judges have given divided judgement and both groups have gone about it correctly, then the judgement of those

must be revoked who have judged less in accordance with law. But if the one group has gone correctly about giving their divided judgement and the other group incorrectly, then the judgement of those who went correctly about giving their divided judgement must stand, even though the others' case was better in substance at the outset. But if neither group has correctly gone about giving divided judgement, the judgement of those must be revoked who in going about giving divided judgement strayed farther from the law; and that judgement must be revoked which seems remoter from the law.

(*Laws I*, 1980 [1260–70]: 88)

It is plausible that the *Lǫgrétta* followed a similar process, that they also strove to revoke the judgement which seemed remoter from the law or strayed farther from it. What is noteworthy here, however, is the implicit recognition that men could be only close or far away from the law, while the law itself could be grasped only with difficulty. The existence of 'divided judgement' did not mean that a single judgement would not be reached at some point, but it was an acknowledgement of the vagaries of the law. The declarations found in *Grágás*, made by claimants and defendants, conform very well with this principle, as these people also needed to swear that they would prosecute their cases or defend themselves in the way they thought 'most true and right and most in accordance with law' (*Grágás-K*, 1850–2 [1250]: 46–7).

The *Lǫgrétta* decided upon what was law 'in the case' after hearing the pronouncements of both claimant and defendant, and thus decisions stemmed from the assessment of particular cases. This process can be compared to case law, and the textual evidence of *Grágás* confirms this, as a great number of provisions seem to have been the product of, or at least based on, case law (Miller, 1990: 223). An analogy can loosely be made with the laws attributed to King Ine of the West Saxons (688–726), in which several provisions are written in convoluted language. One of the possible explanations provided by Patrick Wormald for the intricate syntax is that the provisions responded to particular cases, that law-makers were 'regularly found responding to problems laid before them. Law-making in writing had gone "live"' (Wormald, 2001: 105). The so-called *Lois des Pers dou Castel de Lille* (1283–1308/14) seem to have recorded the remains of the pronouncements of the Spokesmen, members of the law-courts who had legal expertise and did most of the talking in court (Heirbaut, 2007a: 143, 2007b: 258–71). These recorded pronouncements originally contained an elaborate report of the cases, followed by the parties' arguments, the court decision and other notes;

98 Democracy in the 'Dark Ages'

but, as the focus moved to fixed laws instead of the varying arguments, they gradually became a book of legal rules (Heirbaut, 2007a: 149). It is not suggested that identical processes happened in the recording of *Grágás*, but only that similar processes might have taken place and that several of the extant *Grágás* laws are the result of, or based on, case law. If the *Lǫgrétta* could frame the existing laws and make new ones through an independent process from the lawsuits, it is possible that, at least in part, these procedures stemmed from the assessment of lawsuits.[5] The process of law-making would have happened within a dynamic, customary[6] law system which admitted of contradictions, that is, in the context of an acceptance that conflicting interpretations of what was law might co-exist in special circumstances. It was also recognized that the legal system was lacunar, as new laws could be made in response to particular situations.

Contrary to what traditionalists may have once maintained, customary law does not translate into a 'democratic mode of law-making, reflecting the actual convictions of the ordinary people who practice them' (Perreau-Saussine and Murphy, 2007: 2). Indeed, studies have shown that 'notions of customary law as a distillation of popular practices tend to be indefensible, and that the relevant customs prove to be those of an influential group of insiders' (Perreau-Saussine and Murphy, 2007: 2; see also Ibbetson, 2007: 165–6; Schauer, 2007: 31–4). One such group of insiders within the Icelandic legal system were the *goðar*, members of the *Lǫgrétta* with powers to frame the laws and make new ones, but who also chose the Lawspeaker and the men who acted as judges in the courts. Within the laws, the *goði* was a legal officer with various special powers to act in courts and assemblies.[7] A *goði* possessed a *goðorð* (usually translated as 'chieftaincy') which could be sold and inherited, and a *goði* could forfeit his *goðorð* if he did not perform his legal duties. A *goðorð* is described in the laws as a power, 'not property', and it seems to refer to the authority of a *goði* to administer both legal affairs and the affairs of assemblies (*Grágás-K*, 1850–2 [1250]: 255). By being members of the *Lǫgrétta,* the *goðar* already had considerable power in the law-making process, but they also nominated the men who acted as judges in the courts and who in turn were able to make law by creating case law.

The *goðar* nominated judges for the assembly courts and for the *Alþingi* courts, and their number was established by different formulae. For the Quarter Courts, for example, there were thirty-six judges, on the basis of the number of 'full and ancient *goðorð*' – that is, of the *goðorð* in existence when there were three assemblies (*þing*) in each of the four quarters of the country and three *goðar* in each assembly, totalling thirty-six *goðar*.[8] Free men, aged 12 years or older, with a settled home, and who were capable of taking responsibility for what they said or swore were selected by the *goðar* to act as judges in each of the Quarter Courts (*Grágás-K*, 1850–2 [1250]: 20).

The simplicity of the criteria for the selection of judges, though, is only apparent. The judges were chosen by the *goði* among his assembly participants, and these were, in addition to the *goðar*, those who qualified as householders and those called 'to attend the assembly and to provide formal means of proof' (*Laws I*, 1980 [1260–70]: 58). A householder was a landowner or a tenant who owned milking stock, who could freely attach himself to an assembly group. If he did not own milking stock or was not a landowner, he did not qualify as a householder and belonged to the assembly group of the householder into whose care he put himself (*Grágás-K*, 1850–2 [1250]: 81). There were very detailed rules on assembly attachment and household types; for example, men who temporarily lived in fishing boats were attached to the assembly group of the man who owned the land they were living on (*Grágás-K*, 1850–2 [1250]: 81). What is important, though, is that only men with certain material means were free to declare which assembly group they were joining. In the light of evidence from the saga, scholars have argued that this freedom was a dead letter (Karlsson, 1977: 363–4; Vésteinsson, 2007: 133). As Miller points out, 'a farmer living close by a powerful *goði* must have had little real prospect of freely choosing his chieftain' (Miller, 1990: 23). But the law itself seems to account for difficulties in publicly declaring such attachments by allowing a man 'to transfer to another man the business of saying at the General Assembly or a spring assembly that he is joining an assembly group' or to delay his declaration (*Laws I*, 1980 [1260–70]: 132). He could also tell others that he was joining an assembly group and later deny his willingness, although he would be liable to a fine (*Laws I*, 1980 [1260–70]: 132). Even if the power was on the side of the *goðar*, the laws provided a medium of moderation and show that there was plenty of room for manoeuvre.

It is not easy to understand the designs behind all of the rules on assembly attachment, some of which are connected to court procedures (claimants, for instance, needed to know what assembly the man whom they wanted to sue was attached to, so that they could bring their lawsuits to the right assembly court). However, it would perhaps be too simplistic to postulate that the rules aimed to bar from the legal system men with fewer means. As Miller points out, the legal categories into which people were classified – householders who paid dues[9] or did not, tenants, landowners, and so on – 'were not in the strict sense ascribed statuses. People fell into and out of them depending on the vagaries of fortune' (Miller, 1990: 26). The rationale behind the rules could well have been the protection of those who could not leave their farms or of those who, by being too weak or too poor, would not be able to support the penalties which assembly participants acting as judges or witnesses, for example, could incur.

The *goðar* could nominate judges to the courts, but they did not have total control over the selection of these judges, as at least certain men had the freedom to attach themselves to the assemblies from where they could potentially be chosen to act as judges. Gunnar Karlsson argues, on the contrary, that there was nothing in the laws to secure the judges' independence against the legislators (i.e. the *goðar* who sat in the *Lǫgrétta*; Karlsson, 2002: 27–8). But Karlsson is here comparing the appointment of judges in *Grágás* with contemporary Icelandic procedures, which function within independent legislative and judiciary powers. This contemporary structure is dependent on a third pillar, executive power, which is responsible for organizing law enforcement. The structure that emerges from *Grágás*, on the other hand, was not dependent on a centralized executive power: the enforcement of law relied on the parties involved and on society at large (Miller, 1990: 20–1). There is a good deal in the laws that worked as an approximate manifestation of executive power. The *féransdómr*, 'confiscation court', was a type of executive court which was held after a judgement of outlawry had been announced and which concerned the property of the outlaw (*Grágás-K*, 1850–2 [1250]: 48–54, 69, 73). *Grágás* has very elaborate rules to restrict the movement of outlawed men, which were decided by the *féransdómr* but needed the willing participation of the whole society in order of work (*Grágás-K*, 1850–2 [1250]: 52–3).

If the *Grágás* laws represent an effort to produce legal history and constitute a combination of abstract legal rules and material derived, possibly at some remove, from case law, it must follow that they are an idealized construct, even though a great deal of the laws might have been in force at some point. *Grágás* represents the aspirations of thirteenth-century Icelanders as they embarked on the political project of becoming subjects of the Norwegian king and as they reflected upon their new political status. On the other hand, the complexity of the communitarian structures which we see in the *Grágás* seems to reflect a fairly participative and dynamic legal system, even if one ultimately controlled by an oligarchy.

Conclusion

Although it seems that *Grágás* records the relics of an older system, it is difficult to say how far back the laws go, and especially whether the law-making process was implemented when the laws were first written down or long before that. It is possible that this type of law-making had its roots in an ancient assembly system, which later developed into court systems. But the system described in *Grágás* may only have been possible when the laws began to be written down, that is – according to chapter 10 of *Íslendingabók* – around 1117. Chapter 2 of *Íslendingabók* also claims some Norwegian inspiration for the Icelandic laws by recounting that around 930 a certain Norwegian, called Úlfljótr, brought laws from Norway which were mostly taken from the laws of the *Gulaþing* in the west of Norway. Sigurður Líndal observes that at such an early time the laws in Norway were not codified, and thus Úlfljótr did not come to Iceland with an imported legal code but only with information about Norwegian custom (Líndal, 1969: 6–9).

Nineteenth-century scholars firmly believed that the society developed in Iceland had its roots in the ancestral societies of Scandinavia, an idea which endures in modern scholarship: 'For the best idea of what Scandinavian society was like before kingship developed one must go to Iceland' (Lund, 1995: 206). Icelanders also promoted this idea in their sagas, motivated as they were by the political and social circumstances of the thirteenth century, especially the process of negotiation which saw the country's submission to the Norwegian king. A representative number of sagas recount that Iceland was settled towards the end of the ninth century by highborn and powerful Norwegians who wanted to escape King Haraldr inn hárfagri. According to the perception of the sagas, King Haraldr threatened the old social order, which was based on individuals' freedom and power of decision as well as on their ancestral rights. The saga narratives explain how King Haraldr establishes a tyranny in Norway: those who accept his rule accept slavery and oppression, and those who resist him are left to flee the country. Thus noble and powerful landowners left Norway to become the settlers of Iceland, in order to re-establish their ancestral society in a new country, a society which could not be ruled tyrannically by a sole king. In Iceland, the kingless settlers took possession of land and started to organize themselves around social and legal structures which, in the perspective of the sagas at least, reflected that of their Norwegian ancestors. Iceland then emerged as a society of self-governing free men, with

102 *Democracy in the 'Dark Ages'*

a prominent farming oligarchy, responsible for the country's legal and political organization.[10]

Notwithstanding the historical circumstances which partly explain how the idea of an autonomous and kingless society came to be articulated by medieval Icelanders in the sagas, Icelanders did not appear *ex nihilo*; the settlers brought with them their history, laws and mores, which – it is reasonable to believe – they tried to put into practice in the new country. However, the Icelandic laws, in their extant form, are the result of a continuous and changing practice which took place in a very dissimilar society to that of the other Scandinavian countries. We must avoid the excesses of the romantic reconstructions of Scandinavian society, which laid too much emphasis on an immemorial Germanic past and on an idealized model of assemblies of elected men who could freely make their own laws. As Patrick Wormald points out, the democratic fallacy dogged the nineteenth-century understanding of early medieval polities and has ironically obscured discussions about the character of law-making in the North (Wormald, 2001: 4–14). Wormald goes on to note that 'law-making in the North was the business of the community at large, distilled in its most prominent members'; and, although he is concerned with a much earlier historical period than the thirteenth century of the Icelandic *Grágás*, we may cautiously consider some aspects of law-making in Iceland as part of a larger tradition (Wormald, 2001: 94). Studies on the early provincial laws of Sweden, Norway and Denmark have noted some points of similarity with the Icelandic laws as well as with Canon and Roman Law (Bagge, 2001; Sigurðsson et al., 2008; Sjöholm, 1990); but much caution is needed when attempting to reconstruct the law-making process in Scandinavia from what is contained in *Grágás*, as the *Grágás* laws are the product of an oral and written jurisdictional practice specific to Icelandic medieval society.

Medieval Icelandic democracy? The idea would surprise a medieval Icelander as much as it surprises us. But the law-making process described in *Grágás*, as well as the dynamic legal system through which this process operated, also seem surprisingly flexible and open to communitarian participation. The *Grágás* laws present us with evidence of an oligarchic type of society, within which there also existed some diffusion of the power of the few. Perhaps this control remained in the realm of theory, as Icelanders' aspirations for their future, or as their perception of their past – after all, the laws were as engaged as the sagas in recreating, and reflecting upon, the Icelandic past. It does seem, though, that, in the absence of the state, Icelanders developed a system which may have had the law at its centre but community at its very base. It was not an egalitarian society, and the label 'democratic' could only awkwardly be applied to it, but, as Miller points out, the uniqueness of Icelandic society forces us to question our assumptions about law and community (Miller, 1990: 307); it may also force us to question our notions of democracy.

Notes

1. Laws about assembly procedures and juridical procedures are scattered around the provisions of the *Staðarhólsbók* manuscript (see, for example, *Laws I*, 1980 [1260–70]: 205–38). All translations are taken from *The Laws of Early Iceland*, vol. 1 (*Laws I*, 1980 [1260–70]). *Grágás-K* refers to *Grágás* in the *Konungsbók* manuscript and reference is given by section (*Grágás-K*, 1850–2 [1250]).
2. Skálaholt, in the south of Iceland, was one of the two Episcopal sees (the other being Hólar). The Skálaholt bishop presided over the East, South and West Quarters, the Hólar bishop over the North (*Laws I*, 1980 [1260–70]: 35–6). According to *Íslendingabók* Hafliði Másson and other 'learned men' had the laws written down for the first time in 1117. The manuscritps of *Íslendingabók*, 'The Book of the Icelanders', are from the seventeenth century but scholars believe that they are transcripts of a twelfth-century exemplar.
3. Sigurður Líndal argues that the clause 'in this country what is found in books is to be law' indicates that all written records were on an equal footing except for cases of necessity when the books of the bishops prevailed (Líndal, 1993: 62–4, 66–74). He believes that the accounts of men learned in the law were the source of the scrolls mentioned in the provision, the authority of which rested upon the idea of law as ancient custom. The present author argues that the authority of these written records was based upon their immediate usage: they had normative force because they were the product of jurisdictional practice.
4. Attendance at the spring assemblies was compulsory, but only a certain proportion of men of each assembly were called to the *Alþingi*. See note 9 below.
5. Sigurður Líndal considered various scholarly theories of the making of new laws in *Grágás* before concluding that the *Lǫgrétta* agreed to new laws when deemed necessary, following procedures not explained in the *Grágás* manuscripts (Líndal, 1993: 178–9). Others argue that it was only when the *Lǫgrétta* 'corrected' (*rétta*) the law that they considered particular cases (Sandvik and Sigurðsson, 2004: 226).
6. Terms such as 'customary law' can refer to very different legal systems (Simpson, 1987: 359); here, the term is used as a reference to a judicial practice which allowed the decisions reached by the judges on particular cases to become law; in other words, the ability of judges to 'make law'.
7. The term *goði* might have had its origins in religious traditions, but by the time of the writing of *Grágás* the position of *goðar* did not have religious functions.
8. The *Lǫgrétta* and the Fifth Court had 48 *goðar* (Miller, 1990: 17–19).

104　*Democracy in the 'Dark Ages'*

9. *Þingfararkaup*, 'assembly attendance dues', were paid by men who were not attending the *Alþingi* to those who were attending (*Grágás-K*, 1850–2 [1250]: 23). Not all men, though, were liable to pay the dues (*Grágás-K*, 1850–2 [1250]: 89).
10. In the sagas, this landed oligarchy is generally referred to as *hǫfðingi* ('chieftains'). The term refers to individuals who through their political and economic power acted as leaders in their community, but who may not have been *goðar* (Karlsson, 1977: 366; Ingvarsson, 1970: 30). If a *hǫfðingi* happened to hold the office of *goði* he would also have legal power.

7
Democratic Culture in the Early Venetian Republic

Stephen Stockwell

Between the fifth and the thirteenth century CE, from the fall of Rome to the stirrings of the Renaissance, the politics of Europe was monarchical and hierarchical, feudal, brutal and unfair. Throughout this exact period, Venice played a role in keeping democratic tendencies alive. Venice flourished in the so-called 'Dark Ages', economically and intellectually, with a system of government that often fell into oligarchy and sometimes toyed with autocracy, but which nevertheless kept the best traditions of Greek and Roman democratic citizenship alive. The most serene republic – Serenissima, as Venice styled itself – had many democratic virtues: it was founded in equality and frank speech, at play in the liminal and willing to adapt collectively to defend itself and prosper. Venice owes its existence to its location on a large lagoon formed by the estuaries of many rivers to the west and by the long, thin sand islands thrown up by the currents of the Adriatic Sea to the east. Because of its location, Venice could avoid the worst of the barbarian invasions and the wars between empires to keep alive its own republican, and even democratic traditions.

There are many critics of the Venetian state. Some would point to the powerful, central role of the Doge, served as he was by the conspiratorial Council of Ten, and argue that Venice was an autocracy, like a twentieth-century totalitarian regime, with a ruler for life and a brutal secret police force. Other critics argue that Venice was always an oligarchy, ruled by a cabal of a few powerful merchants from even fewer powerful families. Certainly, after Venice closed the books on new citizens at the end of the thirteenth century, it eventually became an aristocracy that ossified into irrelevance until Napoleon put it out of its misery in 1797. But, for its first 800 plus years, from the fifth to the thirteenth century, Venice embraced egalitarianism and free thinking,

106 *Democracy in the 'Dark Ages'*

coupled with a realist approach to politics and a pragmatic system of checks and balances. Its system of governance at that time ensured that, while sometimes slipping into oligarchy, the people were sovereign and had sufficient democratic purchase to reassert their will at key moments, to adapt their government and to prosper. This chapter considers the role Venice played during the feudal period in keeping democratic ideas alive by experimenting with laws and institutions and by allowing the free exchange of ideas among citizens, particularly in large, sovereign assemblies. Those ideas spread through northern Italy, to contribute to the Renaissance and the modern world, and even persisted in the late republic, contributing to its stability and longevity.

The democratic spirit rekindled

The egalitarianism that underwrote Venice's democratic ethos could be seen long before there was a settlement at the Rialto, the islands at the centre of the lagoon that became, and remains, the hub of the city. The city now called Venice began in the fifth century CE, as a scattering of settlements around the extended lagoon between Chioggia and Grado, in the Roman province of Venetia in north-eastern Italy (Lane, 1973: 4). As the western Roman Empire crumbled, successive waves of tribal hordes, Goths, Huns and Lombards laid waste to Venetia. The Eastern Roman (or Byzantine) Empire, based in Constantinople, maintained a territorial claim to the province, but could do little to halt the barbarian invasions (Norwich, 2003: 5–6). Refugees from the destruction, including well-educated Roman citizens, fled to the mudflats of the lagoon and built houses of wattle and daub on planks driven into the mud (Hazlitt, 1966: 3–8). Their economy was based on the mundane activities of harvesting and trading fish and salt, and their politics was marked by equality and independence.

The political system the refugees built bore the influence of Rome and of its almost forgotten republican virtues. While there are claims to an earlier date, there is clear evidence that about a dozen settlements around the lagoon sent tribunes to a representative, co-ordinating council in 466 CE (Hazlitt, 1966 [1900]: 3–8; Norwich, 2003: 6). The tribune had a very particular, historic meaning in the Roman constitutional context. Following a refusal to follow the orders of patrician officers in 494 BCE, Roman plebeians, commoners who owned land, won the right to elect their own officials, called tribunes. They were effectively magistrates from the tribe, but they did not have direct decision-making power; rather, they could use their authority to forestall decision-making processes. They were sacrosanct, and interfering with a tribune was a capital offence, so they could use their bodies to intervene physically in constitutional processes and to veto decisions of the senate, assemblies and magistrates, but only as long as they were present in person (Finer, 1997: 405). Nevertheless, wise and judicial exercise of their powers protected the civil rights of plebeians. Attempts by tribunes from the Gracchi family (133–122 BCE) to redistribute land, open government and extend the power of the tribune via the exercise of a blanket veto on all governmental activity were seen as pushing the tribunes' powers too far and exacerbating the divisions that led to the end of the republic (Finer, 1997: 426–32). The tribunes were an important part of the checks and balances of the Roman system and their re-emergence in the Venetian context clearly bases Venetian politics in the plebeian sphere. It was politics from the people.

The democratic spirit of Venice was clearly evident in 523 CE, when Cassiodorus, secretary to Theodoric, the Gothic king of Italy and the putative head of the Western Roman Empire, wrote to 'the maritime tribunes' of the Venetian lagoon to convince supposed subjects to expedite the shipment of wine and oil from the province of Istria to Theodoric's seat at Ravenna (Cassiodorus, 1886 [523]: *Letters*, 515–18; Norwich, 2003: 6). Cassiodorus (CE 490–484) was aware of the conditions of life of the maritime peoples around the lagoon and praised their equality and independence, concluding that their equal circumstances generated an egalitarian ethos. 'For you live like sea birds, with your homes dispersed, like the Cyclades, across the surface of the water' (Cassiodorus, quoted in Norwich, 2003: 6). This suggests not only the fragility of Venetian homes, but also that they form a ring of strength, like the circle of the Greek Cycladic islands. 'The solidity of the earth on which they rest is secured by osier and wattle; yet you do not hesitate to oppose so frail a bulwark to the wildness of the sea' (Norwich, 2003: 6). This captures the liminal nature of the early Venetian settlements, perched as they were on hard-won land, ready to be reclaimed by the sea. 'Your people have one great wealth – the fish which suffices for them all. Among you there is no difference between rich and poor; your food is the same; your houses are all alike. Envy, which rules the rest of the world is unknown to you' (Norwich 2003: 6). Here Cassiodorus makes the point that the equal battle for economic survival produces Venice's egalitarian world view, which would go on to inform its democratic approach.

By the mid-sixth century, the Eastern Empire had reasserted its authority in Italy and ostensibly over Venice, but the lagoon defended its people against the machinations of the imperial army. The real political

108 *Democracy in the 'Dark Ages'*

power of the Venetian settlements continued in the hands of the con-vocation of elected tribunes, but it was balanced by the emergence of 'periodical conventions...termed in the Venetian dialect *Arrengi,* com-posed of the whole adult male population of the islands...held in the open air' (Hazlitt, 1966 [1900]: 9). While initially the Arengo's meetings were not regular, it continued to be summoned at key moments during the early centuries of Venice's existence. The Arengo, a citizen assem-bly of all the adult males, was the sovereign body that could decide the future of an entire enterprise. During the sixth century, Venice assisted the Byzantine emperor and his generals on a number of occa-sions, participating in blockades and ferrying troops. But the Venetians maintained a distance from Byzantium as well, informing the emperor's representative, according to the *Altino Chronicles*: 'we fear no invasion or seizure by any of the Kings or Princes of this world, not even by the emperor himself' (Norwich, 2003: 9). It was in this spirit that Venice made its first formal arrangement with the eastern empire in the late sixth century and gave its loyalty and service in return for military pro-tection and, much more significantly, trading privileges throughout the empire (Norwich, 2003: 9). So, even when the Lombards, the final wave of barbarian hordes, invaded Italy in 568, Venice, although inundated again with refugees, remained as a string of independent but cooperative trading posts between the east and the west. It was this trade that was to make Venice rich, important and the most advanced, and democratic, city in Europe during the 'Dark Ages'. But, at the start of the seventh century, that rosy future was a long way off and the settlements of the lagoon were often at odds with each other, caught in personal vendettas that turned into brutal civil war.

Raw democracy

During the seventh century Venice remained a very loose coalition of small towns, usually referred to in the plural, *Venetiae* (Norwich, 2003: 12). While the Lombards maintained control around Venice, some towns began to prosper more than others and tensions fol-lowed. Heraclea was formally the provincial capital in Byzantine eyes, but Torcello was the main trading centre. Grado was the seat of the Byzantine patriarch, while Aquileia was home to the Roman Catholic bishop. Tribunes from some settlements were not above exerting their influence in their own interests and in defiance of what the people considered their traditional rights: 'the Tribunes soon felt their power, and soon abused it; each aspired to absolute and undivided authority;

and the nation had frequent cause to complain that their confidence was betrayed by a single magistrate who dared to infringe their dearest privileges' (Hazlitt, 1966 [1900]: 9). Matters were made worse as the eastern (Byzantine) and western (Roman) churches split, and Grado and Aquileia found themselves on different sides of the divide. Differences between adjacent towns led to fighting, and the Byzantine authorities did not have the resources, or interest, to intervene, nor were they interested in assisting the Venetians to band together to resolve matters themselves (Norwich, 2003: 12).

Venetian state mythology claims that the situation changed in 697, in response to 'a cruel ordeal of anarchy, oppression, and bloodshed [as] Tribunes conspired against each other, family rose against family, clan against clan [and] sanguinary affairs were of constant occurrence' (Hazlitt, 1966 [1900]: 16–20). In this context, the patriarch of Grado called together an assembly of all the men of the lagoon at Heraclea. In order to overcome local conflicts and make peace with the Lombards, the assembly is supposed to have elected a single ruler, Paoluccio Anafesto. Unfortunately this history (which is so convenient for those looking for evidence of democratic tendencies in early Venice) is unsupported by anything but clearly unreliable chronicles from many centuries later. However, the revised history, with some basis in fact, has interesting lessons. Things came to a head in 726, over the idolatry of icons and orders from Constantinople for their destruction. Icon worship was not a major issue for the Venetian (and other western) churches, and the people rebelled against Byzantine rule. In 727 the local garrison at Heraclea, constituted predominantly by local soldiers, revolted against Constantinople and elected its own leader, Orso, as Dux, a title which was softened in the local Venetian dialect to Doge (Norwich, 2003: 13).

Within a few years, the iconoclasm from the Eastern Empire was watered down for the west and Orso came to an accommodation with Constantinople, which made him a consul or (*hypatos*), a title that became the family surname (Norwich, 2003: 13). Orso Ipato was the leader for a decade before rebels assassinated him. There was then an interregnum of five years before Orso's son Teodato was elected by the Arengo as the second Doge in 742. He immediately moved the seat of government from imperially sanctioned Heraclea to more republican Malamocco, situated on the Lido and much more central to all the settlements of the lagoon. The Venetian republic had emerged from a period of civil strife between and within its constituent towns with a system of government where individual towns still elected, annually,

110 Democracy in the 'Dark Ages'

tribunes with responsibility for municipal affairs, and the Arengo elected the Doge as a political and religious leader for life. In electing the Doge for life, the Arengo in fact ceded its sovereignty to him for that period. However, the Doge's power was checked to a degree by the *magister militum*, the master of the soldiers, who in other jurisdictions at the time was called captain of the people and who apparently was elected annually, like the tribunes (Hazlitt, 1966 [1900]: 21–3). For a time, this system had its successes in unifying more than a dozen disparate towns and providing stable government. Teodato Ipato stayed in power for thirteen years before dissatisfaction grew, when he was blinded and deposed from power by Galla Gaulo, who suffered the same fate a year later (Norwich, 2003: 16–17).

At this point, in 756, there was a significant constitutional change, the Arengo being empowered to elect annually two tribunes with the specific responsibility 'to prevent the abuse of ducal power' (Norwich, 2003: 17). Thus the Arengo reasserted its sovereignty every twelve months, and this was effective in keeping the Doge responsive to the popular will. Doges were still elected for life and many had great success at unifying the people, undertaking civic works, defeating pirates and managing the diplomatic relationships that fostered Venetian trade. But some Doges also sought to extend their family's power by making their sons or brothers joint holders of the office, so that they could then remain in office after the original Doge's death. While the Arengo acquiesced in these arrangements from time to time, the hereditary regimes that arose were far from satisfactory and broke down in bouts of exile, murder and blinding, which required the Arengo to be convened again. This was far from a perfect system of governance. The introduction of an hereditary element produced factional tensions, particularly between the decentralized settlements, and that factionalism led the Doges to ally themselves with foreign powers, especially the emerging western Frankish Empire of Charlemagne. Nevertheless, when the Doges called on that foreign support, as the Antenori did in 810, the people of the lagoon united themselves under the command of Agnello Participazio, to see off the Frankish invaders. The spirit of unity and the search for greater security after the attempted Frankish invasion led to increased settlement of the comparatively safe and neutral Rialto islands in the centre of the lagoon, where the new Doge, Agnello Participazio, lived, and where Venice stands today (Norwich, 2003: 20–3). The result was a very raw form of democracy, which balanced a high degree of citizen freedom and enthusiastic participation in elections for tribunes and Doges with the emergence of a ducal power based, not on the sovereignty of all the people, but on factions, external support and hereditary claims that led to a politics of violent catharsis. Between the seventh and twelfth centuries, five Doges were forced to abdicate, nine were deposed or exiled, five were blinded and five were murdered (Muir, 1999).

Democratic maturity

The victory over the Franks reaffirmed Venice's status as an ostensible part of the Byzantine Empire. While the city was independent in practice, the connection with the Eastern rather than Western Empire meant that Venice stayed well outside the feudal sphere that arose after Charlemagne's demise, and, while there were family rivalries, the whole fabric of the state was not rent apart by century-long vendettas between Guelph supporters of the papacy and Ghibelline adherents of the Western Empire (Finer, 1997: 986). Venice used its position between the two empires to trade both ways and so to create an autonomous zone, which provided both freedom and relative stability. Venice's distance from the Roman church ensured that Venice was not drawn into the excesses of the Inquisition or into the persecution of knowledge that resulted. Above all, Venice's liminality allowed the persistence of republicanism, with its inherent democratic spirit, in the space between autocratic empires.

During the ninth century the Participazio family ruled effectively and with great political skill, but fell into the Venetian tradition of making its sons join into the Dogeship, which over time had a corrosive effect on even the best of intentions. While Venice was still theoretically a republic, 'the tribunes had declined in importance, the arenghi were never called, and public affairs had become the preserve of whatever little clique chanced to surround the Doge of the day' (Norwich, 2003: 34). In 864 military failures against the Saracens, resurgent piracy in the Adriatic and the early death of the younger Doge in a shared leadership led the older Doge into a series of political mistakes that ended in a conspiracy against him and his assassination. While the new Doge, Orso Participazio, appears to have been from the same family, he was elected by a freshly reconvened and revitalized Arengo and took to the job of resuscitating Venetian democracy with reformist zeal. He introduced a system of elected judges who were high state officials with some ministerial functions, some judicial functions and a full-time watching brief to ensure there was no arbitrary abuse of ducal power (Norwich, 2003: 35). Doges from the Participazio family and their allies in the Candiani

112 *Democracy in the 'Dark Ages'*

family continued to rule with popular support because of their energy, enthusiasm and 'the old, austere republican virtues on which the state had been founded... moral behavior (and) mistrust of personal pomp and ostentation' (Norwich, 2003: 40–1).

For almost a century, the mix of democratically inspired checks and balances and resort to republican virtues worked well. Venetian democracy was maturing and the economy was flourishing. As the rest of Europe was engulfed by feudalism, Venice became a seat of learning and investigation, which translated into technological leadership. Venice became a major maritime power, policing the Adriatic and shipping routes beyond. The maturing democracy saw the benefits of complex controls on power and the growing influence of the judges who, in time, would become members of the senatorial *Curia*, ensuring that the Doge did not become an autocrat and that the interests of all the levels of Venetian society were taken into account in decision-making. Despite these reforms, nepotism around the Doge continued even within new constraints, and this had an adverse effect on the quality of democracy. Thus, when the Arengo elected Pietro Candiano IV as Doge in 959, the limits of the Venetian system quickly became apparent as Pietro emptied the Treasury, married into the Frankish court and became a major feudal landowner in his own right (Norwich, 2003: 41–3).

Pietro Candiani IV and his infant son were assassinated in 976, and he was followed by a string of Dodges who make the worst examples of nepotism: short-term and weak ones, followed by the Orseoli, who had accommodations with foreign powers and a strong belief in their own right to rule. In 1026 Otto Orseolo was deposed and exiled, and in 1032 the Arengo finally took decisive action to end the nepotism by electing Domenico Flabanico as Doge. Flabanico was well known for his anti-dynastic views and had participated in exiling Otto Orseolo. He ended the practice of appointing co-regents who then became successors, and he enforced existing 'legislation providing for the proper election of Doges and giving adequate powers to the popular assembly' (Norwich, 2003: 65–6). In the remaining seven and a half centuries of the Venetian republic, no Doge was ever followed by his son. Flabanico also broadened the base of advice from the elected judges, to include more voices in what eventually would become the Doge's council and the senate (Finer, 1997: 987). For 140 years, Venice flourished under Flabanico's reformed constitution. Venice stalled her entry into the crusades and used good intelligence to turn up at appropriate moments to gain the maximum concessions from the new Christian kingdom of Jerusalem (Norwich, 2003: 79–80, 83–4). The city saw off Norman and

Hungarian intrusions and standardized its shipbuilding efforts into the Arsenal, which became the first production line and the largest industrial enterprise in Europe. Venice used its advanced engineering skills to turn the Rialto settlement into a city, and it even introduced street-lighting centuries before other European cities (Finer, 1997: 1014–15; Lane, 1973: 154–71; Norwich, 2003: 91).

The form of democracy practiced in Venice between the ninth and the twelfth century was not without its problems: elections were often by 'acclamation', and the Doge, elected for life, could only 'fall by popular riot' (Finer, 1997: 987). But in that time the political system gradually emerged, from a 'raw' democracy with regular recourse to blindings and assassinations, into a more mature state, dependent on considered opinion from councils and on a complex set of checks and balances that protected the rights of the still sovereign people. Just as the citizen assembly ceded some sovereign power to the Doge, it ceded more power to his advisory council, so that it could balance the power of the Doge with a close scrutiny of his actions and with an ability to override his decisions. Nevertheless, resort to the Arengo was still an option that allowed the restoration of order and the reconciliation of divergent social views.

Venice had developed a balanced constitution, which managed both ambitions and the potential excesses of popular emotion. When the Holy Roman Empire fractured in 1167, Venice supplied the blueprint for independence to the communes of northern Italy. As Venice reached its zenith as a mature democracy, it was a useful example to other cities that established themselves as communes, many governed by their own councils. They formed the Lombard League, with Venice as a founding member and a sponsor of the accommodation they had reached with the Holy Roman Empire through the treaty known as the Peace of Venice (Norwich, 2003: 103). By the twelfth century, northern Italy was home to a thriving socio-economic and cultural environment, which percolated to cities like Florence and Perugia and gave rise to the Renaissance. The combination of wealthy patrons and intellectual freedom attracted Byzantine scholars, who assisted in the recovery of classical learning about ideas such as democracy and whose teaching spread those notions across Europe. Although the aristocracy often managed the early political machinations of these newly independent city-states, their systems generally evolved into broad-based communes, including the *popolo* (Finer, 1997: 953–4). By the middle of the thirteenth century there were city-state constitutions all across Italy which guaranteed the people their own self-governing political systems. Each of

114 *Democracy in the 'Dark Ages'*

those agreements owed something to the democratic tendencies kept alive and reformed by Venice over the preceding 800 years.

Citizenry solidified into aristocracy

It is ironic that, just as Venice implanted the idea and institutions of democracy into the fertile ground of the Lombard League, Venice itself began the slow shift from a formal democracy with sovereign power in the hands of the people (even if subject to oligarchic manipulation) to a formal aristocracy (although one still without a king). This began simply enough, when a trade dispute broke out with the Eastern Empire in 1171 and Doge Vitale Michiel II set out to avenge Venice's honour, on a wave of popular support. He returned defeated, with sailors carrying the plague, and was assassinated – the first Doge to die in this way for 200 years. It quickly became apparent that the whole adventure had not been subject to required constitutional processes. A review of the catastrophe pointed to a need for less hasty responses to populism and for a more careful consideration of expert opinion by the Doge. The constitutional changes of 1172 started a trend 'to *narrow* the popular base and to *expand* the ruling apex' (Finer, 1997: 988). The Arengo's powers were foreshortened to approving war; the Arengo could no longer choose the Doge, but was limited to acclaiming the candidate already selected. All the other responsibilities of the Arengo shifted to the *Consiglio Maggiore*, the great council of 480 members, which was reviewed annually by itself and quickly became a self-perpetuating oligarchy (Bianchi et al., 1997; Finer, 1997: 987–9).

Initially the Arengo had the responsibility to choose eleven members for the ducal electoral college, but in 1177 that power was trimmed back, so it only elected the four men who chose the new forty-member electoral college – with one proviso, which prevented too much concentration of power: no family could have more than one representative on the electoral college (Norwich, 2003: 119). 'The Forty' consisted mostly of former counsellors to the Doge, who became a *de facto* senate, steering the great council and acting as a court of appeal. The first attempt to present the Arengo with a new Doge as a *fait accompli* led to rioting, but the dissidents were mollified when a minor concession was agreed upon: the successful candidate was presented to the Arengo with the statement 'Here is your Doge, if it please you' (Norwich, 2003: 110). The Doge himself was surrounded by a 'lesser' council of six Signorie, which were the executive of the state (Finer, 1997: 988–9). It was this form of government that turned the Fourth Crusade into a treacherous attack, not on the Saracens of the Levant, but on the Christians of the Byzantine Empire and of Constantinople. The Venetians grabbed three eighths of the empire's domains and became an empire themselves (Norwich, 2003: 127–42). The pretence to democracy was fading fast. It is significant to note that the emerging oligarchy was far from enamoured with the responsibilities of high office: these took up time and energy that could much more profitably be directed to commercial pursuits (Norwich, 2003: 119).

In 1229 the *Pregadi* (senate) was instituted, to run the new Venetian empire by instructing ambassadors, by regulating navigation and, eventually, by managing the legislation to be considered by the great council (Finer, 1997: 989). This was another step along the line of transforming the citizen sovereignty of the Arengo into institutional power and, as the power of the institutions grew, they gradually limited the independent power of the Doge. The Doge remained the chair of all these governmental institutions and retained the position for life. However, the counsellors around him – still limited to annual terms, but now able to move from one body to another and to be annually re-elected – were growing in power. They required new Doges to take more and more restrictive oaths of office – until their salaries were the only public revenue they could accept, they could not play strategically with state secrets and they were not allowed direct contact with foreign powers (Norwich, 2003: 151). By the mid-thirteenth century there was even a system of examining an old Doge's record and of making recommendations about the new Doge's oath of office. The obligations of office were restated afresh for every new Doge, and he swore to observe them (Finer, 1997: 989). Without his councillors, the Doge could do nothing. To ensure that the Doge was not subject to factional or family obligation and to defuse the concentration of power that sat with the electoral college, a new system of choosing the Doge was developed. This complex system involved nine rounds of selection for members of the electoral college; it used both election and chance selection by lot to arrive at a forty-one-member electoral college. The college then decided the successful candidate by a system of nomination, interview and exhaustive elimination (Finer, 1997: 998; Norwich, 2003: 166–7). Even as the oligarchy took power, it sought to do so at an arm's length and with nostalgia for the democratic past. Its members ensured that oligarchy never turned into autocracy and tyranny.

In 1297 a major change was made to the Venetian constitution – a change that finally ended any claim to the republic's life as a democracy: it was legislated that only those who had sat in the great council over the

116   *Democracy in the 'Dark Ages'*

preceding four years and their descendants were eligible for membership of that body and that members sat for life. The Arengo became redundant and formally abolished soon after. The Venetian state effectively became an aristocracy which monopolized political offices and excluded the common citizen. There were a few later additions to the great council – members were added for conspicuous bravery and arduous service to the state – but, to all effects, the council was closed (*serrata*; Finer, 1997: 990). The closure of the great council did not make it smaller. As all male heirs were members, the assembly grew to 1,200 and then to 1,500 members, and thus sovereign power rested in a large, unwieldy assembly subject to factionalism, nepotism and personal ambition.

There were three significant conspiracies against the constitutional arrangements of 1297 and for, ostensibly at least, the restoration of democratic government. First there was a foolhardy attempt in 1300, led by Marin Bocconio. Next there was a more complex effort in 1310, led by the charismatic Bajamonte Tiepolo. Finally there was the coup attempted in 1355 by Doge Marin Falier, who despaired of the arrogance of the young aristocrats and sought a return to older, republican values (Norwich, 2003: 185, 190–7, 223–9). The first two conspiracies were put down by the Doge Gradenigo and their consequence was that the Council of Ten became a permanent, secret service institution to guard the constitution. At first provisional, the Council of Ten became permanent in 1335 and was instrumental in foiling the Falier plot. It maintained an interest in all matters of state security that might unsettle 'the most serene republic' (*Serenissima Res Publica*), down to the fine detail of religious observance (Bornstein, 1993). On the face of it, democracy was over in Venice. Sovereign power had ossified into the aristocracy of the *Maggiore Consiglio*; the Doge occupied the pinnacle of power, assisted by a self-selecting bureaucracy and secret police; and the people were removed from any participation in the government of their own affairs. Despite all this, Venice continued to have some very individual and strangely democratic traits.

A democratic sort of aristocracy

Even when the great council closed its membership and effectively became an aristocracy, Venice found it hard to shrug off its democratic traits of egalitarianism, tolerance and community empowerment. While the great council was large, unwieldy and factional, it retained the responsibility to counter the excesses of state power by calling to account the Doge and his Council of Ten and by releasing those considered unfairly imprisoned. The post-democratic constitution still infused Venice with the spirit of a convoy where the fastest ship had to accommodate the slowest (Lane, 1973; Muir, 1999). The method of investment in the trading missions on which Venice's wealth depended also contributed to the ongoing sense of solidarity: anyone could contribute to a *colleganza* which provided two thirds of the capital for a trading venture to the working merchant's one third, while the returns were split evenly between the *colleganza* and the merchant (Norwich, 2003: 156). It was a most effective system to spread the wealth and the risk while rewarding those from all classes who would take a chance. For a further 200 years after the great council's membership was restricted, until 1506, there was still no judicial distinction between nobles and other citizens and the wealth was a lot more widely spread than supposed. Among the 117 Venetians of 1379 whom we would classify today as millionaires in US dollars, 22 per cent were commoners (Finer, 1997: 992).

In a bid to counter well-founded fears about the emergence of a dominant, 'royal' family and to limit the violent effects of factionalism leading to the emergence of cults of personality, bans were applied to bribery, corruption and a range of network-building activities. The display of coats of arms and other family insignia was proscribed in 1266 (Norwich, 2003: 165). Large banquets, even weddings, were limited to family members only, while god-parenting for factional purposes was outlawed in 1505 (Muir, 1999). The criminalization of the vendetta was another step towards limiting factional violence and building a civil society that could protect all those participating in social activities, aristocrat and commoner alike (Bouwsma, 1968; Ruggiero, 1980). The Venetian approach to elections, too, is strange in the contemporary context, but Venetians were committed to finding the best person for a position not the most popular or well-connected person who might use their personal support-base to make a grab for supremacy, so they banned all forms of political publicity and electioneering generally (Finer, 1997: 997; Lane, 1973: 109).

While a ban on political campaigns would be seen as the abrogation of free speech today, a Venetian from the period might point to our bans on hate speech and suggest that Venetians, too, were seeking to enforce tolerance. Thus insulting words, gestures, pictures, and writing were banned as subversive because they could disrupt thoughtful and considered deliberation and provoke vendettas. Anything lampooning the Doge could end in the artist's losing a hand (Muir, 1999). Yet considered debate was tolerated and prized throughout the aristocratic period: the

118   *Democracy in the 'Dark Ages'*

Republic took a hard line against Vatican restrictions on booksellers and printers spreading new scientific knowledge; provided a haven for the astronomer Galileo; and protected the free-thinking priest Paolo Sarpi, whom the Vatican accused of corresponding with heretics (Bouwsma, 1968: 71–83; Norwich, 2003: 511–12). Petrarch, the 'father of humanism', complained ironically that Venice had 'far too much freedom of speech' and three centuries later Sir Henry Wotton could still report that 'all men speak willingly' (Finer, 1997: 1017). Venice also remained a cosmopolitan city. Trade was always at the heart of its political agenda, and nowhere was that clearer than in its relationship with Jews and Muslims: while elsewhere in Europe the Inquisition persecuted non-Christians, Venice's famous tolerance ensured that the city maintained its grip on the silk, spice and jewel trade throughout the east (Goffman, 2002).

Most significantly in terms of Venice's populist heritage, while the aristocrats controlled the central government, democratic institutions rose spontaneously throughout the city in the *scuole* ('schools'), community collectives which were based on neighborhoods, trades, immigrant groups or supporters of particular saints and which provided common people with their own power bases (Lane, 1973: 105–6). Local and special interests were served by these *scuole*, but members came together in them not only to provide neighborhood social services, but also to discuss broader, common concerns then taken up with higher state officials (Finer, 1997: 1015). This extra level of government brought discussion and debate to the middle and lower classes, gave them an active interest in the state and extended the Republic's democratic tendencies far beyond the ruling council.

Conclusion

While Venice was never a democracy in an ideal form, neither was ancient Athens. Washington, DC today is far from perfect. The problems of oligarchy and elective despotism recur. But certainly in its earlier, democratic years, when the rest of Europe languished in feudalism, and even in its later, aristocratic years, Venice was a beacon of openness, tolerance and free thinking. The Venetians remind us that democracy is more than a grand ideal: it is an accommodation between people and power, between the citizens and the oligarchs. Democracy and the debate it engenders are practical tools by which common people can mould and manage their interactions with power and push the benefits of the state a little their way. The Venetian republic began in equality and frank speech, developed in the liminal and matured as it adapted and learnt. It had, first, a convocation of elected tribunes from settlements around the lagoon; then it became a sovereign state where power was in the hands of the citizen assembly; and finally it shifted again to become an aristocracy with a populist bent.

The possibility of democracy without election campaigns may seem strange to us; but the Venetians remind us, both in their successes and in their failures, of the efficacy of civil conversation. The history of Venice shows how democracy civilizes civil war, allows innovation and invention, and encourages the mix of cooperation and competition in which human endeavour thrives. Perhaps even at its proudest moments, democracy can be no more than an accommodation between circulating elites and the will of the people. If that is the case, then the early Venetian republic, with its experiments and alternative approaches, may be seen not only to have informed emerging Renaissance politics at the time, but also to have lessons for the development of democracy today.

Part III
Indigenous Democracy and Colonialism

8
Africa's Indigenous Democracies: The Baganda of Uganda

Immaculate Kizza

The discourse on democracy often acknowledges the complex nature of this tantalizing concept, starting with the absence of an agreed inclusive definition. George Orwell adds that 'not only is there no agreed definition, but the attempt to make one is resisted from all sides' (Orwell, 1968: 132). One possible explanation for this state of affairs might lie in the concept's universal appeal: it is a label which many entities strive to attach to themselves and to their practices because, as Orwell further explains, '[i]t is almost universally felt that when we call a country democratic we are praising it' (Orwell, 1968: 132).

This discourse becomes even more challenging, and at times provocative, when the elusive concept is debated in the context of Africa, a continent whose nation-states, according to many studies, need help if they are to board the democracy train. As Chinua Achebe says: 'From the period of the Slave Trade, through the Age of Colonization to the present day, the catalogue of what Africa and Africans have been said not to have or not to be, is a pretty extensive list' – and high on that list is democracy (Achebe, 1990: 4). It looks as though, for a long time, the world was convinced that Africans had no democratic practices before encountering the West. This assumption, strengthened by the constant stories of political unrest from the continent, has prompted well-wishers to devise means of making the political systems of African nation-states appropriate this precious concept. On the continent, politicians eager to join the world stage have responded enthusiastically, although few of them practise what they claim they are practising. Various challenges to those African nation-states seeking admittance into the democracy club have been pointed out, including bad leadership and 'deep-seated ethnic rivalries and economic inequalities' (Chege, 1996: 350). Possible solutions also abound; they often include economic sanctions for

124 *Indigenous Democracy and Colonialism*

those states which fail to democratize. Overall, there is no shortage of advice on how Africans should make their administrative systems democratic, but unfortunately most of this advice operates on two misconceptions. The first, as already pointed out above, is that Africans do not know what the concept of 'democracy' means. The second, which is even more rampant, is that democracy is a concept that can be given to those not familiar with it. But, as scholars like Claude Ake remind us, 'democratization is not something that one people does for another. People must do it for themselves or it does not happen' (Ake, 1996: 69).

Something positive, though, has come out of all that lively discourse on how to 'grow democracy' on the African continent: it has prompted Africanists to conduct studies which point out that, contrary to what is often discussed, there were democratic practices on the African continent long before the arrival of Europeans. The widely held notion that democracy as an administrative system was unknown in most African societies until the colonialists introduced it is increasingly brought into question. While it is true that there were several ethnic groups on the continent that seemed lawless, such groups were not in any way confined to Africa, and a good number of African ethnic groups had concrete democratic practices governing their day-to-day activities before the arrival of the colonialists. Joe Teffo, for example reminds us that Africans 'were in the past not ruled against their will' (Teffo, 2002: 1): they always had a voice and representation in their governance through their traditional systems, which included kingships and ruling councils. 'It [therefore] should...not be difficult for an unprejudiced mind to see signs of democracy in traditional African political life' (Teffo, 2004: 446). Francis Deng also cites Dia confirming this point: 'Despite the hierarchical system of traditional governments, most of these were generally governed by consensus and broad participation...through group representation at the central level and village councils at the local level' (Dia, cited in Deng, 2004: 503). Ake too concurs:

> Traditional African political systems were infused with democratic values. They were invariably patrimonial, and consciousness was communal; everything was everybody's business, engendering a strong emphasis on participation. Standards of accountability were even stricter than in Western societies.
>
> (Ake, 1996: 65)

Indigenous democracies in Africa

Ancient Africa was a beehive of activities, with its people, mostly the Bantu, migrating from one part of the continent into another, often in search of better and more farming land. Powerful groups would subdue less powerful ones if they desired their land, and in the process they would destroy or assimilate those people's ways of life and socio-political systems. But there was a good number of strong and firmly established political entities on the continent, similar to others around the globe, by the time Africa had its first encounter with the West. One noticeably unique feature of most traditional African societies was, and still is in many ethnic groups today, the dual nature of their socio-political administrative systems. In this set-up, the social component took care of individuals in kinship groups, giving them a firm sense of security and belonging, ensuring that each person had a voice in the running of the day-to-day affairs in one's society and safeguarding each individual's identity and freedoms. The political segment performed the same duties for the entire ethnic group and safeguarded the security and survival of the group.

The most basic unit in these socio-political administrative systems was the family. Traditionally, African families operated under a 'division of labour' which made every family member a respectable contributor to the well-being of one's family. Under this division of labour setup, each individual had a voice in the overall functioning of one's family and most decisions were reached by consensus, each individual clearly articulating issues related to that person's specific tasks. The second unit was the clan, which operated under the governance of a clan head usually chosen by consensus. All clan members had a voice in the running of the clan, even on matters such as getting rid of clan heads who did not treat clan members with respect. The largest unit was the ethnic group, which was a collection of clans that shared common origins, historical and cultural traditions, language, and a mutually accepted way of life. Although there was a considerable number of kingships among these groups and kings were born into their positions, most of them were aware that they could be deposed if they mistreated their subjects, and 'constitutional checks and dual-sex authority arrangements guarded against unlimited power' (Robinson, 1986: 137). Additionally, most traditional African kingships were people-centered community institutions depending on 'general community involvement and participation' for their functioning (Teffo, 2004: 446). Members had a voice in decision-making at

126 *Indigenous Democracy and Colonialism*

this level mostly through representation, and decisions were made by consensus.

In addition to belonging to lineage groups through which they participated in governance, pre-colonial Africans had other organizational groups they belonged to, such as gender, age and title groups, which gave them further platforms for input into their governance. The importance of gender groups cannot be overstated in any society functioning on a division of labour principle. Since each family member had specific responsibilities, gender groups were schools that prepared individuals for their roles, and also gave them support and encouragement as needed. Additionally, gender groups 'institutionalized the parallel exercise of power by women and men'. Robinson goes on to explain that these systems were particularly of value to women, who were assured of having seats 'among the ranks of monarchs, councillors, title holders, religious dignitaries, political advisors, and lineage heads', thereby participating actively in the governance of their ethnic groups (Robinson, 1986: 136).

Title groups were also popular, mostly as a way to reward achievements, but there were specific obligations to one's society that came with each of those titles, as well as an added opportunity to participate in governance. In *Facing Mount Kenya*, for example, Jomo Kenyatta details specific title groups among the Kikuyu of Kenya, including the council of elders, the council of peace and, probably the most important title group, the religious and sacrificial council, which was the final group into which one could be initiated before joining one's ancestors (Kenyatta, 1962). He also explains each group's specific duties to the Kikuyu people. It is important to stress that any one could earn a title and belong to a specific title group: these were open to all, males and females alike. In many societies, title holders would call meetings and discuss issues pertaining to their respective titles, and they would continue discussing until consensus had been reached.

Probably the most inclusive groups were the age groups, which were open to all through initiation. They started at puberty, the first time when one was initiated into an age group; and the individual in question belonged to that group throughout all of his/her life. These age groups had specific responsibilities to perform for the welfare of the whole group, and such responsibilities increased in importance as a group grew older, until its members reached the most respected age, that of ethnic group elders. Because individuals served their societies in different roles at different times of their lives, through being members of various age groups all the way to old age, each one had a voice and a significant role to play in governance, all the way from puberty through to old age.

Pre-colonial Africa was a colourful landscape, a mosaic of ethnic groups with various lifestyles, which are often grouped into three convenient clusters: hunters and gatherers; herdsmen and pastoralists; and subsistence farmers. These clusters are significant because an ethnic group's administrative system had to suit that group's life style. Hunters and gatherers, like the Bambuti of the Ituri Forest in the Democratic Republic of Congo and the Khoisan or San of the Kalahari Desert in Botswana, had a very well-organized socio-political system, whose basic governing principle was cooperation. Division of labour was practised strictly, the men doing the hunting, mostly of wild game, while the women concentrated on gathering edible plants; but leadership and guidance were duties for all the people in the village. Conflict resolution was a very well-practised technique among these people; affairs regarding the well-being of the group were debated by all, and suggestions and recommendations were fully discussed, until a consensus was reached. Among the herdsmen and pastoralists, like the Nandi of Kenya, age groups were administrative units, the councils of elders were in overall control, and the public had an input to all its affairs by attending village assembly meetings. Most disputes were settled in open discussions in these meetings, and, once again, decisions were reached by consensus.

The third lifestyle cluster in pre-colonial Africa was that of the subsistence farmers, and there are still many around the continent. A number of families in an area constituted a village, which would be in the hands of a clan head if all the families in that village traced descent from a common ancestor. However, if the grouped families shared no line of descent, the village administration would be in the hands of a council of elders made up of heads of families. Although there were many subsistence farming ethnic groups in pre-colonial Africa whose largest political unit was the clan led by a clan head, there was also a substantial number of entities that developed centralized administrative systems by consolidating kinship clans into one entity. That entity would then be led either by a hereditary sovereign or by one selected from that ethnic group's founding clan, from the clan that first moved in the area, or from a conquering clan that had just moved in and imposed power over the other clans. As various scholars have observed, while in theory a sovereign in charge of a whole ethnic group treated their subjects like property and assigned themselves limitless powers, in practice that was not the norm (Dodge, 1966; Robinson, 1986; Teffo, 2004). Generally, African kings ruled through the consent of their people, and with their

128 *Indigenous Democracy and Colonialism*

people, in what Teffo has labelled 'a *communocracy*, insofar as it is a type of governance based on general involvement and participation ... a form of democracy characteristic of many traditional African societies' (Teffo, 2004: 446). There were also many checks and balances on the systems to keep those sovereigns focused on their obligations to their people. Ali A. Mazrui, for example, identifies four levels of checks and balances typical of most kingship administrative systems (Mazrui, 1986). The king constituted the first level; below him was a chief whom he would choose as his principal advisor, and that was the second level. That chief would seek advice and report to the third level in the system, which was represented by an inner council of elders made up of heads of the various clans under the sovereign's leadership. This council of elders would have participated, as its people's representative, in the selection of the sovereign, and its members would advise the sovereign's chief only after consulting with the ordinary members of the clans they represented; and, finally, these ordinary members constituted the fourth level. The council of elders at the third level, in consultation with ordinary members at the fourth level, had the option of deposing any sovereign who seemed incompetent or turning despotic. Governance was by consensus at all levels, and all had a voice in these hierarchical administrative systems, mostly through representation.

The royal administrative systems, together with the clan systems, made up the dual socio-political administrative systems which the West found firmly established in most of the historically known ancient African empires and kingdoms: the Ashanti, Oyo, Benin, Songhai, Mali, and Ngoni in West Africa; Buganda, Bunyoro, and Ankole in East Africa; Mwenemutapa in Central Africa, and the Zulu in South Africa. By no means were all these socio-political administrative systems perfect, and indeed no known socio-political system has ever been so, but the fact remains that there were organized groups of people in pre-colonial Africa with fundamental socio-political administrative systems that embraced various democratic practices to suit individual ethnic groups. Since the governed in most of these systems had a voice in how they were governed, held their leaders responsible for their actions, and were adequately represented at all levels of administration, it is not hard to see why various Africanists are convinced that 'democracy' is not a foreign concept to many Africans. An individual had several avenues for participating in governance: as a member of a family, of a clan, of an ethnic group, of an age-group, of a gender group and, in some cases, of a title group. These peoples' ways of life were materially simple, as Basil Davidson observes; nevertheless they had developed a civilization of dignity and value in its spiritual beliefs, *in methods of self-rule*, in arts such as dancing and singing, in skills that were needed for the solving of the problems of everyday life. It was also, for the most part, *a peaceful civilization*, generally far more so than that of Europe.

(Davidson, 1969: 168, author's emphasis)

Indigenous democracy of the Baganda

As stated above, by the time Europe encountered Africa, the continent had established many political entities with more or less the same administrative systems as those around Europe. In the case of Uganda, for example, 'several nation-states had already developed in the area before the British arrived to award the "stamp of progress" in the form of the protectorate' (Reid, 2005: 325). Whether all the political groupings that the colonialists found in what is now the Republic of Uganda can be described as nation-states is not the central issue of this discussion. The author's focus is on the indigenous democratic practices among the people in the various entities of that region. There were democratic practices in decentralized entities like those of the Karamojong, Iteso, Chiga and Basoga, as well as in hierarchically centralized entities such as the Baganda, Banyoro, Batoro and Ankole people. Even though these people's administrative systems were as different from each other and as unique as the physical features and languages of the people who embraced them, they still shared the dual socio-political administrative feature, which enabled those people to govern themselves democratically.

Although there were several entities in pre-colonial Uganda that had democratic practices, those in Buganda territory exemplified such practices best at that time. The Baganda people's clan, kingdom and judicial systems enabled them to practice a form of democracy based on consensual decision-making and broad participation in governance at all levels, mostly through representation.

The coming of the Baganda people into what is now Central Southern Uganda did not happen all at once; it is said to have been a gradual process of waves of people of various lineages coming into the region between 1000 and 1300 CE, as part of a general Bantu migration south and east due to the desertification of the Sahara and to overpopulation. However, the actual settling of the ancestors of present-day Baganda in this region is estimated to have taken place 'between the thirteenth and sixteenth centuries' (Kiwanuka, 1972: 31). Since these people were, and

130   *Indigenous Democracy and Colonialism*

to a large extent still are, subsistence farmers, they quickly established themselves in this fertile area by clearing land, farming and settling as members of autonomous patrilineal extended family groupings known as *ebika* (clans). Over time, these people turned their individual clans into intricate administrative organizations responsible for a number of activities, including the fostering of solidarity, unity and a sense of belonging among clan members, their protection from attacks, the preservation of the clans' cultural values and traditions and, above all, ensuring that each and every clan member was treated as an equal and that all had a voice in their governance.

The Baganda clan system

The Baganda clan system was, and still is, a hierarchical structure consisting of several units, the smallest of which is the *Nnyumba* (single family), often headed either by a husband/father or by a single mother. Even though a family head was not an elected person, there were checks and balances in place to prevent him or her from being despotic, and one of these was the division of labour. Buganda families, like many African families, traditionally practised the division of labour, as discussed above. In this setup in Buganda, husbands were responsible for the overall running of the family, but each individual adult had a voice in this governance because of the specific duties one had to perform. The husbands were in charge of securing land, building homes and furnishing them, and preparing fields for farming. The wives took care of the homes and all the domestic chores, as well as of planning, planting and maintaining the banana plantations (bananas are the staple food of the Baganda), and also growing other food products and vegetables. Children participated in their respective gender's chores. All adult family members respected each other's duties, knowing very well that, if any one of them neglected his or her responsibilities, the entire family would suffer. Decisions were made by consensus, and disputes were settled in the same way. If any family member, including the family head, mistreated others or neglected his or her chores, that person would be censored by the extended family – amicably, because it was a family. The ultimate punishment for a family head turned despotic, or for any other problematic family member, would be expulsion from the clan, which in effect meant that one had ceased to exist.

Family heads represented their families at the next level in the system, the *Luggya*. The Baganda clan system is patrilineal, so the *Luggya* was the home of brothers turned family heads, and their father, now a grandfather, headed the lot. The *Luggya* was governed in the same way as the family: the grandfather or his successor chose family names for the children, settled disputes among members, ensured that all his people had a voice in the family affairs and preserved his family's traditions. The next lineage level to the *Luggya* was the *Lunyiriri*; this was followed by the *Mutuba*, then by the *Ssiga*; and the final level was the *Ekika* (clan), headed by the *Omutaka* (head of the clan). Every clan member was represented at all levels, and each clan member's voice was heard all the way up the system through this representation. Each level was governed and functioned in the same way as the basic unit, the *Nnyumba*, and the various heads performed the same duties but for more and larger units than the *Nnyumba*. The overall governance of the clan was bottom-up. Decisions were made by consensus at each level and, if one felt dissatisfied with a suggestion, ruling, solution, settlement or any other decision made at any level, that individual was free to take the case higher up, and even all the way to the *Ekika*. The Baganda also have a keen sense of responsibility, a strong spirit of solidarity and kinship, and a love for fairness and justice all of which aided in the smooth running of their units.

Although Buganda historians have several versions pertaining to the founding of the kingdom, they are in agreement that the impressive political entity that European explorers, Henry M. Stanley and James Grant, stumbled upon in search of the source of the Nile in the mid-1800s had its origins in the Baganda people's clan system.

The Buganda kingdom

When Kintu, who is believed to be the founder of the Buganda kingdom, arrived in the area in the late 1300s, there were six very well organized clans permanently settled in the region. These clans were autonomous and considered themselves equal, although every now and then an aggressive clan head would declare himself head of all clans in the area until he was overthrown by an even stronger clan leader. Legend has it that one such clan head by the name of Bemba had established hegemony over the six clans by the time Kintu arrived in the region, bringing thirteen clans with him. Kintu's invasion of the area is said to have been a welcome event, because Bemba was a very harsh and ruthless leader. After defeating Bemba, Kintu added Bemba's six clans to his thirteen and declared himself leader of the now nineteen clans in the locality.

132   Indigenous Democracy and Colonialism

After securing his position as the undisputed leader of the nineteen clans, Kintu invited the clan heads under him to join him in what is often described as the first known 'constitutional' conference in Buganda. During this 'conference', Kintu and the clan heads openly discussed the structure of what later came to be known as the kingdom of Buganda along the same lines as their clan system, with emphasis on governance by consensus and broad participation of all the Baganda under the system. Kintu, who had been a clan head himself, took over the newly structured kingdom as its king (*Kabaka*), but he also retained his position in the clan hierarchy by becoming *Ssabataka* (head of the clan heads). He then created fourteen political offices, including that of prime minister (*Katikkiro*), who was to be his right hand, and he filled these offices with his fellow clan heads, whom he empowered to share political power with him as his administrative team, headed by the prime minister. He also left the clan heads in their positions, just as he had found them, in charge of their respective clans. By retaining the clan heads' positions, Kintu enabled the Baganda people to preserve their clan system and its democratic practices. The kingdom now had a strong dual socio-political administrative structure; the clan system became the social component and the fourteen political offices became the nucleus of the political component.

As the kingdom grew in territorial size and population by conquering and assimilating people from neighbouring political entities, the fourteen political offices were solidified into administrative units, to serve their people better. By the mid-nineteenth century the kingdom had become the largest and best organized political entity in the region, with the *Kabaka* at the top of the system, although the lineage leaders had lost some of their power in the process. There were now six strong political administrative levels in place, which became the political component of the socio-political administrative system still in place today. The smallest political unit in the kingdom was the village (*ekyalo*); a group of villages constituted a parish (*omuluka*); a group of parishes made up a sub-county (*gombolola*); a number of sub-counties made up a county (*saza*). Each of these units was headed by an appointed chief. Village and parish chiefs were appointed by the chiefs above them, and the *Kabaka* appointed the sub-county and county chiefs. The next political level had four political offices, the most important of which was that of the *Katikkiro* (prime minister), followed by that of the *Mujasi* (commander-in-chief), then that of the *Gabunga* (admiral of the navy), and finally that of *Kimbugwe* (overseer of the royal line). These positions were held by officers directly appointed by the *Kabaka*. With the exception of the *Kabaka* position, which was hereditary, all the other political positions were open to all Baganda, and were filled by the *Kabaka* or his representatives on the basis of a merit system 'where excellence in war, demonstration of administrative ability and personal acquaintance with the king were the key to high office' (Gukiina, 1972: 32). Heading the hierarchy was the *Kabaka* himself, constituting the last level in this political administrative system.

This was a bottom-up administrative system in which all Baganda had a voice. The people would be consulted for advice by their village chiefs, who would act on it or pass it along to the parish chiefs, if necessary. That advice would keep going through the various levels, and all the way up to the *Kabaka*, if it was needed at that level. People could also complain about their leaders, and their complaints could go as far as the *Kabaka*. A chief at any level who seemed to be leaning towards becoming a despot could be dismissed from that post by the *Kabaka*. Often chiefs found themselves in delicate positions (Southwold, 1964: 212). For, while they were responsible to their superiors, they needed the consent of their constituents in order to do their jobs efficiently and remain in their positions. Enforcing the will of their superiors, especially unpopular decrees, was not the way to maintain one's authority. Even the *Kabaka* had limits on his power, basically because he governed through councils of clan heads and chiefs at all levels who would seek advice and get input from the people they represented, and the overall governance was by consensus.

Although Buganda was a kingdom, it did not function as most traditional kingdoms around the globe did at that time; this was due to a number of reasons, and in the first place to the absence of a permanent royal residence for the *Kabaka*; this situation enabled him to be in touch with all the people by staying at various locations throughout the kingdom. Secondly, 'succession to the throne was...modelled on the succession system prevalent in the clans and families', which gave all Baganda a chance to participate in the selection of their *Kabakas* (Kiwanuka, 1972: 97). Whenever a *Kabaka* died, the *Katikkiro* would consult with the dead king's mother (*Namasole*), with the clan heads (*Abataka*), and with the chiefs at the various levels; and, with input from all the people, a new *Kabaka* would be chosen from the sons of the deceased one. If there happened to be no sons, then one would be chosen from among the brothers of the deceased or their sons; and, if the people's choice happened to be someone young, the *Katikkiro* would perform his duties and in the process coach him until he came of age. Thirdly, and probably most importantly, there was no patrilineal

134 *Indigenous Democracy and Colonialism*

structured royal clan in Buganda. This was arranged on purpose, to prevent any one clan from being dominant over the others. All clans were, and still are, equal in status, and every clan had a chance to parent a *Kabaka* because *Kabakas* were free to marry from all clans, with the exception of those of their mothers. 'The absence of a royal clan was achieved through what seems to be an elaborate arrangement whereby royal children belonged to their mothers' clans, contrary to the universal patrilineal clan system of the Baganda' (Kiwanuka, 1972: 97).

In addition to the expansion of the political system to serve the expanded kingdom better, there was also growth in size of the clan system. New clans kept being added to the system, so there were fifty-three clans in Buganda at the beginning of the twenty-first century, and clan heads took on additional responsibilities in order to represent their people more efficiently in the new expanded kingdom. In addition to the original duties, each clan head was now also responsible for protecting and sustaining that clan's integrity, identity, traditions, and pride; for hearing and settling disputes concerning mainly land and families of clan members, as well as for representing the clan in inter-clan ceremonies and disputes. Clan heads were additionally responsible for presenting their clan members' needs to the *Kabaka*, helping the *Kabaka* to make appointments to various offices, and recommending and appointing members of their clans to the *Kabaka*'s palace as pages, where some would become chiefs.

The judicial system

In addition to the clan and kingdom systems, the Baganda also had a comprehensive, efficient and impressive judicial system consisting of two components, namely the clan component and the kingdom component. This system allowed individuals to voice their grievances and to get fair treatment. All Baganda were equal before the law. Anyone was free to file a claim, either in the clan judicial component if the grievance was among kindred, or in the kingdom judicial component for all other grievances, especially in criminal cases. To ensure fairness, there were standard procedures for handling all kinds of cases, ranging from murder to casual fights, which were clearly known by all Baganda. Apolo Kaggwa compiled an impressive list of these procedures, potential crimes and related punishments (Kaggwa, 1934 [1905]). Anyone wronged or with a grievance, for example, could take one's case to one's village court, which was the first unit of the kingdom judicial component. The village chief would then summon both the plaintiff and the defendant to appear and state their cases to a jury of peers at the court, in the presence of all villagers interested in that case. After hearing both sides, the village chief, in consultation with all present, would then render a verdict, basing his decision on the well-known laws. The guilty party, regardless of whether defendant or the plaintiff, paid all the fines and costs originating from the case. This was a good way to prevent trivial cases from making it into the courts; it also encouraged people to settle their cases by themselves, if they could, instead of incurring such expenses in courts. If one or both of the disputing parties were not satisfied with the village court's decision, they had the option of appealing that decision in the parish court, and if they were still unhappy they could continue through all the administrative levels up to the supreme arbitrator, the *Kabaka*, whose decisions in such disputes were final.

Conclusion

Since a good number of Africa's ethnic groups, including the Baganda of Uganda, developed elaborate socio-political administrative systems that gave all a voice in governance, emphasized group participation, could get rid of unpopular leaders, privileged consensus over confrontation in decision-making and governance generally, and had efficient judicial systems that safeguarded an individual's rights, freedoms and property, those groups deserve to be included in a history of democracy.

As the discourse on the implementation of democracy in African nation-states continues, scholars should keep in mind two recurring points. First, many Africans are already familiar with democratic practices and there are already in place, in a number of African nation-states, solid democratic infrastructures that can be used as starting blocks in the development of democratic administrative systems. Secondly, efforts to implement democracy in African nation-states should include serious consideration of the role of indigenous democratic systems and institutions in those nations' political systems. This is not, by any means, calling for a total return to the African past; that is practically impossible. But a nation's political system needs to be rooted in that nation's socio-cultural context; and, as Teffo points out, 'there is a suitable tradition of democracy in Indigenous African culture' (Teffo, 2004: 444–5). Those interested in helping African nation-states to chart and implement viable democratic political systems in the age of globalization should consider locating Africa's indigenous experience with democracy centrally in those systems.

9
The Hunters Who Owned Themselves

Philippe Paine

The Métis people of Western Canada are descendants of North American Indians intermarried with French Canadian, Scottish and other fur traders. Since 1670, the Hudson's Bay Company administered a vast region, larger than Europe, known as Rupert's Land. Neither the British Crown nor the Company distinguished between Indians and Métis in law or policy. Both were left to govern their own affairs. Other companies, based in Canada, blithely ignored the Company's legal monopoly of the fur trade, but they all respected the political independence of native peoples.

Métis lifestyle resembled that of the tribes of the forests and plains, especially the Cree, Ojibway and Assiniboine, with whom they had many blood ties. A distinctive Métis ethnicity emerged when independent fur traders, known as Freemen, sought to maintain a strategic social distance from both the fur companies and the tribes they had married into (Foster, 2002). The Métis had their own languages, Michif and Bungee, but also spoke French, English, Gaelic, and a dozen Indian languages (Bakker, 1997). They called themselves '*Otipemisiwak*' ('people who own themselves'). By the mid-nineteenth century the majority were Catholics, but some were Presbyterians, Anglicans and Methodists. Indian ceremonies, such as the Sweat Lodge and Sacred Pipe, were maintained. They considered freedom and self-rule the essential elements of their culture, rather than language, religion or race, anticipating the multicultural ethos that Canadian society embraces today.

The Métis hunted, fished, trapped furs, manned canoe brigades, and traded goods across the plains; but their greatest pride lay in being buffalo hunters. Twice a year, they organized Hunts for meat, hides, and the marketable processed food called *pemican*. Each Hunt deployed a mobile society of hundreds, sometimes over a thousand men, women and children, administered by elected officials chosen among heads of family who considered themselves political equals. Laws were voted by adult males (Giraud, 1945: 143; Ross, 1856: 249–52).

In 1870, the Hudson's Bay Company sold its territory to the newly independent Dominion of Canada. Great changes were afoot: the buffalo herds were dwindling; the fur trade was in decline; a planned transcontinental railroad would render the Métis' skills as traders and guides redundant. The Métis would have to become farmers and cattle-ranchers (Sprenger, 1987). Though most Métis were willing to become Canadians, they assumed they had the right to negotiate the terms of this transition, and were determined that a coherent civil authority, respecting their rights, should accompany settled life. To this end, they formed 'provisional governments', employing the traditional democracy of the Hunt as a template for settled political institutions.

The conflicting values and priorities of the Métis, Indians, settlers, and the Canadian government in Ottawa culminated in the most violent events in Canada's post-Confederation history. In battles between a Canadian expeditionary force and allied Métis and Indian warriors, a total of 128 died. Louis Riel, the principal Métis leader, surrendered and was hung, a result which bitterly divided the country for the next half-century.

The conflict between the Métis and the Canadian State has preoccupied Canadian historians and writers since it began, and even inspired the country's most frequently performed opera, *Louis Riel*. Yet the extraordinary democratic organization of the Métis, though documented well enough, has inspired little interest among historians; Métis political institutions were deemed the preserve of anthropologists.

An invisible achievement

Métis provisional governments, like their settlements and Hunts, always combined Michif, French and English speakers, Catholics and Protestants, Indians and non-Native settlers, all on terms of equality. Despite this, most Canadian historians have discussed the Métis in the context of the two conflicts obsessing Canadians in the East: language and religion. Some have interpreted the key events as a primitive 'millenarian' movement, like the Ghost Dance (Mossmann, 2002). Others have portrayed the Métis as conservative primitives, stubbornly and foolishly resisting modernity (Stanley, 1960).

George Woodcock, a literary critic, was the first to see the democracy of the Buffalo Hunt as historically significant. His biography of

138 *Indigenous Democracy and Colonialism*

the Métis leader Gabriel Dumont drew on Alexander Ross' account of the Hunt to explain the origin of the local provisional government Dumont led in 1873 (Ross, 1856: 249–50; Woodcock, 1975). He did not use sharp critical tools, and his sympathy for the Métis verged on romance. He projected onto the Métis his ideas of European intellectual 'anarchism'. But, since then, at least such Métis institutions have worked their way into some reference works and Métis-related publications (Barkwell, et al., 2007). There is still no analytical or comparative literature on the subject. There has been no effort to place the significance of Métis politics in the context of Canadian, let alone world, history.

Hunt democracy

Contemporary witnesses of the Hunt were astonished by its combination of egalitarian values and efficacious discipline (McLean, 1932: 376). That this discipline was not easily come by is demonstrated in attempts of non-Métis to organize similar operations. Josiah Gregg, who participated in an American wagon train, noted the chaos that ensued when it encountered an Indian war party. In a crisis, '[e]veryone fancied himself a commander, and vociferated his orders accordingly' (Gregg, 1954 [1844]: 58). By contrast, Louis Goulet, a Métis who produced an oral memoir recounting the Hunt, stated:

> The choice of chiefs and members of the council was made with such care that I never encountered any example of favoritism of any kind ... It's unfortunate that transcripts of the activities of these councils were not made and conserved. What interesting chronicles they would be, for us today! All I can say on the matter is that I don't remember experiencing, nor even having heard spoken of, a single case where the authority or the decision of a council was in doubt, or even disputed.
>
> (Goulet, cited in Charette, 1976: 38; author's translation)

Alexander Ross wrote an account of a Hunt he accompanied in 1840. It was the largest one recorded, comprising 1,630 people. Ross was a Scottish trader who retired to farm among the Gaelic-speaking Highlanders of the Red River settlement. He saw himself as a Tory country gentleman, disapproved of the Hunt and disdained democracy, but he conceded that the former was marvellously organized: 'for everything moves with the regularity of clockwork' and the elected Chief,

Jean-Baptiste Wilkie, is described as 'a man of good sound sense and long experience' (Ross, 1856: 228–9).

There are profoundly different attitudes towards such institutions of self-government. Ross wrote that the Métis

> will never become a thoroughly civilized people, nor orderly subjects in a civilized community. Feeling their own strength, from being constantly armed, and free from control, they despise all others; but above all, they are marvelously tenacious of their own original habits. They cherish freedom as they cherish life... They are all republicans in principle, and a licentious freedom is their besetting sin.
>
> (Ross, 1856: 252)

The rationality of its organization is something he readily conceded. Ross' criticism was that the Hunt was *too democratic*. Goulet saw it differently:

> We, of the younger generation, didn't realize that this happy existence, all in spaceous, unembarassed freedom, was to evaporate, like childhood does, like the fine promises of adolescence, virtually overnight. We didn't know that this modern civilization which we greeted with such haste would soon exact such a heavy cost.
>
> (Goulet, cited in Charette, 1976: 41, author's translation)

Henry Youle Hind, who crossed the prairies in 1857–58, left this description:

> After the start from the settlement has been made, and all the stragglers or tardy hunters have arrived, a great council is held, and a president elected. A number of captains are nominated by the president and people jointly. The captains then proceed to appoint their own policemen, the number assigned to each not exceeding ten. Their duty is to see that the laws of the hunt are strictly carried out... All laws are proclaimed in camp, and relate to the hunt alone. All camping orders are given by signal, a flag being carried by the guides, who are appointed by election.
>
> (Hind, 1860: 111)

Contemporary accounts by outsiders like John McLean and the artist Paul Kane, as well as reminiscences of Métis elders collected by

Anguste-Henri de Trémaudan, confirm the democratic governance of the Hunt (Kane, 1859; McLean, 1932; Trémaudan, 1936).

A Hunt would be announced by runners sent to Métis communities. Participants would gather at an announced date and location. In Goulet's account of the 1870s, two chiefs and a council of twelve *Capitaines* were elected, and articles of a Law of the Hunt were voted on and proclaimed (Goulet, cited in Charette, 1976). Trémaudan describes a *Président*, a *Crieur* who relayed commands around the camp, and twelve *Capitaines* (Trémaudan, 1936: 59). He states that candidates presented themselves to voters, who chose by lining up behind them and making themselves directly answerable to the man of their choice. When *Capitaines* acted as military commanders, this direct selection ensured effective command. Each *Capitaine*, in turn, deputized *Découvreurs* (scouts who would ride out to survey conditions) and *Soldats* to act as police and sentinels in the camp. These doubled as officers in combat. *Découvreurs* were selected in pairs, an older experienced man with a young man in training. The council met every evening, hearing reports from scouts and sentinels, and planned the next day's movement. It also served as a judicial body with relatively mild punishments, which usually involved a fine or rebuke (Ross, 1856: 250). When important issues were to be decided, a general assembly of all hunters was convened, and decisions were made by a majority vote taken from them (Trémaudan, 1936: 60). There was a strict separation of powers. *Capitaines* exercised authority only when the expedition was encamped. When the community was in motion, authority rested in the guides who carried the flag, the raising of which signalled the raising of camp. Ross wrote: 'While it is up, the guide is chief of the expedition. Captains are subject to him, and the soldiers of the day are his messengers: he commands all. The moment the flag is lowered, his functions cease, and the captains' and soldiers' duties commence' (Ross, 1856: 249).

Native genesis

To anyone familiar with the culture of the Cree, the native people most closely associated with the Métis, all of these details seem eerily familiar. The various specialized functionaries were the same both in the Métis and in the Plains Cree Hunts (Mandelbaum, 1979: 115–16). Most significantly, Indian hunts employed the same dual division of authority between administration *in loco* and in movement. The Plains Cree equivalent of the Métis guide was an experienced man selected by the band council when the band came together for the Hunt. According to

Kamiokisihkwew ('Fine Day'), a Cree who fought alongside Riel, a new guide was chosen at every monthly council meeting (Fine Day, 1926).

Lex parsimoniae would press the conclusion that the political organization of the Métis Hunt was borrowed from closely allied Plains peoples. The Métis, the Cree and the Ojibway were all forest hunters, trappers and fishermen who gradually moved onto the Plains. They adopted elements of Plains culture, and especially the Buffalo Hunt, from their allies, the Assiniboine and Blackfeet. Tribes were drawn to the limitless food and potential surplus for trade that the buffalo herds could supply. Only those with a disciplined, co-ordinated and versatile political structure could exploit this resource. The archaeological evidence demonstrates that this situation goes back for millennia (Brink, 2008). Before the advent of the horse and gun, Plains tribes constructed 'pounds' and 'jumps', structures of stone, wood, and hide that channelled buffalo herds towards cliffs or corrals. This required the co-operative organization of hundreds of people. Yet it was accomplished using administrative councils, decisions by consensus, voluntary association, and an egalitarian ethos.

While Native North Americans manifested most of the political ideas known to Europeans, they did so in different proportions. Some political concepts were especially prominent among the sub-Arctic forest and plains cultures from which the Métis sprang. Among these were *individual impetus, household autonomy, conciliar flexibility, task-based authority*, and *implied voting by withdrawal*.

Native Canadian egalitarianism did not correspond to that which European scholars imagine, extrapolating from their own religious and utopian traditions. It was a 'level playing field' for the unfolding of individual impetus. Plains and Woodland cultures were extremely competitive. Life was a struggle for the acquisition of property and social prestige. Prestige could be acquired through bravery in war, but the most secure path to it was wealth. Advancement was accompanied by expectations of generosity to friends and by charity to the needy. Wealth had to be acquired to cover these costs and to be seen to be lavishly spent, yet not depleted (Milloy, 1988: 80). 'A Poor Assiniboine Becomes Chief', a story related by Sākäwāw tells of an impoverished man who rose to chiefdom: he began by making arrows and trading them for breeding puppies, and slowly built a fortune by clever enterprise (Bloomfield, 1943: 103–15). Leadership was a side-effect of this individual impetus. The household was the most powerful political unit and no head of household could be compelled by anyone to do anything. Individual households associated with each other in a

142 *Indigenous Democracy and Colonialism*

variety of configurations, usually temporary, but larger, semi-permanent associations formed around economically successful individuals. Such leadership was accepted only so long as it seemed credible. Bands came together in confederations, which required constant conciliation and diplomatic maintenance (Mandelbaum, 1979: 105–6).

Men and women came together in their respective councils, which were the preferred tool for the management of every aspect of life. Key decisions, whether civil, religious, military, commercial or recreational, involved the convening of a council, accompanied by ceremony, speeches, and opportunities for assent or dissent. The temporary and optional nature of Native activities was made possible by a basic template of council-making, which had some universal practices, such as passing the tobacco pipe. This conciliar flexibility lies at the heart of Native politics. The survival and success of the Métis depended on their being adept in such institutions, which goes far towards explaining their behaviour in the Buffalo Hunt.

Division of authority, so that it focused on specific tasks, is one of the hallmarks of Native politics. There were no chiefs with aristocratic authority, but there were war chiefs, religious chiefs, diplomacy chiefs, fishing chiefs, and so on. Outside their particular prerogatives, they could exercise no power. Métis institutions show a similar preference for task-based authority. Anthropologists distinguish between government by consensus and government by voting. It is true that the typical decision-making process involved a circle of councillors, each giving an opinion on an issue, after which the chief would make a decision. However, this type of decision-making occurred when a chief's authority was established and operating. It was not a 'system' alternative to, or opposed to, voting. Native peoples were quite familiar with voting. Voting was known in many contexts, especially in the operation of confederations. Indian agents, for example, were cautioned that it was not sufficient to know the outcome of debates in confederation councils, but subsequently to determine how each band delegate had voted (Atwater, 2009 [1829]). When the Cree of Pelican Narrows, Saskatchewan, entered a treaty relationship with Canada, the Indian Agent was empowered to appoint anyone he chose to be 'chief' in the eyes of the Canadian government. Instead, he told the band he would accept anyone they chose. The Cree immediately fenced off an area to hold an election. Individuals presented themselves as nominees, and each head of a household stood behind the one of his choice (Siggins, 2005: 39). This is identical to the procedure described by Trémaudan for the Métis. But formal voting is not often a necessity in a society where anyone has the option of withdrawal from collective action. The purpose of voting is not to maximize the quality of decisions, but to protect the rights of the individual. Where any party can withdraw consent and is not compelled to obey a group decision, 'voting' is implicit in the option of withdrawal.

Almost every aspect of Buffalo Hunt democracy conforms to what we know of Cree political practice. The weight of the evidence suggests that, in its origins, Indian influences were primary. However, potential European influences must be assessed.

European influences

It is a dubious proposition that there was a great cultural gulf between the European and the Indian ancestors of the Métis, or that today's academic formulae of 'colonialism' applied to the latter. The European ancestors of the Métis were predominantly French Canadians, Orkney Islanders and Highland Scots, usually from impoverished backgrounds. To assume that a Scottish Highlander would have been baffled by a society of bands and clans would be the height of absurdity. Highlanders were Gaelic speakers for whom English was a language of submission. They were looked upon as 'savages' by their own Lowland countrymen. French Canadians had been on intimate terms with Native peoples since 1608. A third of French Canadian males worked in the *pays d'en haut* (the hinterland), among Native peoples at some time during their lives (Franks, 2002). Adopting a Native lifestyle was an ever-present, oft-chosen option. Marriage *au façon du pays* ('by Native custom') was commonplace. Success in the fur trade was better assured if they married the daughter of a wealthy chief, a match usually seen as a social advance for the groom. Canadian youth seeking adventure and freedom set out for Rupert's Land with no more of Europe in them than some old French folksongs. These men of humble origins were not arrogant Pukka Sahibs playing out a game of Imperialist racial domination.

While the Métis descended from Europeans, it is doubtful that this origin exposed them to the ideas that were being debated among the urban elites of Europe. Whatever democratic ideas they received would have been folkloric traditions of clan and village governance, best understood as an underlying commonality between Natives and newcomers. Barkwell has pointed out that Scotland had traditions of small-scale democracy comparable to those of the Métis, which could have been an influence (Barkwell et al., 2007). An examination of the memoirs left by Hudson's Bay Company traders reveals this commonality (Franchére, 1969; Hearne, 1958; Isham, 1949 [1743]; MacKenzie,

144 *Indigenous Democracy and Colonialism*

1801; Rich, 1948; Stewart, 1934; Thompson, 1916; Tyrrell, 1934). It behoves us to read these memoirs with attention, for they display none of the dichotomies demanded by *a priori* theories of cultural contact. Instead, they chronicle hunger and feasting, work and play, friendships and enmities among people who encountered each other as individuals, not as representatives of abstract historical processes.

Adaptations

On 10 December, 1873, the Métis of the South Saskatchewan river valley assembled outside their church, at the village of St Laurent. A public meeting could be called by any Métis. On this occasion, it was Gabriel Dumont, who operated a ferry service and a general store. He had often been elected *Capitaine*, and was a trader and diplomat to the Indian tribes. His call drew every head of household in the region. Dumont's central concern was that three years of Canadian rule had produced no progress. Ottawa's heavy-handed policies had already provoked armed resistance among the Métis and the Scots of the Red River settlement, further east (Morton, 1957). That conflict had prompted the formation of a new Province, Manitoba, a small fragment of the north–west. The remainder, including St Laurent, was governed by a council appointed by the Federal Government. Its proceedings were secret, its decisions vetted in Ottawa. No attempt had been made to establish a police force or much needed land registries, or to deal with the violent American adventurers crossing the border and the tribes who had arrived as refugees from America's Indian Wars. Petitions from Métis and Indians were ignored.

Dumont proposed that they create a permanent civil authority, based on the Hunt, until such time as Canada saw fit to send magistrates to maintain the authority of civil law. As in the Hunt, a *Président*, who did not participate in debate, and a governing council were elected, for a one-year term (Dumont, 2006: 49). The council met monthly, appointed *Capitaines* as marshals and passed twenty-eight laws. These laws empowered the council to act judicially, but constrained it to attempt arbitration before trial; required witnesses to contracts and provided for their enforcement; levied fines for failing to restrain nuisance animals; and mandated redress for unjust dismissal by employers. Dumont was elected *Président* and re-elected for the next term (Woodcock, 1975: 101).

The council attempted to address the issue of declining buffalo herds. The Hunt had always imposed regulations preventing individuals from spoiling the outcome by premature or uncoordinated actions. Now, stiff regulations were needed to maintain the herds. Under this aegis, a mixed party of Métis and non-Métis hunters were fined. One of their number, a Hudson's Bay Company employee, wrote a letter of protest to the Company's Factor at Fort Carlton, who had recently been appointed Justice of the Peace for the Territories by the Territorial Council. In response, he issued a blistering report, claiming that the Métis were in open rebellion. In the meantime, the Canadian government had just created a constabulary, the North West Mounted Police, which was occupied chasing American troublemakers. The 'Mounties' did send a detachment to St Laurent but came to the conclusion that no rebellion was afoot. The Métis council agreed to disband, on the understanding that the government would soon fulfil its obligations. The investigating officer, given a copy of the Métis' laws, concluded that, 'on the Prairie, such regulations are absolutely necessary' (Stanley, 1936: 399).

This was not the first time that the Buffalo Hunt was invoked to address a crisis. Local initiatives of creating constitutions and law codes similar to St Laurent's are claimed for seven other Métis communities – all, significantly, settlements that began as wintering quarters for the Buffalo Hunt (Barkwell et al., 2007). A report from 1845, about the Métis at Red River, describes them as being 'responsible, voluntary, and organized, showing that they could deal with moments of distress on the spot. Their complex hunting party organization required them to be able to handle disorderly conduct' (Laudicina, 2009: 54). The Buffalo Hunt had been employed by Louis Riel to unite the Red River Colony in its struggle for entry into the Canadian Confederation as a Province (Riel, 1985 [1869]). The Hunt would be used again in 1885, to create another Provisional Government, which was hoping to settle issues still unresolved since 1873 (Toussaint, 2005: 178).

This last time, the outcome was tragic for the Métis. They brought Riel from exile to advise them, unaware that he had become mentally unbalanced. Though Riel always observed democratic forms, both those of the Métis and of Canada, he *was* a demagogue, skilled at creating crisis, abruptly upping the ante, and manoeuvring his people into painted corners, in pursuit of ends that were not theirs. The Métis' Cree allies divided on supporting the rebellion. Some hotheads among them attacked the settlers. Anti-Catholic fanatics, powerful in Ontario, imagining a menace at once savage and papist, demanded that the rebellion be crushed. A skirmish with the Mounties prompted Ottawa to send an expeditionary force.

The resulting violence, ending in the execution of Riel, is how the Métis are remembered in Canadian history. Yet the political institutions of the Métis did not entirely fail them. Riel had no power to compel obedience. As his actions became more provocative and his bizarre religious visions emerged, the bulk of his followers and his key Native allies dropped away (Taché, 1885). A more authoritarian movement would have precipitated death on a greater scale. Nevertheless, the Métis did not fare well after the crisis. Voiceless and demoralized, most of them began a process of assimilation into French, English or Indian communities. The word 'Métis' became synonymous with poverty by the turn of the century. Many denied being Métis and gave themselves fictional relatives in Québec (St-Onge, 2004). The Métis did not benefit from romantic images of Native culture. Hollywood films that portrayed Natives as noble warriors cast the Métis as sinister, treacherous weasels. The Métis did not begin to emerge from the shadows and re-assert their ethnicity until the 1970s.

Conclusion

For over two centuries, Europeans and Native Canadians co-existed as political allies and business partners on an equal footing, intermarried and mixed their cultures creatively. In the mid-nineteenth century, ideologies of dominance emanated from the elites of Europe and were mimicked by ambitious converts in Canada. While today's academic fashions proclaim novelty, they are still firmly rooted in nineteenth-century thought. The theoretical dichotomy between the West and the non-West is merely the old orthodoxy of European uniqueness, dressed up in new jargon. Europeans must be seen as uniquely wicked, uniquely noble, uniquely democratic, uniquely 'linear', but they must never be seen as just another group. The Métis' very existence contradicts this dichotomy. Since their institutions illustrate an underlying, global commonality of folkloric democracy, they are an embarrassment to *a priori* theories of social evolution. The Métis were bound to be ignored, and their institutions to be dismissed as 'primitive' and irrelevant.

This process began early on, with their first chronicler, Alexander Ross. The Métis' primitiveness, in his view, consisted in the fact that they ruled themselves (Ross, 1856). Ross was a voice in a growing chorus. The government, the missionaries and those who saw themselves as a potential country gentry believed that 'civilization' was a life devoted to agriculture. A scheme of cultural evolution, in which savages abandoned hunting to become farmers, abandoned freedom to become dependents, and abandoned democracy to submit to their 'betters', was the intellectual formula that unified their otherwise disparate motives. Indians and

Métis were good if they agreed to 'evolve'. If they did not, they were indolent (the word used most often), shiftless, irresponsible, fickle, lazy, backward and primitive. These notions could be held by those who liked and even admired the Métis; and they found expression in a peculiarly patronizing discourse. Marcel Giraud's *Le Métis Canadien* was a dramatic example of this attitude (Giraud, 1945). His picture of happy-go-lucky, child-like semi-savages, representing a quaint past that must be swept away by the stages of history, was imbibed by most of Canada's historians, who relied on him almost exclusively for their impressions of the Métis. Giraud recorded the democratic organization of the Buffalo Hunt, but surrounded it by so many assertions of the Métis' 'child-like' nature and cultural backwardness that no reader would be likely to see in it an example of serious political experience worth investigating. Since the Métis represented, in the eyes of even their most devoted chronicler, a quaint, outdated, and primitive way of life, their political institutions could only be of interest to anthropologists. The facts were not hidden from view, but they were assumed to be irrelevant.

A closer examination of Buffalo Hunt democracy would have been perfectly easy to undertake, since the key evidence was available to Canadian historians from 1850 onward. If it had been, then the received evolutionary notions of democratic history might have been called into question. The Hunt's democratic institutions, including full adult male suffrage, egalitarian social relations, a division of powers to prevent the abuse of authority, and formal recourse to impartial, classless laws, were in place at least by the 1830s. At that time, only one male in seven had a potential political voice in the United Kingdom, and Canadians were just beginning their long struggle for democratic institutions. Contemporary democracy in the United States could not have matched Métis standards, either.

The Métis have reclaimed their democratic traditions. But their experience is not of interest just to themselves. It is relevant to the global history of democracy, and to people anywhere who are struggling for self-government. We do not study the ancient Athenians because they were numerous, nor because they produced a utopian ideal. We study them because their concrete experience, as real men and women, mixing splendid achievements, equivocal confusions and tragic failures, illuminates the human condition. So does the experience of the Métis, and it should be contemplated as part of our common human testament.

10
Aboriginal Australia and Democracy: Old Traditions, New Challenges

Larissa Behrendt

> We bond with the universe and the land and everything that exists on the land. Everyone is bonded to everything. Ownership for the white people is something on a piece of paper. We have a different system. You can no more sell our land than sell the sky.
>
> (Paul Behrendt)

When Europeans arrived in Australia to stay a little over two centuries ago, they did not appreciate the complex and consultative governance and legal structures that existed within the Aboriginal communities that they met. Instead, many Europeans saw a primitive race without developed technology and assumed them to be inferior. This Euro-centric assumption of superiority, eventually bolstered by theories of social Darwinism, would be used to support the doctrine of *terra nullius*, a legal fiction that saw Australia as though it was without a legitimate system of governance. Seen through Europeans eyes, it is not surprising that many outsiders failed to understand the intricacies of our society, especially its complex system of laws and governance.

In fact, the Euro-centric world view may have much to learn from Aboriginal Australia. Through our extended deliberative processes which rely more on consensus than the dictatorship of the bare majority, with our diffused structures of power through clans, 'skin' groups and gendered spheres of knowledge and via their decentralised system of more than 500 sovereign nations, Indigenous Australians had a much more inclusive and participatory model of democracy than the British did at the time. Indeed, the argument could be made that Indigenous

Australians have much more to contribute to the debate about the future of democracy than is generally conceded.

Some non-indigenous authors do appreciate the complexity and democratic intent of Indigenous culture when they refer to the 'egalitarian mutualism' of traditional Indigenous Australian politics (Maddock, 1982 [1972]). This democratic culture became increasingly obvious to the early colonialists as they were at times privy to the negotiation of sophisticated treaties between various tribes or to the consultative and deliberative mechanisms employed in group decision-making. In addition, their response and resistance of the British invasion included petitions and letters that went as far up the hierarchy as Queen Victoria herself (Reynolds, 1995).

Within traditional Aboriginal societies, notions of collective agreement-making that resonate with democracy were pervasive. This can be seen from analysis of traditional practices of decision-making and dispute resolution and from the values inherent in legal and governance systems. This chapter will look at the traditional governance practices in the Eualeyai and Kammillaroi nations of north-west New South Wales to identify ways in which democratic principles permeated notions of governance and collective decision making. It will then look at an example from the Yolngu people in the Northern Territory's Arnhem Land where the contemporary cultural practices of decision-making and conflict resolution also provide evidence of the pervasiveness of democratic principles. The final part of this chapter looks at the way in which contemporary attempts to impose western democratic structures on Indigenous people in Australia have failed. The Aboriginal and Torres Strait Islander Commission (ATSIC) was based on a model of representative democracy that does not resonate with Indigenous communities. Further, scepticism about Indigenous capabilities from the broader Australian community meant ATSIC was without important powers and could not extend democratic principles to grassroots structures to provide co-ordinated representation and timely support for Indigenous people.

The indigenous Australian context

There is evidence that Aboriginal people have lived in Australia for 100,000 years (Lynch et al., 2007: 227). While anthropologists ponder the details, Aboriginal people believe that we have inhabited this country since the beginning of time. At the time of European invasion, there were over 500 different tribal nations in Australia, living in small

150 *Indigenous Democracy and Colonialism*

groups within their tribal areas. They would meet at intervals in larger groups for ceremonies or trade. Some groups were patrilineal but many, like my own tribal group, were matrilineal. These groups were made up of extended families. Some 'aunts' took on the role of mothers, some 'uncles' were fathers, and cousins were brothers and sisters. A person's relationship to others would dictate how to treat them and what a person's obligations to them were. It also determined whom you could and could not marry.

Within these different groups there was similarity and diversity. Groups living in the desert had a vastly different lifestyle to groups living in coastal areas. But in world views, governance structures and philosophy there were strong commonalities across the continent. Aboriginal people were hunters and gatherers and led a semi-nomadic life. Groups had similar technology such as digging sticks and wooden hunting instruments, but these varied between groups according to the climate and conditions. Some used canoes and some did not; some used fish bones to make tools and some did not. All groups had stories about a period of creation, now generally called the Dreaming, when super beings created the world and everything in it. These spirits gave humans ceremonies that explained the rules to live by. In my tribal area, the area inhabited by the Eualeyai in the northwest of New South Wales, this spirit was a serpent. The serpent lived underground and the places where he came up for air were springs and waterholes. This creation story has a similar theme across the continent even though there are regional differences in the specific telling of the story.

Aboriginal culture was oral. Attachment to the land was expressed through song, art, dance and painting. My father explained to me that people 'inherit stories and songs and then become the keepers of those stories and that is how the law passed down'. Boundaries of tribal areas are fixed and explained in the stories told by Elders. Through this story-telling, responsibility for ancestral land was passed on to younger generations. Knowledge created an obligation to protect the land, to take the responsibility of passing the country on to future generations and to maintain the religious ceremonies that needed to be performed there. Thus the landscape was richly symbolic. Mythical stories dictated appropriate modes of behavior and set standards which were enforced by social pressure. Children were taught acceptable modes of behavior through cultural stories and were taught by example rather than by the strict discipline used to rear European children.

This relationship to the land is strikingly similar in all Aboriginal communities on mainland Australia. People have affiliations with tracts of country and the right to hunt and feed in those areas and to perform religious ceremonies in related places. These custodians were also responsible for ensuring that the resources of a certain area were maintained. Aboriginal people knew their relationship to others and the universe through their totems. People had three totems: a clan totem that linked a person to other people; a family totem that linked a person to the natural world (a person considered himself or herself to be descended from the family totem – they would not eat the meat of their totem and would have to ensure that animal's protection); and a spiritual totem that linked a person to the universe. Through these totems Aboriginal people realized that they were one with the land and all that moved upon it. This is the basis for the egalitarianism that infused Indigenous society. The land remains at the heart of Aboriginal political process and is the source of the Indigenous tendency towards democracy.

Conflict resolution in indigenous Australia

The way in which conflict was resolved in Aboriginal society gives an insight into the governance within Indigenous Australia and how they integrated democratic elements into their everyday life. The small size of clans created extreme loyalty and meant that conflict was resolved quickly and to the satisfaction of the community because the disputants were living in close proximity to each other. The closeness of the group and its interdependence meant that the community could use public opinion to encourage people to meet their obligations. This way of pulling family members into line gave a communal aspect to dispute resolution. Unlike Western democracy, power and authority in tribal groups was vested in Elders who were not necessarily the oldest in the group. Elevation to the status of Elder was restricted to the most intelligent and diligent and those who had the most knowledge of religious and ceremonial affairs. Elevation to a leadership position was determined by a fusion of the merit of the individual and the consensus of the group. This resulted in a community that was governed by those who had shown themselves to be consistently wise, dedicated to the continuance of the group and had the capacity to lead. While there was no concept of election within traditional culture, achieving influence or gaining a strong voice in decision-making was effectively granted by the rest of the group.

But while certain people were more influential than others, no one had ultimate power. Continuity was stressed over change. There was

152 *Indigenous Democracy and Colonialism*

no concept of hereditary chiefs that exists in other Indigenous cultures so there was no assumption of leadership simply on the basis of genealogy. The tendency towards democracy was evident in indigenous society because there was an egalitarian diffusion of power rather than concentration of power in one leader. The British, when they first tried to negotiate with Aboriginal Australians, found it hard to deal with this egalitarian system and the lack of Kings and Queens. Early British governors nominated people within Aboriginal communities to act as representatives for the community. They were given breast-plates engraved with titles such as 'King Billy' (Goodall, 2008). The communal decision-making process meant that the members of the community made all the decisions about the community. In itself, this is a form of direct democratic process.

The key characteristics of decision-making and dispute resolution that existed in traditional Aboriginal culture stand in direct contrast to Western culture and governance. While Western culture has a view that people have dominion over land, Aboriginal culture sees people interconnected with their environment and responsible for maintenance of country. Western culture has a written tradition that articulates legal obligations and rights while Aboriginal people have a strong oral tradition of story telling as a way of maintaining behavior, norms and responsibilities. The individual's rights and freedoms are the preoccupation of the West while Indigenous Australia focuses on the community and communal good. Western culture is structured, Aboriginal culture egalitarian. Decision making in the West was adversarial and authoritarian while consensus is to the forefront in Aboriginal culture (Behrendt, 2005; Behrendt and Kelly, 2008).

A key aspect of Indigenous conflict resolution and decision making is that it recognizes that the broader community has an interest in the outcomes of disputes and conflict resolution. There is an inclusive notion of who has a right to speak that extends to anyone who has an opinion that they wish to express. The principle of interconnectedness translates into a process that sees participation extended to anyone who wants to speak or be involved. The process of decision making is not decided by a majority rule or voting, but by an extended and involved process of building towards consensus about the most appropriate outcome. This approach facilitates the participation of the largest number of interested people within the community.

When conflict arose within Aboriginal communities it was often following accusations of sorcery, a breach of marriage or kin arrangements or obligations, failure to observe sacred law or ceremonies, injuring others or neglecting children. Such grievances were resolved in several ways and women played a prominent part in the adjudication and punishment, particularly when a woman had broken the law.

The council of Elders would not just make the decisions for a particular group, but would also intervene in disputes if they had not been resolved between family members. Meetings were usually held at times when groups met for ceremonies. There could be no fighting at ceremonies so the maintenance of order was a duty extended to adjoining tribal groups. Councils of Elders were not judicially formed bodies. No one had a vested power to decide the outcome. 'Although constituted courts did not exist in traditional Aboriginal Australia, there were councils which did much the same thing, although far more informally and less systematically' (Berndt and Berndt, 1999: 348). To cite one example, when two clans of Lower Murray people attempted to settle a dispute, the members of each clan sat facing each other and members of other clans were arranged around the *rupelle* (negotiators or spokespeople for the tribe). The *tendi* (a council) began with a general discussion, then accusers and defendants and their clans spoke, and then witnesses were called (Berndt and Berndt, 1999: 348). This type of procedure was common throughout Australia, and is recorded among the communities of Arnhem land and the Kimberleys.

Nancy Williams gives the example of the community council of the Yolngu, a group living on the Gove Peninsula in the Northern Territory (Williams, 1987). The community council is more important than the town council as the town council's interest in roads and infrastructure had less impact on the community. Decision-making authority is vested in those who would have met together to decide issues in pre-invasion times. Meetings are also held to settle disputes that arise within the community. The order of speaking is governed by seniority, discussion is based on consensus and meetings are held in a familiar and informal outdoor location. Clan groups sit together and people sit reflecting alignment to the disputants. The community council is an assembly of neighbors and kinsmen that decides disputes. Clansmen with authority manage the proceedings, gather and check evidence, obtain admissions of facts, state traditional values and law, and confirm findings and sanctions.

One example Williams uses to demonstrate this process is of a marriage contract that has been breached. First, Elders with jurisdiction over the offenders give statements of the offence and state the relevant traditional law and anyone with status within the community is able to speak. Then the specific allegations of the case are considered. For

154 *Indigenous Democracy and Colonialism*

example, an Elder will state the allegations and the offended person will state how they felt about the wrongdoing and perhaps offer a way that they could be compensated. An Elder then gets the offender to admit wrongful behavior and the offender gets a chance to respond. In the example Williams gives, the Elder, in talking to the offender, stressed the importance of family relationships, respect for parents and the clan. Finally, statements about the appropriate outcome are made including stating what is required for satisfaction of the matter. At this point the Elder, offender and aggrieved all speak (Williams, 1987).

Dispute resolution also occurred at an individual level, beginning with the aggrieved person airing it publicly by shouting or yelling about the offenders and the wrong done to him or her. The aggrieved person would be careful about the time and place because that would affect who the audience was. The aggrieved person would anticipate that wrongdoers would make redress and this method often worked. Women would interfere to prevent violence between the aggrieved and the accused and their kin. This procedure was usually employed where spiritual or kin obligations had been breached.

At all levels of dispute resolution, retaliation, though often a natural instinct, was discouraged and disputants were expected to get their emotions under control before they faced the wrongdoer. The dynamics of a small close-knit community made social pressure an extremely effective sanction to settle a dispute, enforce a punishment or punish negligent behavior. These sanctions were extremely powerful within a group. If a religious law or kin obligation was ignored, redress could include giving the offended person gifts and performing ceremonies to show respect to land. The threat of sorcery was also a powerful way of ensuring people complied with their obligations. Exile or temporary exile was a harsh punishment. It meant being away from the support of the family making physical and emotional survival difficult. Another sanction was spearing. This was often done symbolically and women would intervene to ensure things did not get out of control. However, people did die from this practice. The aggrieved person and sometimes his clan would throw spears and even boomerangs at the offender. My father told me how the men in our area would meet for battle with the men of the clan they were in dispute with and as soon as the first man was injured, they would go home.

Dispute resolution processes reflected the values of Aboriginal culture. These are vastly different to the values of the imposed Western legal system in Australia, but nevertheless have many useful lessons for making justice and governance processes more responsive to human need.

Indigenous disputants could give emotional responses. There are no rules in relation to what evidence can be heard. Aboriginal disputes are mediated and resolved orally. There is a broad view taken within Indigenous dispute resolution about interested parties. Aboriginal culture is imbued with the concept of inter-relatedness. In Aboriginal disputes, people speak for themselves and give their own point of view. These processes predicated on community participation and group decision making constitute a valuable contribution to contemporary dispute resolution. They are still used today by the Youngu and are a reminder that, not only do cultural values and practices that existed in pre-contact society still imbue contemporary Aboriginal cultures, but they continue to embody practices and values that resonate with principles that could revitalize notions of democracy.

Failures of Western democracy

The limits of Western democracy can be seen in the ways it has accepted and assisted the processes of dispossession and colonization has had devastating effects on Aboriginal culture and disrupted and distorted traditional inclinations towards mutualism and democratic tendencies. Life became a battle for survival. The loss of land was crippling to Aboriginal communities. Not only were people less capable of surviving in unfamiliar territory, but religious and cultural life was disrupted. Aboriginal culture was often lost either by the removal of people from ancestral lands so that stories could not be passed down, or when Aboriginal people were massacred. Missionaries did not allow Aboriginal people to use their own languages or practice their ceremonies and attempted to convince Aboriginal people that Aboriginal culture and custom was pagan. Similarly, language and culture could not be exercised or expressed on government reservations. Even today, Australian democracy fails the original inhabitants of the continent as land becomes alienated for the use by pastoral leases, urban development and mining opportunities, diminishing the rights of Aboriginal people to stay on traditional lands.

Despite these events, Aboriginal culture has been adaptable, resilient and strong enough to survive the continual onslaughts of colonization and cultural genocide, finding new ways to build on traditional co-operative and consultative practices. Even though most Aboriginal people have been moved from their lands, land remains important to them. Aboriginal people in urbanized areas continue to maintain their links with the land. The *Royal Commission into Aboriginal Deaths in Custody* noted that Aboriginal people living in urban communities draw a

156　*Indigenous Democracy and Colonialism*

contrast between Aboriginal and non-Aboriginal ways and values. The Commission stated that:

> [Aboriginal] social relations remain focused on the facts of kinship and ties of family. Kin associations permeate most aspects of their life and they feel a great passion about their ties to land and their concern over diminishing access to lands, rivers and coast for hunting and fishing ... Although they cannot now identify particular areas of land as being owned in traditional law by particular ancestors, they have a lively awareness that their forefathers had all those traditional relationships with the land.
>
> (*RCADC*, 1991: 312–13)

Traditional land is needed so that sacred sites that remain can be protected. Australian democracy has allowed and assisted the destruction and defacement of Aboriginal sacred sites due to ignorance and indifference. Destruction of sacred sites causes loss and grief to the Aboriginal custodians. Non-indigenous concern for land is mostly economic. Non-indigenous people do not know and do not understand what is lost when a sacred site is destroyed. Recent legislation finally passed to protect sacred sites provides a superficial commitment to Aboriginal heritage as the final decision as to whether a site will be protected is given to a government minister. Real protection will only be achieved when sites are protected by traditional owners engaged in consultative and cooperative practices with the traditional owners from related sites.

Aboriginal people removed from their traditional land found themselves in artificial communities, forced to associate with other groups with whom they shared little or no deliberative tradition. This led to conflict which was exacerbated by the introduction of alcohol into communities. The continued attachment to ancestral land is shown by the increasing number of out stations. This is a move back to traditional land to look after the country and perform ceremonies. This return to traditional life is not just a move that is culturally satisfying to Aboriginal people; it is also an attempt to avoid conflict in Aboriginal settlements over scarce resources and to avoid the violence in communities where alcohol use and abuse are prevalent.

Despite the fact that Australian Aboriginal people are the only indigenous peoples that have united under one flag, Aboriginal communities remain intensely local. New structures for dispute resolution have developed within communities. These are usually run by younger school-educated Aborigines and are more likely to deal with matters not related to tradition and custom. Such councils usually work by consulting with Elders. Similarly, Land Councils are new bodies that have emerged in Aboriginal communities and are one way in which the community deals with non-community groups and interests. There are examples of communities employing traditional mechanisms to resolve disputes within the community. These have less European influences than the structures that have been created to deal with the non-Aboriginal community and their interests. Despite non-Aboriginal influences, contemporary Aboriginal values have remained faithful to traditional values. The values of informal and emotive expression, a broad view of the issues that can be determined within a dispute and the recognition that a large number of people will have an interest in the outcome of the dispute – and therefore have a right to express their opinion – stand in contrast to the concepts and philosophies that influence adjudication of disputes in dominant Australian democracy.

The population of Indigenous people at the last census was 455,028, or 2.3 per cent of the total Australian population (Australian Bureau of Statistics, 2008: 12). Indigenous people are a political minority and their ability to be able to influence mainstream politics is negligible. There are 226 members of the Australian Federal Parliament at any given time but only two Indigenous people – Neville Bonner and Aden Ridgeway – have ever been elected to the national assembly. Both were elected to the Senate: Bonner in 1971 and Ridgeway in 1996. Ridgeway was a member of the Australian Democrats, a smaller party and arguably more able to influence his party's policies on Indigenous issues. He held the portfolio for Reconciliation. Bonner, on the other hand, was a member of the Liberal Party and was less influential in crafting policy that would represent the interests of Indigenous people. Wyatt is also a Liberal but his impact is yet to be seen. Aboriginal people elected to Parliament are representatives of their political parties, not representatives of Aboriginal people and their views. While there is an expectation from Indigenous communities that an Indigenous person in parliament will be an advocate for their issues, the reality of party politics and the requirements of party loyalty mean that the expectations of the Aboriginal community are rarely met.

Partly in recognition of this, separate bodies that provide a voice for Aboriginal people outside the parliamentary process but with policy making and service delivery responsibilities, have been explored since the federal government was given the power to make laws in relation to Aboriginal people at the 1967 referendum. ATSIC was the most recent attempt to create a national representative structure for Aboriginal people at the national level. The representatives from the Aboriginal and

158 *Indigenous Democracy and Colonialism*

Torres Strait Islander community who sat on ATSIC and on the network of regional councils that were part of the representative model were elected. It has been one of the few bodies for Indigenous people predicated on the principle of representative democracy. It is important to note that the ATSIC structure incorporated concepts prevalent in Western notions of democracy and overlooked the notions of democracy that can be found Aboriginal cultural practices. As will be seen below, ATSIC never became as politically effective as it might have been.

Contemporary Aboriginal politics

ATSIC had two democratic dimensions to its operation. Established in 1989, ATSIC was an elected body with a mandate to give alternative policy advice to government, advice that best reflected the perspectives and interests of Indigenous people. ATSIC's other democratic dimension was a broad legislative mandate to formulate and implement programs, monitor the effectiveness of all bodies and agencies, assist, advise and cooperate with stakeholders, advise the Minister, protect cultural material and information, and collect and publish statistical material, all with a limited budget (*ATSIC Act*, 1989: VII). These functions were designed to assist ATSIC in meeting aims of 'maximum participation', 'the development of self sufficiency and self management', the 'furtherance of the economic, social and cultural development' and the 'coordination in the formulation and implementation of policies... without detracting from the responsibilities of... governments' (*ATSIC Act*, 1989: III). That is, ATSIC supposed to maximize the democratic participation of Aboriginal and Torres Strait Islander peoples in providing an effective policy voice to government while also formulating and implementing programs to improve the Indigenous community.

ATSIC's ability to exercise its functions and meet its aims was impeded by some inherent structural problems. One of the key problems was its lack of executive authority. To fulfil its responsibilities, ATSIC needed the active cooperation and involvement of Commonwealth agencies and State and Territory governments. This in turn required executive authority from the Department of Prime Minister and Cabinet. This authority was never given to ATSIC and the activities of Prime Minister and Cabinet were often contrary to ATSIC's stated policies and intentions. A key weakness of ATSIC included the lack of a state/territory interface in the legislation which impeded ATSIC's ability to work on issues that were shared between the state/territory and federal governments, such as housing, health and education. Another weakness was the undefined relationships between the ATSIC Board, CEO, Minister and Regional Councils; it was not clear how the CEO was to balance his responsibilities to the Board and to the Minister when the two could have opposing views.

When the Federal government finally announced ATSIC's abolition in June 2004, there were several reasons suggested to explain its dismantling. The government claimed that because socio-economic statistics for Aboriginal and Torres Strait Islander people still showed large levels of disadvantage compared to other sections of the population, ATSIC was not working. But ATSIC did not have fiscal responsibility for the areas of health and education and was only a supplementary funding provider on issues such as domestic violence, languages, heritage protection and housing. In addition, almost 80 per cent of the ATSIC budget was quarantined for programs such as the Community Development Employment Program (a work-for-the-dole scheme) and the Community Housing and Infrastructure Program. Misconceptions about ATSIC's role directed attention away from the federal, state and territory government departments with the actual responsibility for Indigenous service delivery (Behrendt, 2003).

Another reason mooted for ATSIC's abolition was its activities as a vocal critic of government performance. ATSIC developed policy on some key areas that reflected the position of Indigenous peoples but that conflicted with the Government's position. One such area was native title. ATSIC funded Native Title Representative Bodies to litigate claims in matters where the Federal Government was a party. ATSIC also lobbied in the international arena where it frequently advocated positions contrary to the Federal Government's agenda. ATSIC maintained a focus on the rights agenda in a period when Federal Government policy was 'practical reconciliation'. ATSIC's position was always that the recognition and enjoyment of Indigenous and other democratic rights are also required if any real, meaningful and sustainable progress is to be attained.

The final reason often put forward for ATSIC's failure was that it did not have the support of the Aboriginal people. Claims of low voter turnout at ATSIC elections were used as evidence that Indigenous people did not support it. But unlike compulsory federal and state elections, voting was voluntary. Nevertheless, in some places that had voluntary local government elections, ATSIC voter turn-out was higher and it was highest in areas where ATSIC's presence was more strongly felt. For example, turn-out was only 4.45 per cent in Tasmania that had few programs, but reached 34.68 per cent in the Northern Territory and 27.70 per cent in

160 *Indigenous Democracy and Colonialism*

Western Australia where ATSIC service delivery was crucial (Behrendt, 2003, 2005). A review of ATSIC recommended greater emphasis be placed on the role of the regions and while it did offer some criticism of ATSIC, it did not advocate its dismantlement (Hannaford *et al.*, 2003). Indeed, it called for increasing democracy within the ATSIC election process, giving more power to the regional councils for policy and service delivery and integrating a state/territory level of representation into the ATSIC structure. Other commentators have taken up this theme and pointed out that Indigenous representation based on the Westminster system has missed opportunities for more appropriate democratic representation drawn from local organizations and traditional tribal groups (Rowse, 2001).

The dissolving of ATSIC meant that Indigenous people no longer had a process to elect representatives to advocate on their behalf at the national level through a body that could democratically influence policy development and program delivery. ATSIC's national body was replaced by the National Indigenous Council (NIC), a government appointed body of 15 individuals. This new body's appointed representatives have no responsibility to represent broader Indigenous interests. The appointees act in an individual capacity and are not accountable to the community whose interests their decisions will affect. The Regional Councils were abolished at the end of June 2005. With them went another layer of the representative structure which Indigenous people could use to advocate their interests. The Regional Councils were required to formulate a regional plan relying on broad consultation and negotiation with various levels of government and regional Indigenous communities. The Regional Councils had an obligation to pass on to ATSIC the views of their constituents about the activities of government bodies in their region and to represent and to advocate on their behalf. These powers and functions provided a grassroots democratic structure at the regional level that served as an important source of advice on policy and priorities at the national level.

Since the abolition of ATSIC there has been an enormous amount of change in Indigenous affairs portfolios – the introduction of Shared Responsibility Agreements, the ideologies of mutual obligation, the reform of major pieces of legislation (including the Northern Territory land rights regime), the out-sourcing of legal services, the increasing over-representation of Indigenous people within the criminal justice system and the mainstreaming of more and more essential services. The refusal of governments to allow Indigenous people a democratic voice has left many Aboriginal and Torres Strait Islanders feeling excluded from debates about policies and programs that directly impact on their lives, families and communities.

Conclusion

The irony of the situation for Aboriginal people in Australia is that, while traditional systems of governance and dispute resolution with strong democratic tendencies have been undermined, marginalized and ignored, there has also been a reluctance to support Western-style government structures that would provide Aboriginal people with new democratic, representative bodies. There has also been a reluctance to devolve power and decision-making to Indigenous people through grassroots democracy despite evidence that policy making is more effective in targeting areas of socio-economic need if Aboriginal people are given a central place in the development of those policies. Aboriginal communities are capable of determining their own methods of dispute resolution, but these have never been recognized. Between the models of governance and dispute resolution that existed in traditional Aboriginal culture and the imposed representative model is another alternative – the exploration of models of self-representation and dispute resolution that find a fluid merging of the distinctive characteristics of Aboriginal cultural governance structures and models of participatory democracy.

The hostility towards ATSIC, despite the fact that it embodied the notion of representative democracy, overlooks the ways in which traditional Aboriginal communities were comfortable, and indeed embraced, an inclusive process of decision making that resonated with notions of democracy. It also overlooks the fact that contemporary Aboriginal cultures that still practice dispute resolution and consultative decision-making remain faithful to those traditional democratic tendencies. The deeper exploration of governance and legal processes embodied in traditional and contemporary Indigenous societies reveal principles of consultation, cooperation, consensus and diffused power structures that provide a way forward for new explorations of democracy.

11
The Pre-History of the Post-Apartheid Settlement: Non-Racial Democracy in South Africa's Cape Colony, 1853–1936

Poppy Fry

As the political underpinnings of South Africa's apartheid regime began to give way in the early 1990s, observers both inside and outside the country expected a major transformation, not just of the scope of the electorate, but also of the character of political and economic life. Having been branded, by American and British politicians as well as by proponents of the apartheid state, as a communist and terrorist organization, the African National Congress (ANC) might easily have been expected to have arrived in power with a revolutionary agenda. As Anthony Butler recalls of the period, 'conservative...scaremongering reinforced radicals' trumpeting of the revolution to come. For visitors, the collapse of the apartheid state seemed to promise (or threaten) revolutionary upheaval' (Butler, 1998: 127). Nor was this expectation of imminent transformation unique to scholarly or privileged observers. 'Mandela has been released, now where is my house?' one woman from a squatter settlement outside Cape Town wrote to a local newspaper (cited in Murray, 1994: 4).

The anticipated revolution, of course, never came. The post-apartheid constitution included extensive anti-discrimination language, but the sanctity of private property was also emphasized. Upon his accession to the office of state president, Nelson Mandela presided over a political dispensation that sought to 'level the playing field' within a fairly traditional Western model. The redistribution that seemingly should have resulted from the enfranchisement of the poor did not take place (Nattrass and Seekings, 2001). Ethnic and cultural differences found no formal expression within the workings of the new government. The

ANC's embrace of the liberal democratic model struck many observers as explicable in only two ways: either the new ruling party had compromised so extensively with the apartheid government as to render itself toothless, or it had been coerced by outside forces (including the United States and the United Nations) into abandoning more radical plans (Johnson, 2003).

Discomfort with the country's liberal democratic tone has continued beyond the 1990s. Even as Thabo Mbeki proclaimed an 'African Renaissance', more than a few South Africans found their own government to be insufficiently indigenous in its form. Part of Jacob Zuma's appeal has been his ability to present himself as 'more African' and less invested in liberal democracy than his colleagues. The perception that liberal democracy – grounded in universalism and equality before the law – has its roots in colonial Southern Africa may be correct, but the implicit claim that the colonial order offered only disenfranchisement to Africans[1] is misleading. The active engagement of Africans with liberal democratic forms and processes is not the product of the 1990s – it has a history that stretches back a century and a half earlier, to a period when political society in the Cape Colony was defined not by race, but by a propertied franchise. While the post-apartheid settlement may not have satisfied large numbers of South Africans, it cannot be understood simply as an outside import or as an artificially imposed equilibrium. In fact, it was the culmination of a long history of liberal democratic ideals and practices.

A 'Secret History'?

The history of non-racial liberal democracy in South Africa is certainly not secret in the sense of being overtly hidden, but rather in the sense of being ignored or marginalized.[2] Nearly all national or regional histories note the existence of a propertied franchise in the Cape Colony. They tend to go on, however, to dismiss the significance of that franchise for the political and social narrative of South Africa. For example, Colin Bundy's seminal work on the South African peasantry carefully charts the economic prosperity of Africans in the nineteenth century, but does not connect that prosperity with the economically based franchise (Bundy, 1988). Robert Ross' history of South Africa, often used as a survey textbook, notes the development of a propertied franchise in the mid-nineteenth century, but goes on to insist that only a handful of constituencies had meaningful coloured and African electorates (Ross, 1999). In his history of twentieth-century South Africa, William Beinart

164 *Indigenous Democracy and Colonialism*

insists that the end of the Cape vote, though it was a death blow to non-racial liberal democracy, was not highly significant (Beinart, 2001). Three related factors help to explain the relegation of liberal democratic forms to the margins of South African history. First, the nineteenth-century political situation in the Cape defies common contemporary expectations about what democracy is and how it operates. Second, those directly impacted by the franchise constitute only a small minority of Africans, and thus cannot be seen as representative of the African experience more broadly. Finally, there seems to exist, among South Africans and scholars alike, a discomfort with the elitist, exclusionary roots of the ANC and potentially with the post-apartheid dispensation.

To those outside of South Africa and without specific education in the country's history, it seems almost impossible that the same place that experienced apartheid could, almost a century earlier, have had thousands of black voters. De Tocqueville's assertion that, in democracies, electorates will inevitably widen may have seeped into public consciousness, making the idea of an increasingly bounded electorate counter-intuitive (De Tocqueville, 1864 [1835]: 55). As Hermann Giliomee notes, 'the temptation is strong to see democratization as a broad, inexorable process which swells to establish ever greater rights and freedom' (Giliomee, 1995: 199). This perspective, while understandable, cannot account for the dramatic contraction of rights and freedoms within South Africa's democratic system. The Cape Colony's experience also challenges the intuitive dualisms of colonial rule. It is probably difficult for the casual observer to reconcile the existence of an African electorate with the essentially exploitative process of colonial conquest and administration. That an individual could be among both 'the colonized' and 'the colonial political elite' demands a nuanced understanding of agency and identity. In the contemporary world, furthermore, democracy is generally defined in universal terms – 'government by all the people or their [direct] representative' (Bickford-Smith, 1995: 443). By those standards, the United States could only be considered to have a democratic history of perhaps fifty years. Defining democracy in such a limited manner marginalizes the variety of ways in which democratic practices have been understood throughout history.

The reason that historians often cite for discounting the Cape franchise is its apparently limited resonance. The overwhelming majority of those African residents in the Cape Colony did not qualify them to vote, nor could they reasonably hope to qualify them. This must be acknowledged. The franchise did not, furthermore, represent a universal (or even coherent) commitment to non-racialism among government officials and European settlers. The narrowness of the franchise's practical application or its framing should not, however, negate its significance. The intent of those framing the legislation is of perhaps less interest than the ways in which it was understood and received, both by voters and by others. The history of liberal democracy in southern Africa is by no mean *the* organizing narrative of the region, it is *a* narrative that serves to demonstrate the complexity of African experiences in British colonial society as well as the convolution of British thought and policy. As will be shown below, the ethos of liberal democracy impacted a segment of southern African society which is far larger than just those who registered to vote.

Perhaps the most challenging obstacle to foregrounding the history of liberal democracy in the Cape Colony is its contemporary political implication. If the ANC, and the African political elite who created it, are in fact the product of a democratic tradition grounded in the nineteenth-century franchise, then present-day South Africa owes its shape as much to British colonial rule as to radical anti-racism. This connection constitutes a major problem for the 'liberation narrative' of South African history, which posits the ANC as representative of the poor and disenfranchised. As early as 1984, the ANC itself sought to distance itself from its own liberal past. Writing in the *Canadian Journal of African Studies*, future President Thabo Mbeki insisted that, within the ANC, 'the black working class must play the leading role, not as an appendage of the petty bourgeoisie but as a conscious vanguard class' (Mbeki, 1984: 612). It is worth noting that Mbeki's own background put him squarely in the category of the petty bourgeoisie. In order to bring together a broad-based anti-apartheid movement, the ANC necessarily offered a selective reading of its own meaning and history.

It is perhaps not coincidental that the two most prolific historians of the Cape franchise, Stanley Trapido and J. L. McCracken, came from a liberal – rather than radical – historiographical tradition and that they both wrote during the 1960s, just as the ANC began to transform its image into that of a liberation movement. Disposed to support the anti-apartheid movement and hopeful for a successful post-apartheid South Africa, scholars have been hesitant to link the new democratic model explicitly to the ANC's 'liberal modernist sensibilities':

> Throughout much of its history the ANC remained an elite – and very often an elitist – organization. As is well known, its critique of the state was less radical than reformist, that all individuals should have access to the state irrespective of race ... Segregation, from the

166 *Indigenous Democracy and Colonialism*

1920s, and apartheid, from the 1950s, was wrong because they denied Africans rights within, and democratic access to, the modern state ... This was a classically liberal, indeed Lockean, politics that ultimately justified violence – revolution even – in the name of bourgeois modernist rights.

(Crais, 2002: 143–4)

Although the leadership of the ANC, as well as its members and sympathizers, certainly shifted and adapted both philosophically and strategically over the course of the anti-apartheid struggle, the organization remains the heir to a potent tradition of bounded liberal democracy. Attempts to grapple with the ANC's 'left turn' must reflect upon the legacies of its earlier directions. It is only by taking into account the history of liberal democracy – and, in particular, the non-racial franchise – that the disjunction between democratization and redistribution in South Africa can be fully understood.

The non-racial franchise in South Africa's Cape Colony

The Cape Colony's tendency to define political inclusion in non-racial terms developed well before the 1853 constitution established a colony-wide franchise. Beginning in 1828, when Ordinance 50 decreed the equality of all free subjects before the law and new jury regulations were applied to landholders and tax payers regardless of race, it became increasingly clear that potential participation in governance would be bounded by property and income (and of course gender), rather than by membership in a particular racial or ethnic community. In 1836, the ordinance creating municipal bodies allowed the right to vote to all those who occupied houses of the yearly value or rent of £10 and who paid at least six shillings per year in taxes. The 1843 ordinance for the establishment of road boards allowed that franchise to the owners of immovable property should be valued at £50 or upwards (McCracken, 1963: 64). By mid-century, a variety of different economic qualifications existed, but the principle of economic (rather than racial) qualification was well established.

The creation of an economically defined political class in the Cape Colony intersected with a broader discourse about inclusion in and exclusion from the British world. Ordinance 50, in particular, has been understood as an important component of British attempts to 'Anglicize' territory previously dominated by Dutch, German and French settlers. In seeking to render the colony a more direct reflection of its colonial master, the Anglicization project brought to southern Africa a set of ideas that were percolating within British society – ideas about what rendered an individual fit for engagement with the political world. These ideas found metropolitan expression in the Reform Act of 1832, the New Poor Law of 1834 and the general abolition of slavery in 1838. Each of these pieces of legislation was grounded in the claim that social and political inclusion hinged on economic rationality. Only through individual engagement with the market could a man be considered free, and only through the accumulation or maintenance of economic assets could he be considered sufficiently rational for political life (Bayly, 2004: 115–16).

Gaurev Desai argues that the question 'Is the African capable of rational thought?' underwrote all attempts by colonial powers to make sense of their subjects (Desai, 2001: 22). The non-racial franchise suggests that, in practice, the answer in the early nineteenth-century Cape Colony was understood to be affirmative. Richard Elphick has described liberalism in the Cape as putting faith not so much in Africans' reason as in their 'reasonableness' (Elphick, 1987: 72). In other words, educated and prosperous men of any racial or ethnic background might be expected to engage with one another in a moderate and measured way. Although settlers and government officials in the Cape spent a substantial amount of time fearing the Africans, that fear did not extend – for the most part – to those who could qualify as voters. These latter were seen, at least by the government, as sufficiently comprehensible to be absorbed into colonial political society.

In 1853 the franchise qualifications took on a new significance when a representative government and a constitution were to be introduced in the Cape Colony. The exact amount of property necessary for someone to qualify as a voter was the focus of significant controversy, but neither the metropolitan government nor the local settlers seem to have objected to enshrining further the principle of a non-racial electorate. William Porter, Attorney General of the colony, argued that voters of African origin were likely to be as fit, if not fitter, than those of Dutch origin. Eastern Cape settlers, in spite of their general suspicion of any policy that might benefit Africans within the colony, seem to have been rather enthusiastic about the new political dispensation. British army officer Edward Wellesley wrote to his brother from the notoriously illiberal outpost of Grahamstown that settlers had nothing but high hopes for the constitution:

> Like Holloway's Ointment or [Pan's] Life Pills it is expected to heal and keep in vigor all the ills of this crazy carcass of a Colony & I believe people are so sanguine that bald headed Independents even

168 *Indigenous Democracy and Colonialism*

think it would make their hair grow again like Macassar oil and smoky Radicals that it will give their teeth 'that pearly appearance much desired' like the Odonto.

(Carver, 1995: 111)

The franchise qualifications of 1853 remained in force even as the Cape Colony transitioned to responsible governance in the 1870s. The added gravity of responsible politics seems to have turned some settlers against the idea that the political community could be defined on economic rather than racial grounds. An organization calling itself the Kaffrarian Vigilance Association publicly declared that it was 'absolutely necessary that the principle of special legislation for the Native population should be openly adopted' (McCracken, 1963: 87). This was an even more aggressive claim than that raised one year earlier by the Congress of Farmers' Associations, which proposed that educationally qualified voters ought to be required to fill out their own registration paperwork (*Resolutions and Proceedings*, 1877: 65). These statements highlight two things about the situation in the late 1870s: first, that some individuals in the Cape Colony felt the existing franchise to be out of step with colonial realities; and, second, that those individuals found expression for their sentiments outside formal politics. That the letter of the law and the reality of practice were different is evidenced by Cape politician Saul Solomon's statement that he 'had no fear of the colony ever sinking to the level of preventing by law any coloured man from having the right to vote for members of parliament' (McCracken, 1963: 87). Solomon seems to have valued the principle of equality before the law while recognizing the existence, and perhaps even the necessity, of inequality in practice. Although African voters might have been experiencing racial discrimination within the electoral process, franchise qualifications remained explicitly non-discriminatory. It would not be until the 1880s that concerns about the 'native vote' would be sufficiently forceful to be considered by Cape politicians.

The discovery of gold on the Witwatersrand in the mid-1880s set in motion a transformation of southern Africa's political economy, and one of its most immediate effects was a change in the tone of political life in the Cape Colony. Since the British takeover in 1806, the Cape had been of limited interest to the metropolitan government. The discovery of diamonds in Kimberley in 1867 began to change the attitude of benign neglect, and the rise of gold mining further raised the economic (and political) stakes for the British government and for residents of the colony. There was a widespread sense that Britain's control of the region needed to be rationalized and regularized. The conditions of the franchise, previously ignored by many, now became the object of discussion, a discussion which culminated in parliamentary debate in the late 1880s.

Given its intention to reconsider franchise qualifications, the 1887 Voters Registration Act proved to bring surprisingly limited shift. The prospect of a racially defined electorate remained a distant one. The Voters Registration Act, along with several other pieces of legislation, limited the ways in which an individual's economic situation could be measured for the purpose of the franchise and added to the paperwork needed in order to vote. Although the act did not propose a qualitative change in the way the Cape Colony's political community was defined, it did have a dramatic quantitative effect. Almost a quarter of the colony's voters were to be struck off the electoral rolls, although the new legislation does not seem to have been implemented in all constituencies (Mbeki, 1992). The majority of these were made up of African voters whose communally held land no longer qualified them to vote; but the disenfranchised also included several hundred German immigrants (Odendaal, 1983: 137). The impact of the legislation for those disenfranchised ought not be underestimated, but the standard of a non-racial franchise remained essentially untouched.

The 1887 dispensation would not last long. The more active and intense tone of Cape Colony politics meant that the franchise issue would be revisited much more frequently than it had been in the mid-nineteenth century. In 1892, legislation backed by Cecil Rhodes raised the basic economic qualification for the franchise from £25 to £75. The impact of this change paled, however, in comparison to the long-reaching implications of the 1894 Glen Grey Act. This act represented a major shift in the way Africans were to be represented within the colony. It established a separate 'native' political sphere, local in focus and 'traditional' in structure. After 1894, the established system of non-racial liberal democracy would be challenged by a racialized alternative. No longer could a universalist conception of political society be assumed as the starting point for governmental discourse.

The Glen Grey Act marked a tipping point in the political history of the Cape Colony and it set a precedent for the twentieth century and, in particular, for the unification of South Africa. The 1902 Treaty of Vereeniging, which ended what is now known as the South African War, also foreshadowed the marginalization and ultimate destruction of the Cape's propertied franchise. This trend manifested itself more fully in the Act of Union, which in 1910 created a unified South African state.

170 *Indigenous Democracy and Colonialism*

The act specifically rejected any attempt to create a non-racial electorate outside of the Cape, rendering liberal democracy an anomaly in the new unified order. The power of African voters, and of those white voters steeped in the idea of a non-racial electorate, figured dramatically less prominently in the political calculus of the Union of South Africa than it had in the Cape Colony. After 1910 it was perhaps inevitable that the propertied franchise would be marginalized and eventually eliminated, as the new state moved towards regularized voter qualification.

The dilution of a limited number of African voters within a much increased white electorate only intensified with the enfranchisement of women 'of European descent' in 1930. Politicians launched a more direct assault on the non-racial franchise a year later by introducing the Franchise Laws Amendment Bill. This bill sought to increase the number of white voters while moving non-white voters to a separate electoral roll. D. F. Malan, then minister of the interior and a major supporter of the bill, explicitly stated that 'a difference will be made in the Cape Province between White and non-White voters in respect of the franchise which did not exist before. The Whites will be qualified on a different basis to non-Whites' (Tatz, 1962: 63). This was the kind of explicit legal discrimination which had been unthinkable within the Cape Colony fifty years earlier.

It took five years for the provisions of Franchise Laws Amendment Bill to be accepted by a majority of the assembly and enacted as law. From this point, political representation for non-white South Africans existed only outside the parliamentary system, in 'traditional' councils explicitly under parliamentary authority. 1936 marked, for all practical purposes, the end of any substantive liberal democracy for those South Africans who could not identify themselves as white. Prime Minister J. B. M. Hertzog would make good on his 1929 declaration towards 'natives': 'only one thing will get the franchise for them, and that is a revolution; yes, force only will obtain it' (Hertzog cited in McCracken, 1963: 81).

African voters and the African National Congress

Before the revision of franchise qualifications in 1887, the electorate of the Cape Colony included approximately 80,000 voters, of whom at least 20 per cent were 'non-European'. This group included both so-called coloured voters and the kind who would have been described at the time as 'natives'. Even as late as 1907, after a number of measures designed, at least in part, to limit the ability of Africans to qualify for the franchise, there were 8,418 'native' voters, constituting 6 per cent of the total electorate (McCracken, 1963: 92–3).[3] These voters were not equally distributed across the colony; rather, they seem to have been concentrated in the eastern 'frontier' region. This meant that, while not every local electorate was substantially multi-racial, individual constituencies could see proportions of African voters much higher than that of the entire colony. Although the Cape's franchise regulations certainly did not produce an electorate representative of the colony's demography (nor were they intended to), they did produce enough African voters to make them both a factor in elections and a substantial community.

Both those who supported the Cape franchise and those who opposed it seem to have agreed that African voters constituted a not inconsequential factor in elections. Following the arrival of responsible government in 1872, John Gordon Sprigg (who would later become prime minister of the Cape Colony) reflected with a certain amount of approbation on a number of cases in which 'the successful candidate had been elected to parliament with the support of the Native voters, while the defeated candidate had polled a larger number of European votes' (McCracken, 1963: 87). As far as Gordon Sprigg was concerned, the only politicians who objected to non-European voters were those who could not harness such voters to their own cause. The 1869 election of Gordon Wood to the Grahamstown local council seems to have been due not simply to the 'African vote', but to the support of one particular 'tribal' community, while James Rose Innes attributed his success as a politician during the 1880s and 1890s to the support of 'a Native electoral association' (McCracken, 1963: 71–2). In the eastern Cape, at least, political candidates seem to have taken the African vote seriously and to have addressed African voters as an important part of their constituencies.

As late as the first decade of the twentieth century, when the non-racial franchise had already been undermined by the Glen Grey Act and marginalized by the move towards regional unification, observers noted that electoral success in the eastern Cape required at least some engagement with African voters and their concerns. Some members of the Native Affairs Commission of 1903–5, anticipating the regularization of 'native policy' across British territories, noted with concern that, 'if a Native has a vote and a white man wants to be elected, it is still necessary for him to appeal to that Native' (*South African Native Affairs Commission*, 1904: 490). The commissioners drew this conclusion after interviewing magistrates from the area around Kingwilliamstown – men with some personal experience of political realities. Even as the legal foundations of the non-racial franchise became increasingly shaky, the

172 *Indigenous Democracy and Colonialism*

lived experience of candidates and voters continued the momentum of a decades-old practice.

African voters certainly experienced the problem of racial prejudice in very real ways, but that should not negate the reality of their experience of political inclusion. Even as politicians and white activists argued over the principle of the non-racial franchise (and even as racialism and scientific racism gained ground in the minds of settlers and colonial officials), African voters proceeded to polling places, found their names on the same electoral rolls as their neighbours and, in many cases, saw 'their' candidates elected. Over the course of the second half of the nineteenth century, those men who qualified for the vote had good reason to think of themselves as part of the British project in southern Africa. In the institution of the franchise and in the economic prosperity that made enfranchisement possible, 'the mid-Victorian "code-words" *progress* and *improvement* had a material reality' (Marks, 1986: 47). Regardless of whether or not the representatives of British governance in South Africa intended the franchise to allow Africans substantive power, African voters experienced it as much more than an anomaly or a gloss on colonial exploitation.

Nor was it only voters, or even potential voters, who took seriously the meaning of the franchise. The relatives and neighbours of voters experienced a kind of vicarious connection with the political arena. In particular, the wives, daughters and sisters of voters seem to have shared their political values (if not always their political views). As Shula Marks has pointed out, an entire class of Africans – including, but by no means limited to, those with the right to vote – constructed their worldview 'out of the mid-Victorian vision of a "progressive world order", based on the virtues of free labor, secure property rights linked to a free market in land and individual tenure, equality before the law, and some notion of "no taxation without representation"' (Marks, 1986: 48). The statistics on African voters, therefore, do not adequately describe the community bound together by a liberal ethos. For every thousand voters, there will have been several thousand other individuals equally steeped in the principle of a non-racial franchise.

Even those prosperous and educated Africans who found themselves outside the Cape Colony seem to have understood politics through the lens of liberal democracy. The Bud Mbelle family demonstrates how political consciousness was not limited to the Cape. Isaiah Bud Mbelle spent the 1920s as a civil servant in Pretoria, but he identified himself with the African voters he had encountered during his childhood in the eastern Cape. His sister Elizabeth and her husband Sol Plaatje also lived outside of the Cape Colony, but oriented themselves in relationship – both familial and political – to the Cape electorate (Cobley, 1990: 71). From 1853 through to the 1920s, the Cape franchise served as a touchstone for politically minded Africans across southern Africa. After 1936, the recollection of a political order represented by the non-racial franchise took on the character of 'an increasingly romanticized folk memory' (Cobley, 1990: 75). For at least some South Africans, the democracy they longed for during apartheid would be the limited liberal democracy of their reminiscence.

The intensity of Africans' engagement with the Cape's electoral system is perhaps best evidenced by the repeated attempts to defend that system against qualitative change. As early as 1864, one rural community insisted that any attempts by the government to change the citizenship certificates that marked them as residents of the colony and as potential voters would be met with violent resistance (Brownlee, 1897: 160). As vernacular newspapers developed in the later part of the nineteenth century, the defense of the non-racial franchise would constitute a major topic of reports and editorials. The political orientation of these journals veered not so much towards broad-based democracy or universal rights as towards a liberalism bounded by ideas of economic rationality. As Andre Odendaal has pointed out, Andrew Gontshi, the editor of the *Manyano nge Mvo Zabantsundu* newspaper, actually supported the Voters Registration Act of 1887, because it did not discriminate against black people *per se* but instead discriminated on the basis of class and wealth (Gontshi, cited in Odendaal, 1983). Gontshi's opinion highlights an implicit (and often explicit) elitism that would linger as part of the folk memory of liberal democracy.

Conclusion

As late as 1910, many African political leaders remained convinced that the Cape's electoral system ought simply to be returned to its early nineteenth-century form (and extended to other parts of the Union). J. T. Jabavu, editor of the *Imvo Zabantsundu* newspaper, described the Act of Union as 'illiberal' in introducing distinctions of colour, as opposed to those of class. Jabavu further insisted that the Act resulted from the 'unreasoning and unreasonable' prejudices of those outside the Cape Colony (Jabavu cited in Odendaal, 1983: 152). His choice of words reflects the fundamental faith of earlier Cape liberals in the shared 'reasonableness' of all qualified voters.

174 *Indigenous Democracy and Colonialism*

The ANC grew out of this ongoing defense of the non-racial franchise. From its foundation until well into the 1950s, support for and engagement with the ANC came almost exclusively from people and groups who had adopted the liberal ethos associated with the propertied franchise. Robert Ross describes the founders as 'white-shirted, dark-suited, mission-educated... most of them voters for the Cape Parliament' (Ross, 1999: 83). The initial goal of the ANC was essentially conservative – the preservation (or restoration) of the nineteenth-century franchise. That it should be 'protective, paternalistic and even discriminatory in seeking to maintain existing rights and privileges' should not be surprising (Switzer, 1993: 247). The liberalism espoused by African voters necessarily discriminated against those deemed unfit for political life. The liberal tension between inclusion and exclusion runs deep in the history of the ANC.

From Pixley Seme to Nelson Mandela, the majority of ANC leaders came from white-collar professions and turned to protest only when the government thwarted their own bourgeois political ambitions. At an earlier period, Mandela (born and raised in the eastern Cape) could have been a voter. The narrative of lost opportunity – of a lost world of political possibility – underpinned his early experiences. As the mythology surrounding Mandela continues to grow, it is worth pointing out that part of his legacy overlaps with the history of liberal democracy in southern Africa. The arc of Mandela's life serves as a reminder that the post-apartheid dispensation in South Africa was grounded not only in the anti-apartheid struggle, but also in a longer history of African political engagement.

Notes

1. This chapter uses the term African to refer to individuals who would today be called black. The latter term is an anachronism for nineteenth century history, while the former is preferable to 'native' (the most commonly used nineteenth century term).
2. In particular, the experience of black, African voters has been neglected. The history of the franchise for the coloured community (made up of Malay, Indian and mixed-race descendants) has been explored in some depth (Bickford-Smith, 1995).
3. The Colony of Natal, by way of comparison, had only six 'native', 150 Indian and 50 coloured voters in 1907. Natal did not automatically permit non-Europeans to qualify for the voter; would-be voters had to petition the government, which had no obligation to grant their requests (Tatz, 1962: 4).

Part IV
Alternative Currents in Modern Democracy

12
Birthing Democracy: The Role of Women in the Democratic Discourse of the Middle East

K. Luisa Gandolfo

> It had to begin at the beginning: The Woman! A nation cannot be liberated whether internally or externally while its women are enchained. In the very midst of this earthquake, in this crazy desire for Liberty for a whole nation my feminist movement was born.
>
> (Shafiq, cited in Nelson, 1996: 142)

For the better part of the twentieth century, women's rights in the Middle East and North Africa (MENA) have been afflicted by a dual malaise: from within, through questionable patriarchal state and legal mechanisms; and from external sources via the 'fetishization of Islam' (Lazreg, 1988: 95).[1] In the haste to seek solutions that would ameliorate the circumstances of women in the MENA region, existent notions of democracy have been overlooked and the source of gender discrimination attributed to the theological aspect, with less regard for the historical and socio-economic context. The notion that '[r]eligion cannot be detached from the socio-economic and political context within which it unfolds' yields a new perspective in which to study the early women's movements of the nineteenth and twentieth century (Lazreg, 1988: 95). In recent years, women's organizations in the MENA region have inspired vigorous debate within the field of gender studies, rather than in that of political studies. Nevertheless, their early struggle provided the foundations not only for a democratic future for subsequent generations, but also for a harkening back to religious and social practices and beliefs that have become mired in the re-Islamization of society. Thus, while calls for democratic change emerge *ad infinitum*, this chapter will explore the manner in which women have inspired and

178   *Alternative Currents in Modern Democracy*

directed political and social developments in the Middle East and in the process transcended gender roles to facilitate democratic practices.

Democracy is about suffrage, freedom and the protection of human rights; it is fickle, but also malleable and capable of redefinition within the context of the MENA according to the social, economic and religious elements of each country. Rather than exacting a Western model, customized democracy provides a framework within which support and representation for all citizens is viable. Thus, just as the women's organizations of the late nineteenth and early twentieth century called for universal suffrage and equal representation, so too were they (re)igniting the democratic process of the region and ensuring that a form of democracy suitable for the countries in question would become attainable. Central to the democratic debate is gender and empowerment. Given that the two concepts determine the extent to which a society implements democratic principles, the terms must be further defined. For Marysia Zalewski, gender theory is traceable to the core question 'Who are women?' and through multiple responses like 'woman is not man', 'woman is lack', 'woman/mother', 'women are sex objects', 'women are whores', or 'women are pure' (Zalewski, 2000: 41). Women, like democracy, are subjective according to the political climate, social milieu and economic circumstances and, as a result, they 'have tended to become subjects only when they conform to specified and calculable representations of themselves as subjects, for example as (good) mothers, wives or daughters' (Elam, cited in Zalewski, 2000: 42). The notion of women exuding goodness in their gender-ascribed roles shall be analysed further, through the works of Qassim Amin (1863–1908), for whom gender equality also denoted dutiful domestic conduct. It is possible, then, to define gender as a social construct in which individuals ascribe behaviours and expectations predicated on the basis of male and female roles. Similar to democracy, gender determines the extent to which an individual participates in society and how he or she does so; it is dependent on socio-economic conditions; and it is variable and responsive to political and social upheaval. Accordingly, gender empowerment can be defined as the 'expansion of assets and capabilities of individuals to participate in, negotiate with, influence, control, and hold accountable the institutions that affect their lives' (MENA Development Report, 2004: xviii). With aspects of accountability, participation and variability according to socio-economic, social and political environs, gender empowerment and democracy become irrevocably juxtaposed. The resultant mélange makes the early feminist campaigners and movements of the Middle East the forerunners of the (re)implementation of democratic practices in the region. After all, the absence of gender equality renders democracy but a barren and redundant notion.

Democratic voices: Gender and equality in the Middle East

By the end of the nineteenth and the beginning of the twentieth century, activists for women's rights and universal suffrage increasingly vocalized their calls for suffrage through the written medium. Foremost among those advocating gender equality were Amin, Zainab Fawwaz (1850–1914), Doria Shafiq (1908–75), Huda Shaarawi (1879–1947) and Ghada Samman (1942–). While the region continues to yield a wealth of male and female campaigners, only three will be studied in this paper: Amin, Fawwaz and Samman. Drawn from Egypt, Lebanon and Syria respectively, the campaigners promulgated their views through women's journals, periodicals and national newspapers, circulating articles that at times were akin to manifestos: point-by-point arguments for enhanced educational, professional and social roles for women. Often looking to the past for examples of women who excelled in business, war and governance – examples that would equal those of the male counterparts – they cited Cleopatra, Zenobia, Khadija, Aisha and Elizabeth I (Fawwaz, 2004 [1891]: 224). For each of the campaigners, a single work remains: their legacy, an inspired and influential *magnum opus* that exudes the original zeal for the eradication of gender inequality.

Amin, galvanized by his experiences of Ottoman domination and Western colonialism and by his involvement with the nationalist reform movement, was spurred to compile two publications, *Tahrir al-Mar'a* (*The Liberation of Women*) and *Al-Mar'a al-Jadida* (*The New Woman*), which appeared in 1899 and 1900 respectively. A feminist essayist, novelist, poet and dramatist, Fawwaz emerged as the protégée of the writer and newspaper publisher Hasan Husni Pasha al-Tuwayrani, in whose newspaper, *Al-Nil*, she published, in the early 1890s, essays that emphasized women's abilities and called for equality, most lucidly through *al-insāf* (fair and equal treatment). Lastly, Samman's article 'Let Us Pray for the Slave Who Is Flogged', published in *Jaridat al-Nasr al-Suriya*, laments the reluctance of women to become involved in political processes and issues a rallying cry for female citizens to exercise their rights, while ceaselessly striving for enhanced emancipation and equality.

A French-educated *qadi* (judge) in the Egyptian Court of Appeals and a prominent advocate for the emancipation of women, Amin passed his first year of practicing law at an educational mission at Montpellier, where he remained for four years, before returning to Egypt in 1885.

180   *Alternative Currents in Modern Democracy*

While in France, Amin had become engrossed in the history of Western thought and upon his return infused his existing knowledge of Islam with elements of Herbert Spencer, John Stuart Mill, Karl Marx, Friedrich Nietzsche and Charles Darwin (Zeidan, 1995: 15–16), in addition to the novel reinterpretations of Islam by ideologues such as Muhammad Abduh (1849–1905) and al-Afghani (1838–97).[2] Stirred by his experiences of Ottoman domination and Western colonialism, Amin became involved in the nationalist reform movement and, while the discourse surrounding female emancipation in Egypt had, until the end of the nineteenth century, focused on education, Amin and Abduh broadened the scope of women's rights, extending them from school to marriage, polygamy, divorce and the veil. The role of women in the struggle against colonialism became apparent, and in 1899 Amin penned *Tahrir al-Mar'a* (*The Liberation of Women*), to be swiftly followed by *Al-Mar'a al-Jadida* (*The New Woman*) in 1900, which elaborated further on the concepts defined in *Tahrir al-Mar'a*.

In *Tahrir al-Mar'a*, Amin indicated not only the flaws in the status of women of the period, but also the measures to be taken, both for the benefit of women and for that of wider Egyptian society. Divided into five sections – 'The Status of Women in Society: A Reflection of the Nation's Moral Standards', 'The Education of Women', 'Women and the Veil', 'Women and the Nation', 'The Family' – the publication lamented the subjugation that women had been exposed to throughout history, as 'men crushed their rights, despised them, treated them with contempt, and stomped on their personality' (Amin, 2000: 9). For Amin, the progress of society depended on the status of its women: as American, British, German and French women enjoyed enhanced rights, so too did their civilization flourish. More significant is the role of women in Islam, a point that Amin recurrently returns to in order to compound the necessity for equality and emancipation:

> the Islamic legal system, the Shari'a, stipulated the equality of women and men before any other legal system. Islam declared women's freedom and emancipation, and granted women all human rights during a time when women occupied the lowest status in all societies.
>
> (Amin, 2000: 7)

Amin challenged the traditional stance, which advocated seclusion – 'a form of execution' – and the limitations placed on a woman's right to education. Women, he contended, could only be independent through education: widows, mothers with no sons, and divorced or single women with no relatives could become self-sufficient rather than be compelled to undertake immoral professions or 'a parasitic dependence upon generous families' (Amin, 2000: 7). *Tahrir al-Mar'a* broke boundaries in debating aspects of society that had previously been unquestioned, and, in the process, emancipation was held aloft, as a remedy for the ills of society – a national, religious and economic cause that could benefit all (Gandolfo, 2011).

While *Tahrir al-Mar'a* triumphed on a contentious issue, the approach by Amin nevertheless attracted criticism. Branded by Ahmed 'the son of Cromer [the British consul general] and colonialism', he sustained an apologetic stance vis-à-vis the European wars and colonialism, while condemning the veil as an Islamic tool of oppression (Ahmed, 1992: 163). His stance did not pass unnoticed: two of Egypt's prominent nationalists, Talaat Harb (1867–1941) and Mustafa Kamel (1874–1908), vehemently opposed Amin's theories on the grounds that they were 'foreign to Egypt', while Harb contended that 'the emancipation of women [was] just another plot to weaken the Egyptian nation and disseminate immorality and decadence in its society' (Hassan, 2000).

Ironically, Amin expressed a bitter vitriol for the women he sought to liberate, variously describing them as 'too clingy', 'accustomed to idleness' and indiscreet:

> While with friends and neighbors, her deep sighs ascend with the cigarette smoke and coffee steam as she talks loudly about her private concerns: her relationship with her husband, her husband's relatives and friends, her sadness, her happiness, her anxiety, her joy. She pours out every secret to her friends, even those details associated with private behavior in the bedroom.
>
> (Amin, 2000: 32)

An additional dimension of Amin's critique comprises class and social status. In the above passage he is primarily assessing the shortcomings of seclusion, yet the role of the servants – with whom the mistress of the house socializes, in an endeavour to alleviate the tedium of daily life – in stirring the garrulous nature of the mistress is regarded negatively. Indeed, Amin goes as far as to cite seclusion as a 'source of moral corruption', as it prompts upper-class women to mix with their lower-class compatriots and 'talk freely to peddlers', actions that contradict Amin's vision of the liberation of women (albeit solely bourgeois women). Accordingly, while at one level Amin campaigned for the rights of women, at another he remained desirous of a nation of good wives

182 *Alternative Currents in Modern Democracy*

and mothers for whom class ties would triumph over kinship, in a world where capitalism would dichotomize the public and private realms and women would tend to their immediate families without having external distractions from friends and relatives (Abu-Lughod, 1998: 261). According to Leila Ahmed, by virtue of his status as a man, Amin would have had limited exposure to a wide range of women, and hence his depiction of Egyptian women as backwards, ignorant and lagging behind their European counterparts was based on limited evidence (Ahmed, 1992). Nevertheless, Amin's position as a judge and as an aristocrat rendered his advocacy of female emancipation significant, as he 'held the reins of interpretive shari'a and reformist Islamic politics of the highest form' (Abisaab and Abisaab, 2000). In spite of the criticism leveled at Amin's ideologies, his role as a leading promulgator of women's rights in Egypt encouraged a wave of activists for emancipation, including Safiya Zaghlul (1912–37), and Shaarawi, who would proceed to establish the Egyptian Feminist Union (EFU) in 1923. Moreover, as Anouar Majid notes, the publication of Amin's tomes and the ensuing reactions to them developed a 'precursor or prototype' of the subsequent debate, which placed the feminist agenda in the discursive debate of cultural and political sovereignty (Majid, 1998: 337). Through *Tahrir al-Mar'a* and through its counterpart, *Al-Mar'a al-Jadida*, Amin contributed towards the fledgling struggle that would ultimately scale greater heights under the guidance of Shaarawi and Shafiq.

By contrast, Fawwaz approached the issue from an egalitarian orientation: born to an illiterate and poor Shi'ite family in Tibnin, Jabal Amil, in southern Lebanon, she differed from contemporaries such as Warda al-Yaziji, Alice al-Bustani and Aisha Ismat al-Taimuriya, who could claim prominent or elite status. Following her first marriage, Fawwaz emigrated from Lebanon to Egypt, where she became a prominent writer on gender issues in the nationalist press, contributing to journals like *al-Fatah, al-Muayyad, al-Nil* and *al-Anis al-Jalis*. In 1894 she composed the first biographical dictionary dedicated to famous women, *al-Durr al-Manthur fi Tabaqat Rabbat al-Khudar* (*Pearls Scattered Throughout the Women's Quarters*), to be followed by three novels and a collection of essays and articles titled *al-Rasail al-Zaynabiyya* (*Zaynab's Letters*) in 1897. Throughout the collection Fawwaz countered that women should be accorded political rights equal to those enjoyed by their male contemporaries, and she refuted the notion that women's lives should be restricted to the domestic realm.

In 1891, through the article *al-Insāf* ('Fair and Equal Treatment'), Fawwaz called for the recognition of women's abilities and for their being treated equally to men. There Fawwaz was responding to an argument expressed by Hana Kasbani Kurani (1870–98) in her article 'Women and Politics', published in the newspaper *Lubnan*. In an eloquent riposte to Kurani's theory that 'woman cannot perform work outside the home while at the same time fulfilling the duties incumbent upon her to serve her husband and children', Fawwaz countered that, since women were intellectually equal to men, they were fully entitled to pursue equivalent avenues of professional endeavours to those of their male counterparts, including careers in politics. 'Fair and Equal Treatment' consequently bears substantial association with 'Women and Politics', both Fawwaz and Kurani assuming a polemic stance on the issue of religious, social and historical interpretations of the roles of women in society – in the West and the Middle East like. Since women excelled academically in fields as diverse as philosophy and engineering, law and mathematics, Fawwaz ruled that womankind could dedicate itself and triumph in such fields, only to encounter impediments to its continued success due to women's gender (Gandolfo, 2011). Such restrictions made women be forever excluded from 'the ruling group' – a group that otherwise would be enriched rather than hindered by the presence of women. Far from being an unnatural element, as Kurani postulates, the equal participation of women would realize the fact that women are rendered in an equal likeness to man in terms of their capabilities, as Fawwaz demonstrates by drawing on the example of pre-modern rulers and early Muslim women. The act of preventing women from scaling the heights of politics and other professional fields through reasoning such as that expressed by Kurani was in itself atypical.

Fawwaz's assertion that women could excel just as much as their male contemporaries, if not more, drew scorn from political and religious quarters. Raising the issue of Shari'a and of the role of the veil as an impediment to women's progress in realms such as politics, Shaikh Ahmad Arif al-Zayn (1884–1960), the founder of the Beirut magazine *al-'Irfan*, countered that women could not perform the functions of men and condemned Fawwaz's response to Kurani. In response, Fawwaz once more reiterated the crucial point of her article:

> I did not violate the legal claims of Islamic jurisprudence . . . Your idea that women cannot perform the functions of men is wrong, because Western women have exceeded men by far. As for us, the veil does not prevent us from doing men's jobs.
>
> (Ibrahim cited in Zeidan, 1995: 65)

184 *Alternative Currents in Modern Democracy*

The works of Fawwaz, including *al-Rasail al-Zaynabiyya* and *al-Durr al-Manthur fi Tabaqat Rabbat al-Khudar*, proved bold and original in their stance and facilitated future calls for the liberation of women and for the provision of equal rights for women in the Middle East. Moreover, *al-Durr al-Manthur fi Tabaqat Rabbat al-Khudar* substantially contributed towards the transformation of the traditional perception of women as mere vessels for marriage and children. Prior to the book's publication in 1894, no record of the lives of renowned women had been published in Arabic; subsequently, the publication provided a source of information for future *Shahirat al-Nisa* (*Famous Women*) columns, though Fawwaz's work remained frequently unacknowledged (Booth, 1997: 841). Just as Fawwaz drew upon the ancient rulers Cleopatra and Zenobia, the biographies of renowned women published in magazines served to make readers aware of the necessity to struggle and advance the circumstances of women. Likewise, Fawwaz succeeded in recording the nascent stirrings of a movement towards suffrage and equality, though nothing would happen for many years to follow; the actions of women in the past inculcated hope for the future. Far from idling beneath the perceived yoke of religion, women had always been active and their need for democracy continued to course through society until the mid-twentieth century brought a degree of realization to their objectives.

As the twentieth century progressed, the endeavours of feminist activists such as Fawwaz and Amin began to bear fruit: women had gained the vote in Egypt in 1956, in Lebanon in 1964 and in Syria in 1949, which was subsequently rescinded, before being reinstated in 1953. Born in 1942 in Al-Shamiya, Syria, Ghada Samman is a Syrian fiction writer and author of a number of articles pertaining to cultural identity, conflict, and the role of women in society. While Samman has been publishing for over forty years, the tenacity that has rendered her a luminary of the feminist literature movement in the region has remained undiminished, as the article, 'Our Constitution – We the Liberated Women' attests.

Published in *Jaridat al-Nasr al-Suriya* in November 1961, the article was also known by the title 'Let Us Pray for the Slave Who Is Flogged' and expresses Samman's disdain for the women of Hama in Syria, who refused to vote in elections. Structured into three sections – 'It's a Crime for a Slave to Love her Bonds', 'Our Constitution – We the Liberated Women' and 'They Will Not Plant Us in Cocoons of Fog after Today' – the essay commences with condemnation of women's spurning of suffrage, a rejection that Samman likens to a woman held in a cave who 'melted her chains...[and] reunited them for a master to re-tie her because she's afraid to live, because she is too cowardly to bear the responsibility of living' (Samman, 2004 [1961]: 138). In response to the women of Hama who invoked Islamic faith as a reason not to vote, Samman raises the example of Aisha, the second wife of the Prophet Muhammad, who was accused of adultery and later vindicated. By relinquishing their right to participate as human beings, women were committing a treacherous deed, akin to the betrayal 'of the eye-lashes to the eye, of the fingernail to the finger, of the hand to the arm' (Samman, 2004 [1961]: 140). In the second section Samman details the characteristics of the liberated woman, notably that she 'believes that she is as human as a man' and recognizes that the difference between a man and a woman is 'how, not how much', and that 'they are equally human [and] they must have equal human rights' (Samman, 2004 [1961]: 140–1). While Samman's critics denounced her endorse-ment of freedom, she retorts: 'Choice is the one thing which produces responsibility and the one thing that gives a moral code its true value' (Samman, 2004 [1961]: 141). Thus freedom, and choice, empower and morally guide a woman in a manner that cannot be developed while one is constrained by religious, social, or political conventions. In the final section Samman censures Arab society and those who claim that Arab women who do not modernize in the Western way have failed and are therefore incapable of changing, since '[i]t is better that we investigate the reasons for the Arab woman's backwardness instead of returning her to her chains in the cave and saying that she is only fit for its darkness' (Samman, 2004 [1961]: 142).

Through the article Samman addressed a contentious socio-political issue, which drew condemnation from the religious conservatives. In response, she reiterated her stance through a subsequent essay bearing the combative title 'Let Us Demand Emancipation for Men Too'. At the time of publication of the article, Syrian women were at a crossroads: briefly granted suffrage in 1953, only to have it rescinded until 1972, Samman expressed the frustration of the period, as women remained divided on the issue of suffrage. By challenging the role of Islam in the emancipation and freedom of women, Samman provided a new perspec-tive, which made freedom an opportunity exist morally and according to the precepts of Islam, while the person who had them was enjoy-ing full rights as a Syrian citizen. As Samman's foremost article, the essay established a focus and tone that has endured through her later works: the passion for women's rights, cultural identity, and the clash between tradition and progress. Through these concepts the theme of

186 *Alternative Currents in Modern Democracy*

'a cry for freedom' is evident both in 'Our Constitution – We the Liberated Women' and her later works. This cry is particularly tangible in the former, as the recurring 'Let us pray' lends a religious tone to a socio-political lament. Thus, for Samman, the desire for freedom is linked to the issue of women's emancipation. In this respect, Samman provided a contentious, yet pertinent, insight into the political circumstances – and choices – of Syrian women during the interim period before they attained full and lasting suffrage. Despite the length of time since its publication, the article has not lost its tone of urgency and remains a pertinent critique of the role of women in the socio-political framework of a state.

A new democracy: Islamic feminism, secularism and gender participation

Islam has been central to debate of both nineteenth-century and contemporary campaigners for women's rights, within the Middle East and beyond. Faith has been cited both as a force for progress, with activists indicating egalitarian aspects within the Quran, and as a force of oppression, with calls for a return to the period of *jahiliyya*, the pre-Islamic period broadly defined as the time of ignorance. In recent years a new form of feminism has emerged that neatly merges the two and promotes a view of Islam juxtaposed with gender equality through Islamic feminism. Although a relatively new movement, this feminism has splintered into four branches: Sufi-based Islamic feminism; feminists who believe that Quranic norms should be treated as ethical injunctions, not as legal stipulations; feminists who seek to dispel the notion of the hijab as a tool of oppression; and radical Muslim feminists, who reinterpret the Quran so as to discern benefits for womankind (Lapidus, 2002: 864–5). For Islamist feminists, the Quran provides a source of inspiration that would ameliorate the circumstances of women: rather than denouncing Islam as acting to the detriment of women's rights, these feminists point to the historical conditions of society as a force behind the subjugation and oppression of women. Early Islam, they counter, elevated the status of women in Arabian society; prior to that, women were regarded as chattel, within a patriarchal system predicated on clans and lineages. Indubitably, this varied by clan, since not all women were denied independence – the wife of the Prophet, Khadija, was an independent businesswoman, for example. The Quran bridged the two eras, providing women with rights in terms of property and divorce, while women also assumed pertinent roles within the family, brokering marriages, liaising with other families and teaching the Quran to the young of the household (Lapidus, 2002: 854). Their involvement spanned the socio-economic divide; upper-class Ottoman women became property owners through inheritance and they endowed *waqfs* and held *timars*, tax-farms and business partnerships. Similarly, women of the lower classes participated in animal husbandry, crafts, pottery and agriculture (Lapidus, 2002: 854).

By mid-twentieth century, Arab women were bringing the Islamic dimension to the fore through the questioning of the religious authorities on their ever hardening stance against women in education, professions and the law. In 1952 Doria Shafiq penned an attack on the then Mufti, Shaikh Hasanain Makhluf, through the article 'Islam and the Constitutional Rights of Woman'. Shafiq called upon her fellow humans to defend not only the country of Egypt, but also their faith, against the notion that 'woman was created merely for *fitna*... this is not in keeping with the generous tenets of Islam regarding women' (Shafiq, 2004 [1952]: 354). Rather she pointed to the viewpoint of the previous Mufti, Shaikh Alam Nassar, who emphasized the egalitarianism inherent in Islam:

> Islam looks at the woman as it looks at the man with respect to humanity, rights and personality... Woman and man in the judgement of Islam are equal. A man is condemned to death if he kills a woman and a woman is condemned to death if she kills a man, therefore the two are equal... Islam also gave the woman the freedom to choose her headband and to contract and consummate marriage as long as she is of age. This is proof that Islam has made guarantees to the woman in the most important aspect of her life.
>
> (Shafiq, 2004 [1952]: 355)

According to Shafiq's argument, the limitations placed on women that inhibited their access to education and the professions also ran contrary to national interests. As nationalism fused with feminism, the emancipation of Egyptian women joined denunciations of gender segregation, arranged marriages, polygamy and repudiation, which had featured on the agenda of *fin-de-siècle* equality campaigners as an impediment to national progress. In this manner, by combining feminist discourse with Islamic rhetoric, women's rights activists such as Shafiq seized the very weapon with which the patriarchal system sought to subdue them and deployed it against their ideological opponents.

For the contemporary feminist writers Fatema Mernissi and Nawal El Saadawi, conservative Islam has born a negative impact on the freedom and rights previously enjoyed by women during the period of

188   *Alternative Currents in Modern Democracy*

jahiliya and early Islam. As El Saadawi indicates, women have with time become synonymous with *fitna* (chaos) and pleasure has resulted in the conditioning of 'Arab men's ambiguous attitude and inhibited their adequate examination of the tragedy of women in their cultures' (El Saadawi, 1980: 165–7). Harkening back to an era of liberty is echoed by Mernissi, for whom democracy is redefined as a mode of *shirk* (disbelief in the form of equating another deity with Allah), and *jahiliya*, as an era of discussion and human rights (Mernissi, cited in Majid, 1998: 329). *Jahiliya* is thus transposed from being a negative entity associated with ignorance to being a period that deserves emulation; by contrast, Islam is perceived as anti-historical, anti-feminist and strident in the crusade to 'veil anything that threatens their faith, whether it be Western democracy, history . . . or simply any form of change' (Majid, 1998: 329). Nevertheless, while Mernissi and El Saadawi look to the pre-Islamic era for examples of women's freedom, Majid counters that it was less the imposition of Islam that curtailed women's liberties and more the socio-economic transformation and the power of oral culture in the Arab world. Living in a homo-social society, women were at ease to sustain orality free from repression, as is evidenced by Muslim women in Islamic Spain during the eleventh and twelfth centuries, who exhibited their erotic freedom through poetry and personal lifestyles that beguiled their European contemporaries (Majid, 1998: 336; see also Walther, 1993: 144–9). That this lurid oral culture has become more sanitized as a result of the diminishment of homo-social settings is questionable: the fact that modern writers turn more frequently towards Europe in search of literary expression does not denote a lessening of the impact of their works or of the potency of Islam as a cosmopolitan positive force for progress. As the tussle for democratic progress in the context of gender equality continues into the twenty-first century, a new ideological battleground has emerged in which Islamist feminists vie against conservative Islamists, each seeking to redefine the tenets of Islam according to their own agenda. For Mernissi, the fact that the new onslaught focuses on the dress, mobility and status of women is a manifestation of the contemporary Islamic identity in turmoil, as social transformation raises challenges to the existing patriarchal authority (Kandiyoti, 1991: 9–14).

Conclusion

Despite the endeavours of campaigners in the realm of women's rights in the Middle East, there remains a significant number of reforms to be done in the realm of citizenship, nationality and human rights.

The chasm opened by their conspicuous absence undermines not only democratic principles in the context of the MENA region, but also the essential Islamic tenets, which are egalitarian. For all the campaigns and vociferous calls by activists, the twentieth century has brought comparably scant progress. Just as citizenship laws are contravened to by patriarchal personal laws that bestow primacy upon men in marriage, divorce, custody, maintenance and inheritance, tradition consistently undermines the value of women through lenient legal responses to honour crimes (Davis, 1999; Hasso, 2005; Joseph, 2000; Kandiyoti, 1991). Nevertheless, the sustained struggle for gender equality – coupled with the rise of Islamist feminism – provides hope for a renewed feminist onslaught in the region.

While women have often assumed crucial roles in national struggles, both as symbols of the community and as fighters – notably in the Palestinian uprising (1936–39) – their involvement has ebbed and flowed with time. After 1948 the pressure to conform to moral and cultural norms resulted in a lessening of female participation in providing medical care, arms smugglings and fund collection. With the onset of the first *Intifada* (uprising) from 1987–93 and the subsequent Al Aqsa *Intifada* in 2000, the Israeli occupation of the West Bank and Gaza Strip galvanized Palestinian women towards conflict through roles in politics, as heads of families, households and the community, and as suicide bombers. Nevertheless, to infer that national struggle slackens the bonds of patriarchy would be overly optimistic: though the gender roles fluctuate, patriarchy continues to beat steadily beneath the furore. Just as Palestinian feminists feared that women will eventually be returned to their archetypal gender roles, this worry is being realized in contemporary Gaza. According to the Palestinian Center for Human Rights Report about the impact of Operation Cast Lead (December 2008–January 2009) on the female population of Gaza, women have become increasingly susceptible to marginalization, poverty and suffering (Palestinian Center for Human Rights, 2009: 5). In the aftermath of war, a rising tide of fundamentalism has enhanced restrictions on women's dress and education, to the point that, at the start of a new school year, girls were turned away from school gates for not donning the *jilbab* ('Gaza: Rescind Religious Dress Code for Girls', 2009). The strict – yet 'unofficial'[3] – implementation of the Islamic dress code has cast a pall over Gaza, as it emerges as a forerunner of stauncher measures taken through the 'virtue' campaign initiated by Hamas in July 2009. Mernissi notes that the focus of the new Islamist agenda commences with dress, to be followed by the mobility and status of women. In the same way, the

190 *Alternative Currents in Modern Democracy*

'virtue' campaign abrogates the Palestine Basic Law, which guarantees freedom of thought, conscience, and expression, while heralding bleak prospects for women's rights in Gaza. For, as the fledgling 'virtue' campaign unfurls, Gaza appears to be emulating Iran through crackdowns, infringements of human rights, abuse and deprivation, all committed in the name of 'virtue': one cannot help comparing the tactics enacted by Hamas and those used by the Iranian *basiji* in recent years.

Democracy is not unobtainable in the Middle East; but it must be a democracy born of the history, culture and religious faith. Most of all, it must be an inclusive democracy in which women are placed legally, socially and politically on an equal standing with their male counterparts. The foundations are there: the works of Amin, Fawwaz, Shafiq, El Saadawi and Mernissi demonstrate that Islam and democracy are far from being awkward bedfellows. Resisting the (re)Islamization programmes promulgated by the fundamentalist organizations has become a priority. Certainly, it often seems that for every step of progress there are two accompanying steps in the opposite direction – the very nature of the region, afflicted as it is by conflict, poverty and the traditions entrenched in the country, provides obstacles that challenge the endeavours of reformers and campaigners. The solution, once more, resides in mirroring the forces that work against women's emancipation: if those in favour of preserving the patriarchal structures interpret Islam according to their objectives, a redefined Islam must be promoted, one that capitalizes on Islam's inherent ability to interact and contribute at a panglobal level, politically, and culturally, on an inter-faith basis, gender equality being central to the agenda. Then, and only then, will women forge ahead in the struggle for equality and democracy, being free from the connotations of Westernization.

Notes

1. The works of authors such as Tahar ben Jelloun, Driss Chraibi and Salman Rushdie have been cited as examples of the fetishization of Islam (Lazreg, 1988: 95).
2. Sayyid Muhammad Ibn Safdar al-Husayn (1838–97), better known as al-Afghani, and Muhammad Abduh (1849–1905) are regarded as the founders of Islamic Modernism (Amin, 2000: 1–109).
3. While the imposition of the Islamic dress code on women in Gaza has not been legally ratified, Hamas police in the area have ensured that the suggestion is not interpreted as optional.

13

The Streets of Iraq: Protests and Democracy after Saddam

Benjamin Isakhan

Since the US led 'Coalition of the Willing' invaded in 2003, the streets of Iraq have featured prominently in media and political discourse. Overwhelmingly, this coverage has emphasized the disorder and chaos found on these streets, and has done so through depictions of horrific violence in the forms of suicide bombings, kidnappings, mortar attacks, improvised explosive devices, sectarian hostility and the threat of all-out civil war. One might argue that the tendency of the Western media, academics and other commentators to emphasize the daily atrocities of post-Saddam Iraq has largely obfuscated the positive political developments and has seen successful stories of Iraq's fledgling democracy buried beneath a seemingly endless reel of bloodshed and chaos. Where attention has been paid to the political landscape in Iraq, this attention has tended to privilege disagreements and disunities between Iraq's myriad ethno-religious factions over the complexity of Iraqi politics and the highly inclusive and progressive nature of the democratic deliberations being conducted.

In addition, much of the coverage has argued that Iraq simply lacks the social and political prerequisites necessary for building democratic forms of governance (Isakhan, 2007b, 2008a). For example, in 2006 *USA Today* published an editorial by former US army officer Ralph Peters, in which the author brings to the fore classically Orientalist[1] rhetoric about the incompatibility between the Middle East and democracy, while at the same time he all but absolves the United States of any wrong-doing. He writes:

> Yet, for all our errors, we did give the Iraqis a unique chance to build a rule-of-law democracy. They preferred to indulge in old hatreds, confessional violence, ethnic bigotry and a culture of corruption.

192 *Alternative Currents in Modern Democracy*

It appears that the cynics were right: Arab societies can't support democracy as we know it...Iraq was the Arab world's last chance to board the train to modernity, to give the region a future, not just a bitter past. The violence staining Baghdad's streets with gore isn't only a symptom of the Iraqi government's incompetence, but of the comprehensive inability of the Arab world to progress in any sphere of organized human endeavor. We are witnessing the collapse of a civilization.

(Peters, 2006)

While balanced assessments of the intractable problems that Iraqi democracy faces, along with an open acknowledgement of the failures of the Iraqi government and of the deep-seated corruption which plagues the nation are not in themselves Orientalist, it is instructive to note how often such assessments are seen as being indicative of a deeper problem. Here Peters connects such problems to 'culture', 'Arab societies', 'a bitter past', 'civilization' and 'the comprehensive inability of the Arab world to progress in any sphere of organized human endeavour'. This suggests a degree of Iraqi (or, more broadly, Arab or Muslim) exceptionalism, which forgets the long toils and tribulations upon which Western democracy is built, as well as a degree of cultural primordialism and stagnation, which assumes that Iraq is trapped in the inviolable web of an anti-democratic legacy. Clearly, such Orientalist coverage of Iraq and of its purported inability to democratize relies on assumptions not only about the despotic nature of the Orient, but also about the Occident and its tendency towards democracy. That the Iraqis are unable to democratize is not seen as the fault of the invading and occupying forces of the West, or of the political system they tried to install, but as indicative of the backward and barbaric nature of the Iraqi people.

However, there is in fact an entirely 'secret' history to democracy in post-2003 Iraq. There is much evidence to suggest a return to a civic culture in Iraq, where the streets of the nation have concurrently developed into a locus for varied deliberation, debate and discourse. For example, following the fall of the Ba'athist regime, a complex array of political, religious and ethno-sectarian factions formed political parties and civil society movements, many of which have written policy agendas, engaged in complex political alliances and debated and deliberated over the key issues facing the state (Davis, 2004: 1, 3, 2007: 3). Most of these political factions also sponsor their own media outlets which have been enthusiastically read by a populace thirsty for uncensored news, even if it is partisan. This was particularly true in the lead up to the elections and referendum conducted across Iraq in 2005, where Iraq's many media outlets fulfilled their function as the Fourth Estate, providing the Iraqi citizens with a rich array of information on key policies, politicians and parties (Isakhan, 2006, 2008b, 2009). This was followed by the events of the elections themselves, which saw millions of Iraqi citizens – young and old, Sunni and Shia, Kurd and Arab, Christian and Muslim – risk threats of further violence to line the streets of the nation, patiently waiting for their chance to take part in the first democratic elections held in Iraq for many decades. These trends continued at the time of the January 2009 provincial elections in Iraq, which saw colourful campaign posters glued to walls all over Iraq, while party volunteers handed out leaflets at security check-points. Other volunteers used more traditional tactics, such as going door-to-door, doing radio interviews or calling public assemblies where ordinary citizens were invited to grill leading candidates on their policies (Isakhan, 2011).

Building on the above discussion of the democratic currents within Iraq, this chapter seeks to document and examine the Iraqi people's exercise of their right to protest and the influence these protests have had on the political landscape of the post-Saddam era. Since 2003, the Iraqi people have frequently taken to the streets *en masse*, to air their concerns about everything – from the ongoing US-led occupation to the government's failure to provide basic security and infrastructure and to the airing of 'indecent' programmss on Iraqi television. This paper concludes by arguing that Iraqi citizens who play an active role in their own governance and participate in democratic mechanisms such as elections and mass demonstrations are helping to create a more robust democracy.

Grassroots democracy

The lesser known story of democracy in Iraq begins immediately after the fall of Baghdad in April 2003, when the nation witnessed a whole series of spontaneous elections. In northern Kurdish cities such as Mosul, in majority Sunni Arab towns like Samarra, in prominent Shia Arab cities such as Hilla and Najaf and in the capital of Baghdad, religious leaders, tribal elders and secular professionals summoned town hall meetings where representatives were elected and plans were hatched for local reconstruction projects, security operations and the return of basic infrastructure. Such moves were initially supported by the occupying forces and there are records of US troops having played a facilitating role in the process, while even the head of the Coalition

194 *Alternative Currents in Modern Democracy*

Provisional Authority (CPA), Lewis Paul Bremer III, had initially planned to convene a national assembly in which representatives from all sectors of Iraq's complex society would elect an interim council (Klein, 2007: 362).

However, the United States was quick to quell such indigenous drives towards democratization and to exert its own hegemony over Iraq. Fearing that the people of Iraq would elect certain 'undesirables' such as military strongmen or political Islamists, Bremer decided that he would appoint the members of the Interim Iraqi Government (IIG) and, by the end of June, he had further ordered that all local and regional elections were to be stopped immediately (Klein, 2007: 363–5). This effectively meant that any decisions made by local councils were revoked, and the mayors and governors who had been elected by their own constituents were replaced by hand-picked representatives, sometimes former Baathist cronies (Booth, 2003; Booth and Chandrasekaran, 2003). Not surprisingly, such moves met with staunch opposition across Iraq and prompted some of the earliest protests of the post-Saddam era. In the Shia holy city of Najaf, for example, hundreds of peaceful protestors took to the streets, demanding that the installed mayor be removed and replaced by a representative selected via free and fair elections. Several protestors carried placards reading 'Cancelled elections are evidence of bad intentions' and 'O America, where are promises of freedom, elections and democracy?' (cited in Booth and Chandrasekaran, 2003). Much larger demonstrations were conducted in Baghdad and Basra, where thousands banded together to chant the words 'Yes, yes, elections. No, no, selections' (cited in Hendawi, 2003).

Shia Arab protests

Despite such warnings, the CPA attempted to go ahead with its plan to install a puppet government in Baghdad. Once again, such anti-democratic moves were widely contested across Iraq, particularly amongst the Shia Arab population, where senior religious figures such as Grand Ayatollah Ali Al-Sistani[2] were able to mobilize thousands of Iraqis in protests that called for a general election prior to the drafting of the Iraqi constitution (Davis, 2005a: 115–17, 2005b: 59; Klein, 2007: 365). Al-Sistani, a member of the quietist branch of the Shia faith, took the unprecedented step of issuing several politically motivated *fatwas*, urging his clergymen to get involved in local politics and encouraging the faithful, including women, to protest around key decisions and to vote in elections (Al-Rahim, 2005: 50). Reasoning that a greater involvement of the Shia Arab majority in Iraqi politics would rectify the power imbalance that had swung in favour of the Sunni Arab minority since the inception of the state in 1921, Al-Sistani began his religio-political campaign on 25 June 2003 by issuing a *fatwa* that read:

> These [occupation] authorities do not have the authority to appoint the members of the constitution writing council. There is no guarantee that this council will produce a constitution that responds to the paramount interests of the Iraqi people and expresses its national identity of which Islam and noble social values are basic components... There must be general elections in which each eligible Iraqi can choose his representative in a constituent assembly for writing the constitution. This is to be followed by a general referendum on the constitution approved by the constituent assembly. All believers must demand the realization of this important issue and participate in completing the task in the best manner.
>
> (Al-Sistani, cited in Arato, 2004: 174)

As Ruel Marc Gerecht has pointed out, such *fatwas* were less of a religious edict and more of a 'flawlessly secular proclamation that clearly and consistently established "the people" as the final arbiters of Iraq's political system' (Gerecht, 2004). This tendency to put 'the people' first garnered Al-Sistani considerable momentum in his campaign to get democratic elections in Iraq. When the cleric called for the protestors to join the cause in mid-January 2004, more than 100,000 Shia marched through Baghdad, while a further 30,000 took to the streets of Basra (Walker, 2005). Put simply, they demanded democracy. They called on the US occupation to conduct free and fair national elections, which would enable the people of Iraq to nominate an Iraqi legislature. They waved flags and chanted: 'Yes, yes to unification! Yes, yes to voting! Yes, yes to elections! No, no to occupation!' (cited in Jamail, 2004). Some carried banners with slogans such as 'We refuse any constitution that is not elected by the Iraqi people', while one protestor told reporters: 'If America won't give us the democracy they promised, we will make it for ourselves' (cited in Jamail, 2004). Demonstrating the power of Al-Sistani, these protests remained peaceful, in accordance with his instructions; and, when the cleric announced that he had agreed to wait for a UN inspection team to study the situation, the protestors disbanded just as quickly as they had been assembled (Finn, 2004).

However, if it was Al-Sistani who was to have the most impact over the political landscape of Iraq during the first few months of the occupation,

196 *Alternative Currents in Modern Democracy*

it was the younger, more radical Moqtada Al-Sadr[3] who was to gain both notoriety and political influence in the years that followed. This arguably began when the CPA forced the closure of two organs produced by Al-Sadr, *Al-Hawza* (the name of a particular Shia seminary in Najaf where a number of leading clerics teach) and the quarterly journal *Al-Mada* (*The View*). Both of these publications appear to have represented Al-Sadr's political and theological ideology, advocating an Islamic republic for Iraq and featuring vitriolic critiques of Israel and of the American-led occupation (Rosen, 2004). Specifically, *Al-Hawza* was targeted for featuring articles with headlines such as 'America Hates Islam and Muslims', and its closure prompted thousands of protestors to gather at the paper's office in central Baghdad. Despite being relatively peaceful at the time, the protestors chanted slogans such as 'No, no, America!' and 'Where is democracy now?', also vowing to avenge *Al-Hawza*'s closure (Al-Sheikh, 2004; Gettleman, 2004). In a twist of irony, it was the forced closure of *Al-Hawza*, rather than anything printed across its humble pages that ultimately garnered Al-Sadr's renewed reverence amongst his already loyal followers and arguably incited his Mahdi Army to violence (Al-Marashi, 2007: 132).

Indeed, throughout 2004 Al-Sadr led several military uprisings against the occupation. These events brought Al-Sadr a sudden notoriety, they helped to refine his mastery of anti-occupation political rhetoric and they distinguished him from Al-Sistani as a strong militant religious leader who had both the strength and the gall to take on the United States. However, when his military campaigns consistently failed, Al-Sadr employed a new arsenal of weapons in his struggle against the occupation from 2005 onwards. These included a dramatic shift in approach from armed resistance to (mostly) non-violent political struggle, an evolution in rhetoric that saw him change from fire-brand pro-Shia Islamism to calls for tolerance, national unity and social inclusion, and the effective transformation of the Mahdi Army from militia to social welfare organization (Yaphe, 2008: 3). As part of this shift, Al-Sadr, following in the footsteps of Al-Sistani, began to capitalize on his enormous support base and mobilized it regularly in co-ordinated protests across Iraq. For example, on the second anniversary of the invasion of Iraq (April 2005), Al-Sadr effectively orchestrated massive protests in Baghdad. His supporters marched the 5 kilometres from Sadr city to Firdos square, where the United States had torn down the giant bronze statue of Saddam, in an attempt to look like liberators, and not like the invaders of Iraq in 2003. Thousands travelled from all over the nation to attend these peaceful protests, which made them one of the largest political rallies in Iraqi history (Jasim, 2005). They chanted anti-occupation slogans, while a statement read on behalf of Al-Sadr claimed: 'We want a stable Iraq and this will only happen through independence…There will be no security and stability unless the occupiers leave…The occupiers must leave my country' (cited in Al-Khairalla, 2005b).

What was particularly interesting here was that Al-Sadr ordered his followers to wave only Iraqi flags, and not flags of the Mahdi Army or of other Shia Arab organisations. This was a self-conscious attempt to move the protests beyond the level of a pro-Al-Sadr, Shia-backed movement, into more of a nationalist struggle against occupation, something which would appeal to Iraqis of all persuasions. At the time, a spokesperson for Al-Sadr, Sheikh Abdul-Hadi Al-Daraji is reported to have said: 'Many of our brothers, including Sunnis, have welcomed the call and will take part' (Al-Daraji, cited in 'Anti-US Protest Marks Anniversary of Saddam's Overthrow', 2005). This was to prove true for a number of Sunni Arabs attending the Baghdad protests, as well as for a small contingent of Iraqi Christians. Concurrent protests were also co-ordinated by the Association of Muslim Scholars in the Sunni city of Ramadi and attended by around 5,000 protestors (Carl, 2005). These massive anti-occupation protests, organized by Al-Sadr, have become an ongoing annual event in Iraq, with successful and largely peaceful demonstrations having been conducted each year since 2005 (Ahmed, 2009). In addition, the followers of Al-Sadr have also organized several other demonstrations concerning more pragmatic problems. For example, in the Sunni Arab-dominated city of Samarra hundreds of Al-Sadr's followers have repeatedly demonstrated against the lack of basic infrastructure and public services such as electricity, fuel and potable water, against the high cost of ice and against the increasingly bleak employment market.

Following up on the strength of these protests, Al-Sadr has further demonstrated his keen political instincts and acute knowledge of democratic mechanisms. For example, in 2005, he instructed his followers to collect the signatures of one million Iraqis in a petition that asked the US and Coalition troops to leave the country immediately. More recently, in March 2008, Al-Sadr launched a nation-wide civil disobedience campaign in response to a series of raids targeting the cleric's offices and to the subsequent arrest of a number of members of his organization. In several key Baghdad neighborhoods such as Mahmoudiya and Yusufiya, members of the Mahdi Army marched in a show of force, while in Abu Disher the streets were emptied, the stores closed and the schools vacated in protest (Tawfeeq et al., 2008). Then, in October 2008,

198 *Alternative Currents in Modern Democracy*

thousands of Iraqis took to the streets of Sadr city and in the south-eastern province of Missan, in support of Al-Sadr's expressed concerns about the parliament's consideration of a new draft of the US–Iraqi Security pact, which would extend US troop presence until 2011 ('Sadr Supporters Protest Planned US–Iraqi Security Agreement', 2008). When the Iraqi government ignored the protests and signed the deal, Al-Sadr's followers re-appeared in the streets and a senior supporter of Al-Sadr read a message the cleric had written at the rally which stated:

> This crowd shows that the opposition to the agreement is not insignificant and parliament will be making a big mistake if it chooses to ignore it ... The government must know it is the people who help it in the good and the bad times. If it throws the occupier out, we will stand by it.
>
> (Al-Sadr cited in Chulov, 2008)

Sunni Arab, Kurdish and Christian protests

It is undeniable, however, that the key reason why the Shia Arab protests have been so effective is the fact that they make up the majority of Iraq's population. This is not true of smaller minorities in Iraq, such as the Sunni Arab (around 20 per cent), the Kurds (around 20 per cent) and the Iraqi Christians (around 3 per cent), who simply cannot command such impressively large demonstrations. Nonetheless, these smaller minorities have also been able to utilize the power of the streets in order to air their concerns and advocate political change. For example, the Sunni Arab minority conducted some of its earliest protests in the form of general strikes in resistance to US blockades of Sunni cities. In Ramadi, for example, the entire town shut down for two days, as US troops launched a major offensive across the Sunni region. As Sheikh Majeed Al-Gaood described it, 'a call came from the mosques for a general strike in Ramadi and neighboring towns. Schools, markets and offices shut down in protest at the blockade' (Al-Gaood, cited in Assaf, 2005). Such Sunni Arab protests were to gather increased momentum as members of the former ruling minority found themselves increasingly ostracized by the Shia Arab- and Kurdish-dominated central government. In 2005, Sunni Arab demonstrations were held in the towns of Hit, Ramadi, Samarra and Mosul, in protest of the fact that the US and the Iraqi government was planning a nation-wide referendum in October 2005, which was designed to ratify the Iraqi constitution drawn up by the government. Again, the Sunnis felt that they had had little say in this constitution and took to the streets *en masse* to air their concerns (Nasr, 2005). In addition, the Sunni Arab population of northern cities such as Kirkuk and Mosul has frequently taken to the streets in protests against what it sees as the Kurdish domination of Nineveh's regional administration (Nourredin, 2005). Most recently, 2008 saw the Sunni Arab population of the Baghdad suburb of Adhamiyah protest against moves by Kurds to incorporate the oil province of Kirkuk into the autonomous Kurdish region ('Hundreds Protest in Baghdad over Kirkuk's Status', 2008).

At around the same time, the Kurds were also conducting their own protests regarding Kirkuk. Thousands gathered in cities such as Sulaymanyah, Arbil, Kirkuk and Dohuk after the Iraqi Parliament passed a law that would see a power-sharing arrangement devised for Kurdistan's multi-ethnic cities ('Hundreds of Kurds Protest in Northern Iraq', 2008). In both Sulamanyah and Dohuk, the protestors submitted a warrant of protest to the UN Secretary General, the Iraqi president, the president of the Kurdistan Regional Government (KRG) and the Iraqi Parliament, asking the law to be revoked ('Duhuk Eemo Ends by Presenting Warrant of Protest against Elections Law', 2008; 'Protestors in Sulaimaniya Present Warrant of Protest against Election Law', 2008). However, the Kurds have also rallied against the inequities they see across their own region. For example, during March and August 2006, and more recently in August 2008, a series of largely peaceful demonstrations broke into angry protest against the KRG and its failure to provide basic public services to the region (Hama-Saeed, 2007; Ridolfo, 2006).

Caught in the political and sectarian cross-fire of post-Saddam Iraq, smaller ethno-religious minorities such as the Turkomans, the Faili Kurds (Shiite Kurds) and the Christian minority of Iraq (made up mostly of Syriac-speaking Assyrians and Chaldeans) are often forgotten alongside the three larger ethno-sectarian groups. Sadly, these small Iraqi minorities have been the victims of much violence and harassment, many having left the country, fearing for their lives. However, they have nonetheless been politically active, some minor successes occurring through their inclusion in various allegiances and coalitions with the larger groups, through their small number of media outlets and through the handful of political protests they have staged since 2003. For example, in 2008, hundreds of Iraqi Christians demonstrated across key towns in northern Iraq such as Qosh, Karabakh, Tell-esqope and Dohuk (among others). They chanted slogans and carried banners expressing their indignation at not being able to elect their own representatives in the provinces in which they live, and they also called for autonomy

200 *Alternative Currents in Modern Democracy*

in their ancestral homeland. The president of the Assyrian-Chaldean-Syriac Council, Jameel Zito, spoke to the crowds in the following terms: 'Our rights to elect our own representation has been denied therefore we demand our right to self-government, because this is the only way to ensure our rights in our homeland' (Zito, cited in Hakim, 2008).

Civil rights and workers' protests

However, not all of the protests of post-Saddam Iraq have been conducted along ethno-religious lines. Indeed, Iraq has also seen a variety of civil movements emerge that are not so much concerned with issues regarding ethno-religious rights, their resistance to occupation or their rejection of state policy, but the plight of normal Iraqi citizens – ordinary people who demand better working conditions, higher salaries, safer environments and better infrastructure. While many of these protests have occurred in very specific ethno-religious areas and are at times issued entirely by one particular ethno-religious group, their common element is the people's struggle for a more inclusive and equitable future. For example, the Iraqi people have repeatedly protested against corruption and nepotism in their local and national governments and called for the resignation of several senior officials ('Dozens Rally Demonstrations to Protest Corruption in Muthana', 2008; 'Mass Protest over Basra Insecurity', 2008).

Women's rights have also become a particular concern in post-Saddam Iraq, Iraqi women of all ethnicities and religious persuasions having come up with their own powerful protest campaigns after the invasion in 2003. For example, various women's rights and social justice activists joined forces in a group known as 'Women's Will', which has organized a boycott of the US goods that have flooded the Iraqi market since the invasion. One of the leaders of the group is reported to have argued:

> We are now living under another dictatorship, you see what kind of democracy we have, seems more like bloodocracy. You see what kind of liberation they brought: unemployment, murder and destruction. We must resist this, it is the right of any occupied people to resist. Especially the women, we can use the simplest weapons of resistance, a financial boycott.
>
> (Carr, 2005)

Along similar lines, June 2005 saw massive protests organized by various Islamic human rights and women's rights organizations in Mosul, to press for the immediate release of all Iraqi women in US custody. So effective was this campaign that the United States was forced to release twenty-one Iraqi women in Mosul who had been held as a bargaining chip against relatives suspected of resistance (Al-Din and El-Yassari, 2005).

In addition to protests against corruption, nepotism and women's rights, Iraq has also seen a collection of powerful workers' movements emerge in recent years. Iraqi doctors, nurses, taxi drivers, university staff, police, customs officers and emergency service personnel have repeatedly used non-violent protests, strikes, sit-ins and walk-outs. They have done so in order to draw attention to important issues such as their poor working conditions, the interference they are subjected to from various forces, the pressures under which they work, unfair dismissals, ineffectual government regulation and the dangerous nature of their jobs (Al-Dulaimy and Allam, 2005; Al-Khairalla, 2005a; Assaf, 2005; Hassan, 2005). Perhaps the best example of such civil protests in Iraq have been those co-ordinated by the nation's largest and most powerful independent union, the General Union of Oil Employees (which was later renamed the Iraqi Federation of Oil Unions (IFOU)). The union is led by President Hassan Jumaa Awwad Al-Asady and has over 26,000 members. The IFOU began really to flex its political muscles in May 2005, when it held a conference against the privatization of Iraq's oil industry. Aiming directly at the complicity of certain Iraqi politicians with US plans to privatize Iraqi oil, the conference called upon 'members of Parliament...to take a firm stand against political currents and directives calling for the privatisation of the public sector in Iraq' ('Iraqi Oil Workers Hold 24-Hour Strike – Oil Exports Shut Down', 2005).

By June 2005, around 15,000 workers conducted a peaceful twenty-four-hour strike, cutting most oil exports from the south of Iraq. This particular strike was in support of demands made by Basra Governor Mohammad Al-Waili that a higher percentage of Basra's oil revenue be invested back into the regions deplorable infrastructure. At the time, Al-Waili is quoted as saying: 'Faced with a pathetic and unjust situation, our moral responsibility leads us to demand in the name of our people a fair share of resources' (Al-Waili, cited in 'Iraqi Oil Exports Suspended for Few Hours by Strike', 2005). In addition, the IFOU also demanded the removal of fifteen high-ranking Ba'ath loyalists in the Ministry of Oil as well as a salary increase for the workers ('Basra Oil Workers out on Strike', 2005).

Two years later, in May 2007, the IFOU threatened to strike again, but this was delayed when a meeting with Iraqi Prime Minister Nouri

202 *Alternative Currents in Modern Democracy*

Al-Maliki resulted in the formation of a committee tasked with working on finding solutions acceptable to both sides ('IRAQ: Oil Workers on Strike in Basra', 2007). However, when the government failed to deliver on any of its promises by June, the oil workers went on strike across southern Iraq, bringing an immediate halt to the free flow of oil products, kerosene and gas to much of the country. A few days later, the Iraqi government responded by issuing arrest warrants for leaders of IFOU, including Awwad, in an attempt to clamp down on industrial action. At the time, Sami Ramadani, who runs IFOU's support committee in the United Kingdom, pointed out: 'Issuing a warrant for the arrest of the oil workers' leaders is an outrageous attack on trade union and democratic freedom' (Ramadani, cited in 'Iraq Government Orders Arrest of Oil Workers' leaders', 2007). In the face of such intimidation the union held firm, taking the further step of closing the main distribution pipelines, including supplies to Baghdad. After several days of meetings and much political deliberation, Awwad released a statement which claimed: 'Finally the workers have won in demanding their legitimate rights ... And after deliberations ... the two sides agreed to halt the strike and to use dialogue in dealings to resolve the outstanding issues' (Awwad, 2007).

Conclusion

There are several very interesting points to be made about the series of protests occurring across Iraq in the years that have elapsed since 2003. First, these indigenous, localized and highly co-ordinated movements reveal the strength of the Iraqi people's will towards democracy and the fact that, when given the opportunity to make this will a reality, they are more than capable of utilizing democratic mechanisms independently of foreign interference. The movements also indicate the degree to which democratic practices and culture are familiar to the people of Iraq. The latter are far from being alien to them or somehow uniquely Western. The Iraqi people implicitly understand that, by taking to the streets, they force their newly elected democratic government to take their opinions into account. Another important point is that the actions of key religious figures such as Sistani and Al-Sadr directly contradict the common belief that Islam is incompatible with democracy. Similarly, the protests conducted by the Sunnis, the Kurds and the Christians reveal that Iraqi culture, in its many rich and divergent guises, is open to democracy. Indeed, the fact that Iraqi citizens of all ethno-religious persuasions and professions have actively utilized the mechanisms of democratic deliberation to voice their concerns effectively and to influence politics is at odds with the overwhelming view that the streets of Iraq are solely the locus of spontaneous acts of violence and barbarity.

It is also worth noting that the Iraqi protest movements have been able to use successfully protests against the United States and against its self-proclaimed status as a harbinger of democracy in the Middle East. That the United States was so determined to shut down the original grassroots democratic impetus is also revealing, in that it demonstrates the US administration's desire to exert its hegemony over the Iraqi people via an installed government rather than to foster and encourage genuine democratic reform. Beyond this, when the United States attempted to eschew democracy in favour of a puppet government, it was the power of the Iraqi people that put in motion a series of events that led to the formation of an Iraqi government elected by the people, in free and fair elections.

While the Iraqi citizenship's participation in, and engagement with, democratic mechanisms such as elections, an independent press and mass demonstrations do not themselves qualify Iraq as a robust and stable democracy, they are positive milestones towards such an end. Specifically, a strong protest culture is not only crucial in re-establishing a participatory and engaged public life, but it can also help to abate the many conflicts across Iraq and thereby to aid the shift towards a free, egalitarian and democratic nation.

Notes

1. See the works of Edward Said, particularly his seminal *Orientalism* (Said, 2003 [1978]).
2. Iranian-born Grand Ayatollah Ali Al-Al-Sistani comes from a long line of well-respected Shia theologians. He has gradually ascended the ranks of the clergy to become the pre-eminent Shia cleric in Iraq today. Despite the fact that quietist Shia clerics generally abstain from politics, Al-Sistani has become a central player in the post-Saddam political landscape and continues to have an enormous impact over key decisions and policies.
3. Moqtada Al-Sadr has no formal religious training, his renown being inherited from his father and former Grand Ayatollah Mohamad Sadiq Al-Sadr, who was assassinated by the Ba'ath in 1999. In addition, Al-Sadr holds no official political position within the Iraqi government. Despite these limitations, he continues to have enormous influence over Iraqi politics due to his legion of loyal followers, his political faction the *Sadr Trend* (or Sadrist Movement), the military strength of his *Mahdi Army* and the collection of media outlets his organisation controls.

14
Monitory Democracy? The Secret History of Democracy since 1945

John Keane

This chapter proposes a fundamental revision of the way we think about democracy in our times. Its starting point is the observation that the history that is closest to us is always the hardest to fathom: the living characters, institutions and events that shape our daily lives like to keep their secrets, to hide their long-term historical significance by submerging us in a never ending flow of random developments, which impair our sense of perspective and weaken our ability to understand where we have been, what we are currently doing and where we may be heading. This knack of recent history to hide its significance from us, its ability to pass cleverly unnoticed right under our noses, is the target of this chapter. It tries to tell a secret. It pinpoints an epochal transformation, which for some decades has been taking place in the contours and dynamics of democracy, without much comment or conceptualization. It reveals something striking: from roughly the mid-twentieth century, representative democracy as our parents and grandparents experienced it has been morphing into a new historical form of democracy. The chapter rejects dead or zombie descriptors such as 'liberal democracy', 'capitalist democracy' or 'Western democracy'. It also supposes that Fukuyama-style 'end of history' perspectives and Samuel Huntington's 'third wave' are too limited to grasp the epochal change – too bound to the surface of things, too preoccupied with continuities and aggregate data to notice that political tides have begun to run in entirely new directions (Fukuyama, 1992; Huntington, 1991). The claim is that our world is now living through an historic sea change, one that is taking us away from the old era of representative democracy towards a brand new form of 'monitory' democracy, defined by the growth of many different power-scrutinizing mechanisms and by their spreading influence within the fields of government and civil society, both at home and abroad, in cross-border settings that were once dominated by empires, states and business organizations. Concentrating in the final part on the growth of media-saturated societies – or communicative abundance – the chapter raises questions about the causes and causers of this new historical form of democracy, its advantages and disadvantages, and why it has profound implications for how we think and practice democracy in the coming decades.

Monitory democracy

It is hard to find an elegant name for the emergent form of democracy, let alone to describe and explain in a few words its workings and political implications. The strange-sounding phrase 'monitory democracy' is the most exact for describing the great transformation that is taking hold in regions like Europe and South Asia and in countries otherwise as different as the United States, Japan, Argentina, Australia and New Zealand.[1] The opening conjecture is that monitory democracy is a new historical type of democracy, a variety of 'post-electoral' politics defined by the rapid growth of many different kinds of extra-parliamentary, power-scrutinizing mechanisms. These monitory bodies take root within the 'domestic' fields of government and civil society, as well as in cross-border settings. In consequence, the whole architecture of self-government is changing. The central grip of elections, political parties and parliaments on citizens' lives is weakening. Democracy is coming to mean more than elections, although nothing less. Within and outside states, independent monitors of power are beginning to have tangible effects. By keeping politicians, parties and elected governments permanently on their toes, these monitors complicate their lives, question their authority and force them to change their agendas – and sometimes smother them in disgrace.

Whether or not the trend towards this new kind of democracy is a sustainable, historically irreversible development remains to be seen; like participatory and representative democracy before it, monitory democracy is not inevitable. It did not have to happen, but it did; whether it will live or fade away and die remains untreated in this chapter (the subject of counter-trends and dysfunctions of monitory democracy is taken up in Keane, 2009). Certainly when judged by its institutional contours and inner dynamics, monitory democracy is the most complex form of democracy yet. It is the not fully formed successor of the earlier historical experiments with assembly-based and representative forms of democracy. One symptom of its novelty is the altered

206 *Alternative Currents in Modern Democracy*

language through which millions of people now describe democracy. In the name of 'the public', 'public accountability', 'the people' or 'citizens', power-scrutinizing institutions spring up all over the place. Elections, political parties and legislatures neither disappear, nor necessarily decline in importance; but they most definitely lose their pivotal position in politics. Democracy is no longer simply a way of handling the power of elected governments by electoral and parliamentary and constitutional means, and no longer a matter confined to territorial states. Gone are the days when democracy could be described (and in the next breath attacked) as 'government by the unrestricted will of the majority' (von Hayek, 1979: 39). In the age of monitory democracy, the rules of representation, democratic accountability and public participation are applied to a much wider range of settings than ever before. Here is one striking clue for understanding why this is happening: the age of monitory democracy, which began around 1945, has witnessed the birth of nearly one hundred new types of power-scrutinizing institutions unknown to previous democrats.[2] As we shall see, defenders of these inventions often speak of their importance in solving a basic problem facing contemporary democracies: how to promote the unfinished business of finding new ways of democratic living for little people in big and complex societies – a matter in which substantial numbers of citizens believe that politicians are not easily trusted and in which governments are often accused of abusing their power or of being out of touch with citizens, or simply unwilling to deal with their concerns and problems. By addressing such concerns, the new power-scrutinizing inventions break the grip of the majority rule principle – the worship of numbers – associated with representative democracy. Freed as well from the measured caution and double-speak of political parties, some inventions give a voice to the strongly felt concerns of minorities that feel left out of official politics. Some monitors, electoral commissions and consumer protection agencies, for instance, use their claimed 'neutrality' to protect the rules of the democratic game from predators and enemies. Other monitors publicize long-term issues that are neglected, or dealt with badly, by the short-term mentality encouraged by election cycles. Still other monitory groups are remarkable for their evanescence; in a fast-changing world, they come on the scene, stir the pot, then move on like nomads or dissolve into thin air.

Collectively, these inventions have the combined effect of raising the level and quality of public monitoring of power, often for the first time in many areas of life, including power relationships 'beneath' and 'beyond' the institutions of territorial states. It is little wonder that the new power-monitoring inventions have changed the language of contemporary politics. They prompt much talk of 'empowerment', 'high energy democracy', 'stakeholders', 'participatory governance', 'communicative democracy' and 'deliberative democracy'; and they help to spread, often for the first time, a culture of voting into many walks of life. Monitory democracy is the age of surveys, focus groups, deliberative polling, online petitions and audience and customer voting. Whether intended or not, the spreading culture of voting, backed by the new mechanisms for monitoring power, has the effect of interrupting and often silencing the soliloquies of parties, politicians and parliaments. The new power-scrutinizing innovations tend to enfranchise many more citizens' voices, sometimes by means of *unelected representatives* skilled at using what Americans sometimes call 'bully pulpits'. The number and range of monitory institutions point to a world where the old rule of 'one person, one vote, one representative' – the central demand in the struggle for representative democracy – is replaced by the new principle of monitory democracy: 'one person, many interests, many voices, multiple votes, multiple representatives'.

Caution must be exercised when trying to understand these new methods of restraining power. The new monitory inventions are not exclusively 'American' or 'European' or 'OECD' or Western products. Among their more remarkable features is the way in which they have rapidly diffused around the world, from all points on the globe. They mushroom in a wide variety of different settings – participatory budgeting is a Brazilian invention; truth and reconciliation commissions hail from central America, while integrity commissions first sprang up with force in Australia – and there are even signs, for the first time in the history of democracy, of mounting awareness about the added value of the art of invention – as if the democratic ability to invent is itself a most valuable invention.

Monitory mechanisms are not just information-providing mechanisms. They operate in different ways, on different fronts. Some scrutinize power primarily at the level of *citizens' inputs* to government or civil society bodies; other monitory mechanisms are preoccupied with monitoring and contesting what is called *policy throughputs*; still others concentrate on scrutinizing *policy outputs* produced by governmental or non-governmental organisations. Quite a few of the inventions concentrate simultaneously upon all three dimensions. Monitory mechanisms also come in different sizes and operate on various spatial scales, ranging from 'just round the corner' bodies with merely local footprints to global networks aimed at keeping tabs on those who exercise power over

208 *Alternative Currents in Modern Democracy*

great distances. Monitory institutions are also committed to providing publics with extra viewpoints and better information about the operations and performance of various governmental and non-governmental bodies. Monitory mechanisms are also geared towards the definition, scrutiny and enforcement of public standards and ethical rules for preventing corruption, or the improper behaviour of those responsible for making decisions, not only in the field of elected government, but in a wide variety of settings. The new institutions of monitory democracy are further defined by their overall commitment to strengthening the diversity and influence of citizens' voices and choices in decisions that affect their lives – regardless of the outcome of elections.

What is distinctive about this new historical type of democracy is the way *all fields of social and political life* come to be scrutinized, not just by the standard machinery of representative democracy, but by a whole host of *non-party, extra-parliamentary and often unelected bodies* operating within, underneath and beyond the boundaries of territorial states. In the era of monitory democracy, it is as if the principles of representative democracy are superimposed on representative democracy itself. Just as representative democracies preserved the spirit and form of ancient assemblies, so monitory democracies preserves representation, elections, civil society and watchdogs. But such is the growing variety of inter-laced, power-monitoring mechanisms that democrats from earlier times, if catapulted into the new world of monitory democracy, would find it hard to understand what is happening. Indeed, the following sections considers the consequences monitory democracy has had for the ways in which we understand and practice these traditional mechanisms of representative democracy and the profound changes the latter have undergone. It also considers many of the widely held misconceptions about monitory democracy.

Representative mechanisms in a monitory age

To begin with, it is worth noting that monitory democracy thrives on representation. It is often mistakenly thought that the struggle to bring greater public accountability to government and non-government organizations that wield power over others is in effect a struggle for 'grassroots democracy', 'participatory democracy' or 'popular empowerment'. Such metaphors rest on a misunderstanding of the trends. The age of monitory democracy is not heading backwards; it is not motivated by efforts to recapture the (imagined) spirit of assembly-based democracy. Many contemporary champions of 'deep' or 'direct' democracy still speak as if they were Greeks, as if what really counts in matters of democracy is (as Archon Fung and Erik Olin Wright put it) 'the commitment and capacities of ordinary people to make sensible decisions through reasoned deliberation . . . empowered because they attempt to tie action to discussion' (Fung and Wright, 2003: 5). The reality of monitory democracy is otherwise, in that all of the new power-scrutinizing experiments in the name of 'the people' or citizens' empowerment rely inevitably on *representation*. These experiments often draw their ultimate legitimacy from 'the people';[3] but they cannot be understood merely as efforts to abolish the gap between representatives and the represented, as if citizens could live without others acting on their behalf, find their true selves and express themselves as equals within a unified political community no longer burdened by miscommunication, or by misgovernment.

Another misconception, to do with the changing status of elections, prevents many people from spotting the novelty of monitory democracy. It is vital to grasp that this new type of democracy does not dispense with questions of suffrage, or voting in national or local elections. This is not an age that has settled once and for all the issue of who is entitled to vote, and under what conditions (think of the emerging legal and political controversies about who owns the software of unreliable electronic voting machines pioneered by companies such as Election Systems and Software). In fact, some people, for instance felons, have their votes withdrawn; others, including members of diasporas, minority language speakers, the disabled and people with low literacy and number skills, are disadvantaged by secret ballot elections; still other constituencies, such as women, young people and the biosphere, are either poorly represented or not represented at all. Struggles to open up and improve the quality of electoral representation are by no means finished. Yet in the era of monitory democracy the franchise struggles that once tugged and tore whole societies apart have lost their centrality. As the culture of voting spreads, and as unelected representatives multiply in many different contexts, a brand new issue begins to surface. The old question that racked the age of representative democracy – who is entitled to vote and *when* – *is* compounded and complicated by a question for which there are still no easy answers: are people entitled to representation between and outside elections and, if so, through what representatives?

Another remarkable feature of monitory democracy is the way power-scrutinizing mechanisms gradually spread into areas of social life that were previously untouched by democratic hands. The extension of

210 *Alternative Currents in Modern Democracy*

democracy downwards, into realms of power beneath and cutting across the institutions of territorial states, has the effect of arousing great interest in the old eighteenth-century European phrase 'civil society'; for the first time in the history of democracy, these two words are now routinely used by democrats in all four corners of the earth. The intense public concern with civil society and with publicly scrutinizing matters once thought to be non-political is unique to the age of monitory democracy. The era of representative democracy (as Tocqueville and others spotted) certainly saw the rise of self-organized pressure groups and schemes for 'socializing' the power of government, for instance through workers' control of industry (De Tocqueville, 1864 [1835]). However, few of these schemes survived the upheavals of the first half of the twentieth century, which makes the contrast with monitory democracy all the more striking. The trend towards public scrutiny is strongly evident in all kinds of policy areas, ranging from public concern about the maltreatment and legal rights of children and about bodily habits related to exercise and diet, through to the development of habitat protection plans and alternative (non-carbon and non-nuclear) sources of energy. Initiatives to guarantee that the future development of nanotechnology and genetically-modified crops is governed publicly in the interests of the many, not the few – efforts to take democracy 'upstream' into the tributaries of scientific research and technical development – are further examples of the same trend. Experiments with fostering new forms of citizens' participation and elected representation have even penetrated markets, to lay hands on the sacred cow of private property. Following the near-collapse of banking systems during 2007–08, many new proposals are now on the political table to extend monitoring mechanisms into the banking and investment sectors of global markets that previously operated with little or no regulatory restraint.

The vital role played by civil societies in the invention of power-monitoring mechanisms seems to confirm what might be called James Madison's Law of Free Government: no government can be considered free unless it is capable of governing a society that is itself capable of controlling the government (Madison, cited in Rossiter, 1961 [1788]: number 51). Madison's Law has tempted some people to conclude – mistakenly – that governments are quite incapable of scrutinizing their own power. The truth is otherwise. In the era of monitory democracy, experience shows that governments, unlike ducks and turkeys, sometimes vote to sacrifice themselves for the good of citizen guests at the dinner table. Government 'watchdog' institutions are a case in point. Their stated purpose is the public scrutiny of government by semi-independent government agencies. Scrutiny mechanisms supplement the power-monitoring role of elected government representatives and judges, even though this is not always their stated aim; very often they are introduced under the general authority of elected governments, for instance through ministerial responsibility. In practice, things often turn out differently. Especially when protected by legislation, being well resourced and well managed, government scrutiny bodies tend to take on a life of their own. Building on the much older precedents of royal commissions, public enquiries and independent auditors checking the financial probity of government agencies – inventions that had their roots in the age of representative democracy – the new scrutiny mechanisms add checks and balances on the possible abuse of power by elected representatives. Often they are justified in terms of improving the efficiency and effectiveness of government, for instance through 'better informed' decision-making that has the added advantage of raising the level of public trust in political institutions among citizens considered as 'stakeholders'. The process contains a double paradox. Not only are government scrutiny mechanisms often established by governments who subsequently fail to control their workings, for instance in cases of corruption and the enforcement of legal standards; the new mechanisms also have democratic, power-checking effects, even though they are normally staffed by un-elected officials who operate at several arms' length from the rhythm of periodic elections.

Communicative abundance

Now that we have tackled some misconceptions about the contours and main dynamics of monitory democracy, let me pause finally to ask one short question: how can its unplanned birth be explained? This is not an easy question to answer. The motives behind the vast number of inventions associated with monitory democracy are complicated; as in earlier phases of the history of democracy, generalizations are as difficult as they are perilous. But one thing is certain: the new type of democracy has had both its causes and causers. Monitory democracy is not a monogenic matter – a living thing hatched from a single cell. It is rather the resultant of many overlapping and intersecting forces. But one force is turning out to be the principal driver: the emergence of a new galaxy of communication media.

No account of monitory democracy would be credible without paying heed to the way in which power and conflict are shaped by new media institutions. Think of it like this: assembly-based democracy in

212 *Alternative Currents in Modern Democracy*

ancient Greek times belonged to an era dominated by the spoken word, backed up by laws written on papyrus and stone, and by messages dispatched by foot, or by donkey and horse. Representative democracy sprang up in the era of print culture – the book, pamphlet and newspaper, and telegraphed and mailed messages – and fell into crisis during the advent of early mass communication media, especially radio and cinema and (in its infancy) television. By contrast, monitory democracy is tied closely to the growth of multi-media-saturated societies – societies whose structures of power are continuously 'bitten' by monitory institutions operating within a new galaxy of media defined by the ethos of communicative abundance.

Compared with the era of representative democracy, when print culture and limited-spectrum audio-visual media (including public service broadcasting) were much more closely aligned with political parties and governments, the age of monitory democracy witnesses constant public scrutiny and spats about power, to the point where it seems as if no organization or leader within the fields of government or social life is immune from political trouble. The change has been shaped by a variety of forces, including the decline of journalism proud of its commitment to fact-based 'objectivity' (an ideal born of the age of representative democracy) and the rise of adversarial and 'gotcha' styles of commercial journalism driven by ratings, sales and hits. Technical factors, such as electronic memory, tighter channel spacing, new frequency allocation, direct satellite broadcasting, digital tuning, and advanced compression techniques, have also been important. Chief among these technical factors is the advent of cable – and satellite-linked, computerized communications, which from the end of the 1960s triggered both product and process innovations in virtually every field of an increasingly commercialized media. This new galaxy of media has no historical precedent. Symbolized by one of its core components, the Internet, it is a whole new world system of overlapping and interlinked devices that, for the first time in human history, integrate texts, sounds and images and enable communication to take place through multiple user points, in chosen time, either real or delayed, within modularized and ultimately global networks that are affordable and accessible to many hundreds of millions of people scattered across the globe.

All institutions in the business of scrutinizing power rely heavily on these media innovations; if the new galaxy of communicative abundance suddenly imploded, monitory democracy would not last long. Monitory democracy and computerized media networks behave as if they are conjoined twins. To say this is not to fall into the trap of supposing that computer-linked communications networks prefigure a brand new utopian world, a carnival of 'virtual communities' home-steading on the electronic frontier, a 'cyber-revolution' that yields to all citizens equal access to all media, anywhere and at any time. Hype of this kind was strongly evident in the *Declaration of the Independence of Cyberspace*, a document drawn up by the self-styled cyber-revolutionary John Perry Barlow, former lyricist of a famous rock band known as the Grateful Dead, simultaneously campaign manager for an infamous American vice-president, Dick Cheney. The *Declaration* proclaimed the end of the old world of representation within territorial states. Making hype seem profound, it claimed that computer-linked networks were 'creating a world that all may enter without privilege or prejudice accorded by race, economic power, military force, or station of birth' (Barlow, 1996).

Such utopian extravagance prompts a political health warning, not least because the new age of communicative abundance produces disappointment, instability and self-contradictions, for instance in worrying patterns of closure or 'privatization' of digital networks that restrict their generativity, or in the widening power gaps between the rich and the poor in matters of communication: the latter seem almost unneeded as communicators or as consumers of media products (Zittrain, 2008). The majority of the world's people is too poor to make a telephone call; only a tiny minority has access to the Internet. The divide between media rich and media poor citizens blights all monitory democracies; it contradicts their basic principle that all citizens are equally entitled to communicate their opinions, and periodically to give elected and unelected representatives a rough ride.

Yet, despite such contradictions and disappointments, there are new and important things happening inside the swirling galaxy of communicative abundance. Especially striking is the way in which the realms of 'private life' and 'privacy', and the wheeling and dealing of power 'in private' have been put on the defensive. From the point of view of monitory democracy, that is no bad thing. Every nook and cranny of power – the quiet discriminations and injustices that happen behind closed doors and in the world of everyday life – become the potential target of 'publicity' and 'public exposure'. Routine matters such as birth and death, diet and sex, religious and ethnic customs are less and less based on unthinking habit, on unquestioned, taken-for-granted certainties about 'normal' ways of doing things. In the era

214 *Alternative Currents in Modern Democracy*

of communicative abundance, no hidden topic is protected unconditionally from media coverage and from possible politicization; the more 'private' it is, the more 'publicity' it seems to get.

Helped along by red-blooded journalism that relies on styles of reporting concerned less with veracity than with 'breaking news' and blockbusting scoops, communicative abundance cuts like a knife into the power relations between government and civil society. It is easy to complain (as many do) about the methods of the new journalism. It hunts in packs, its eyes on bad news, egged on by the newsroom and by bloggers' saying that facts must never be allowed to get in the way of stories. Professional and citizens' journalism loves titillation, draws upon un-attributed sources, fills news holes – in the era of monitory democracy news never sleeps – spins sensations, and concentrates too much on personalities rather than on time-bound contexts. The new journalism is formulaic and gets bored too quickly; and it likes to bow down to corporate power and government press briefings, which helps to explain why disinformation (about such matters as weapons of mass destruction and excessive leveraging of risks within financial markets) still whizzes around the world with frightening speed and power.

But these trends are only half the story. For, in spite of all the accusations made against it, red-blooded journalism helps to keep alive the old utopias of shedding light on power, of 'freedom of information', of 'government in the sunshine' and of greater 'transparency' in the making of decisions. Given that unchecked power still weighs down hard on the heads of citizens, it is not surprising, thanks to the new journalism and new monitoring inventions, that public objections to wrongdoing and corruption are commonplace in the era of monitory democracy. Thanks to journalism and the new media of communicative abundance, stuff happens. There seems to be no end of scandals; and there are even times when '-gate' scandals, like earthquakes, rumble beneath the feet of whole governments.

Conclusion: Viral politics

The profusion of '-gate' scandals reminds us of a perennial problem facing monitory democracy: there is no shortage of organized efforts by the powerful to manipulate people beneath them and, hence, the political dirty business of dragging power from the shadows and flinging it into the blazing halogen of publicity remains fundamentally important. Nobody should be kidded into thinking that the world of monitory democracy, with its many power-scrutinizing institutions, is a level playing-field – a paradise of equality of opportunity among all its citizens and their elected and unelected representatives. We still live in the age of the put-on. The combination of monitory democracy and communicative abundance nevertheless produces permanent flux, an unending restlessness driven by complex combinations of different interacting players and institutions, permanently pushing and pulling, heaving and straining, sometimes working together, at other times in opposition to one another. Elected and unelected representatives routinely strive to define and to determine who gets what, when and how; but the represented, taking advantage of various power-scrutinizing devices, keep tabs on their representatives – sometimes with surprising success.

There is something utterly novel about the whole trend. From its origins in the ancient assemblies of Syria–Mesopotamia, democracy has always cut through habit, prejudice and hierarchies of power. It has stirred up the sense that people can shape and reshape their lives as equals, and – not surprisingly – it has often brought commotion into the world. In the era of monitory democracy, the constant public scrutiny of power by hosts of differently sized monitory bodies with footprints large and small makes it the most energetic, most dynamic form of democracy ever. Various watchdogs, guide dogs and barking dogs are constantly on the job, pressing for greater public accountability on the part of those who exercise power. The powerful consequently come to feel the constant pinch of the powerless. In the era of monitory democracy, those who make decisions are subject constantly to the ideal of public chastening.

When they do their job well, monitory mechanisms have many positive effects, ranging from greater openness and justice within markets and blowing the whistle on foolish government decisions to the general enrichment of public deliberation and to the empowerment of citizens and their chosen representatives through meaningful schemes of participation. Power monitoring can also be ineffective, or counter-productive, of course. Campaigns misfire or are poorly targeted; power wielders cleverly find loopholes and ways of rebutting or simply ignoring their opponents. And there are times when large numbers of citizens find the monitory strategies of organizations too timid, or confused, or simply irrelevant to their lives as consumers, workers, parents, community residents and young and elderly citizens.

Despite such weaknesses, the political dynamics and overall 'feel' of monitory democracies are very different from those of the era of representative democracy. Politics in the age of monitory democracy

216 *Alternative Currents in Modern Democracy*

has a definite 'viral' quality about it. The power controversies stirred up by monitory mechanisms follow unexpected paths and reach surprising destinations. Groups using mobile phones, bulletin boards, news groups, wikkies and blogs sometimes manage, against considerable odds, to embarrass publicly politicians, parties and parliaments, or even whole governments. In the age of monitory democracy, bossy power can no longer hide comfortably behind private masks; power relations everywhere are subjected to organized efforts by some, with the help of media, to tell others – publics of various sizes – about matters that previously had been hidden away, 'in private'. This denaturing of power is usually messy business, and it often comes wrapped in hype, certainly. But the unmasking of power resonates strongly with the power-scrutinizing spirit of monitory democracy. The whole process is reinforced by the growing availability of cheap tools of communication (multi-purpose mobile phones, digital cameras, video recorders, the Internet) to individuals, groups and organizations; and communicative abundance multiplies the genres of programming, information and storytelling that are available to audiences and publics. News, chat shows, political oratory, bitter legal spats, comedy, infotainment, drama, music, advertising, blogs – all of these, and many more, constantly clamour and jostle for public attention.

Some people complain about effects like 'information overload'; but, from the point of view of monitory democracy, communicative abundance has, on balance, positive consequences. In spite of all its hype and spin, the new media galaxy nudges and broadens people's horizons. It tutors their sense of pluralism and prods them into taking greater responsibility for how, when and why they communicate. In addition, message-saturated democracies encourage people's suspicions of unaccountable power. Within the world of monitory democracies, people are coming to learn that they must keep an eye on power and its representatives, that they must make judgements and choose their own courses of action. Citizens are tempted to think for themselves; to see the same world in different ways, from different angles; and to sharpen their overall sense that prevailing power relationships are not 'natural', but contingent.

There is, admittedly, nothing automatic or magical about any of this. In the era of monitory democracy, communication is constantly the subject of dissembling, negotiation, compromise and power conflicts – in a phrase, a matter of politics. Communicative abundance for that reason does not somehow automatically ensure the triumph either of the spirit or of the institutions of monitory democracy. Message-saturated societies can and do have effects that are harmful for democracy. In some quarters, for instance, media saturation triggers citizens' inattention to events. While they are expected as good citizens to keep their eyes on public affairs, to take an interest in the world beyond their immediate household and neighbourhood, more than a few find it ever harder to pay attention to the media's vast outpourings. Profusion breeds confusion. There are times, for instance, when voters are so pelted with a hail of election advertisements on prime-time television that they react frostily. Disaffected, they get up from their sofas, leave their living rooms, change channels, or turn to mute, concluding with a heavy sigh that the less you know the better off you are. The coming age of IPTV (internet protocol television) is likely to deepen such disaffection; and, if that happens, then something more worrying could happen: the spread of a culture of unthinking indifference. Monitory democracy certainly feeds upon communicative abundance, but one of its more perverse effects is to encourage individuals to escape the great complexity of the world by sticking their heads, like ostriches, into the sands of wilful ignorance, or to float cynically upon the swirling tides and waves and eddies of fashion – to change their minds, to speak and act flippantly, to embrace or even celebrate opposites, to bid farewell to veracity, to slip into the arms of what some carefully call 'bullshit'.

Foolish illusions, cynicism and disaffection are among the biggest temptations facing citizens and their elected and unelected representatives in existing democracies. Whether or not the new forms of monitory democracy will survive their deadly effects is for the future to tell us.

Notes

1. The adjective 'monitory' derived from the medieval *monitoria* (from *monere*, to warn). It entered Middle English in the shape of *monitorie* and from there it wended its way into the modern English language in the mid-fifteenth century to refer to the process of giving or conveying a warning of an impending danger, or an admonition to someone to refrain from a specified course of action considered offensive. In more recent years, not unconnected with the emergence of monitory democracy, 'to monitor' became a commonplace verb to describe the process of systematically checking the content or quality of something, as when a city authority monitors the local drinking water for impurities, or a group of scientific experts monitors the population of an endangered species.
2. The list includes: citizen juries, bioregional assemblies, participatory budgeting, advisory boards, focus groups and 'talkaoke' (local/global talk shows broadcast live on the internet). There are think tanks, consensus conferences,

218 *Alternative Currents in Modern Democracy*

teach-ins, public memorials, local community consultation schemes and open houses (developed for instance in the field of architecture) that offer information and advisory and advocacy services, archive and research facilities and opportunities for professional networking. Citizens' assemblies, democratic audits, brainstorming conferences, conflict of interest boards, global associations of parliamentarians against corruption and constitutional safaris (famously used by the drafters of the new South African constitution to examine best practice elsewhere) are on the list. So too are the inventions of India's 'banyan' democracy: railway courts, lok adalats, public interest litigation and satyagraha methods of civil resistance. Included as well are consumer testing agencies and consumer councils, online petitions and chat rooms, democracy clubs and democracy cafés, public vigils, peaceful sieges, protestivals (a South Korean speciality), summits and global watchdog organizations set up to bring greater public accountability to business and other civil society bodies. The list of innovations extends to deliberative polls, boards of accountancy, independent religious courts, experts councils (such as the 'Five Wise Men' of the Council of Economic Advisers in Germany), public 'scorecards' – yellow cards and white lists – public planning exercises, public consultations, social forums, weblogs, electronic civil disobedience and websites dedicated to monitoring the abuse of power (such as Bully OnLine, a UK-based initiative that aims to tackle workplace bullying and related issues). And the list of new inventions includes self-selected opinion polls ('SLOPs') and unofficial ballots (text-messaged straw polls, for instance), international criminal courts, global social forums and the tendency of increasing numbers of non-governmental organisations to adopt written constitutions, with an elected component.

3. The point can be put like this: if the principles of representative democracy turned 'the people' of assembly democracy into a more distant judge of how well representatives performed, then monitory democracy exposes the fiction of a unified 'sovereign people'. It could be said that monitory democracy democratizes – publicly exposes – the whole principle of 'the sovereign people' as a pompous fiction; at best, it turns it into a handy reference device that most people know to be just that: a useful political fiction.

Conclusion: Democratizing the History of Democracy

Benjamin Isakhan and Stephen Stockwell

The aim of *The Secret History of Democracy* has been to open debate on a larger view of democratic practice than that encapsulated by its well-known standard history. The book came about from a concern that, while democracy was experiencing an ascendancy that began in the aftermath of the Second World War and intensified with the end of the Cold War, the global uptake of this particular form of governance came at the very moment when its limitations were becoming clearer: in its European and American heartlands there was less interest in participating in democracy; Clinton began in hope but ended in scandal; 9/11 was a victory for intolerance precisely because Western democracy restricted its own freedoms; the Bush, Blair and Howard governments became less relevant to their constituents and waged unpopular wars; the global financial crisis revealed democracy's dependence on a flawed economic model; and difficulties in dealing with the global impact of climate change showed the limitations of national democracies, hostage to sectional interests. The exemplars of democracy were not having an easy time.

Beyond these immediate concerns, there lurked a deeper crisis about what democracy is and how it should be conducted. Listening to political professionals like foreign policy pundits, hawkish bureaucrats, campaign directors and press secretaries, one could be left with the impression that democratization movements in eastern Europe, Asia, Latin America and the rest were predominantly business opportunities. The people were there as cannon fodder when big demonstrations were required to bring the tyrants down; but then they disappeared. As the world turned to democracy, democracy revealed itself as a stage-managed ritual, which allowed the rotation of elites as long as they did not threaten to do too much. The Obama phenomenon, while based in

220　*Conclusion: Democratizing the History of Democracy*

optimism about new ways of doing democracy, quickly returned to business as usual. While Obama was successful at letting democracy do what it does best – motivating the masses towards the peaceful removal of a failed leader – it remains unclear whether he, or anyone else, can make grassroots democracy work beyond the heady days of the campaign trail. The great democratic contribution of the Obama administration may yet be in its ability to address the question that so often plagues modern representative democrats: how can the people get more involved in politics *after* the final ballot is cast?

It was in this context that *The Secret History of Democracy* was conceived. Each chapter discussed a different attempt at democracy, which had a few glorious moments of success and then failed for the same old reasons: the democrats lost their nerve; intolerance and factionalism split the people; the citizens got bored or had to make a living; the oligarchs tightened their grip; democracy remained only in name; autocracy returned. But together, as a whole, the chapters of this book remind us of the value of constantly rethinking democracy's history, to look for opportunities to improve, grow and make it more effective. By stimulating further discussion and debate on the history of democracy, this book seeks to open up new ways to do democracy, to excite people with the possibilities of democracy, to give them the real sense that, while elites will always be with us, the real power in a democracy rests in the hands of the people just so long as they choose to grasp it.

The individual chapters of this book open up disregarded historical periods and milieus, to see what contribution they made to the development of democracy and what contribution they can continue to make to rethinking and remodelling democracy in the future. First, the practices of various ancient Asiatic and Mediterranean assemblies were considered to appreciate that popular governance has a much broader geographical base than previously supposed. Moving forward, the book explored cases of democratic experimentation during the so-called 'Dark Ages' of medieval history and offers further evidence of the resilience of popular governance under Islam and on the margins of feudal Europe, in Iceland and Venice. The third part of this book sought to understand how democracy flourished in various tribal councils through dispute resolution methods and non-racial governments and to demonstrate that, even in the worst periods of colonial domination, such methods continued to adapt to the new conditions under which they found themselves operating. The final section of this book looked at more modern trends by examining the sphere of influence carved out by women's voices in Islam, the texture of democratic politics in post-2003 Iraq and the emergence of monitory democracy. While the whole is diverse in context, scope and approach, each of these chapters is useful in taking the discussion of democracy back to where it all begins, in an active citizenship sufficiently skilled and motivated to use all the channels at its disposal so as to create a voice which, with sufficient support, can become the voice of the people.

Concerns and limitations

However, any thorough reader must by now have a host of concerns about these 'secret' histories. To begin with, there is a danger that this work merely establishes an alternative standard history of democracy and that, by genuflecting to India, Iceland or Iraqis, the history of democracy has been sufficiently expanded and the problem of democracy's limited forbears is solved. Rather, the editors would argue, this is but the start to a much broader slate of work, which will probe back further in history and across more societies, on other continents and in different epochs, to explore how often democratic tendencies have occurred in human history, how they have interacted with despotism – at times undermining it, at other times being overcome by it – with a view to making people fully informed about the complexities of history and the possibilities to create democracy anew.

Another concern with this project is that both the standard and the secret histories are over-glorifying the past. There is a danger that the passing of time allows us to sugar-coat the experiences of earlier peoples and forget that moments of individual equality and collective concern came amidst centuries of tyranny and despair. For every Mesopotamian council there were a dozen despots with deep disregard for their subjects; for every Chinese liberal, there were a thousand peasants starving to death as war lords fought their forgotten battles. Even in their more democratic moments, most of the societies discussed in this book exploited women and slaves, were suspicious and violent towards foreigners, had a propensity towards colonialism and imperialism, were riven by factionalism and did not trust each other. The challenging question in this context is: how do moments of common decency, group solidarity and positive democracy emerge at all?

Another danger with this discussion of the secret history of democracy is that any historical precedent – whether genuine, fabricated or the result of careless investigation – might be seized by decidedly *un*democratic people to justify their particular form of oppression. The 'secret' histories of democracy could easily fall prey to the kind of abuse

222 *Conclusion: Democratizing the History of Democracy*

common among tyrants and fundamentalists, who are keen to wear the achievements of the past like masks that cover the despotism of the present. Saddam Hussein was always ready to equate his regime with that of the ancient city-states of Mesopotamia, just as right-wing Christian Phalangists in Lebanon have been enthusiastic about usurping aspects of the Phoenician heritage for themselves. In a similar vein, the Democratic People's Republic of Korea and the Democratic Republic of the Congo display anti-democratic sentiments, while the old (East) German Democratic Republic was a model of tyranny. The hi-jacking of history is a common concern where there is little robust critique connecting past democracy and present conditions, but despots are not often limited by history and, where the facts do not fit their requirements, they will simply make it all up. The most effective antidote against those who would comandeer history for their own ends is not to deny the history that is there, but rather to insist that present-day despots live up to the claims they draw from the past.

The concern about the undermining of democratic histories by despots and oligarchs connects to a wider concern about what can properly be called democracy. It would be a genuine shame if *The Secret History of Democracy* encouraged haphazard and inexact scholarship of the kind that may allow vested interests to call it a 'democracy' any time a king listened to a courtier, or oligarchs consulted amongst each other. The word 'democracy' would quickly lose any salience, any pragmatic use and any desirability if it were to be applied too liberally. The editors encourage people everywhere to look within their own cultures and histories to unearth some of the other 'secret' histories of democracy that lay hidden, but there is also concern that this must be done with the appropriate rigour. It is important that the evidence be sifted carefully, to gauge whether collective decisions were made with free debate, whether government consultation included a broad participation of equals, whether the democracy was a creature of the people or mere window-dressing by the one or few really in charge. This book does not hold out one form of democracy as right and other attempts as not democracy at all, but it does suggest that rigorous investigation and debate will assist people in understanding what is good and bad about democracy in its different forms and will help them to make better democracy now and into the future.

The final concern is that this book might suggest that democracy is a panacea for all the world's ills. Winston Churchill's response is perhaps most useful: 'democracy is the worst form of government except all those other forms that have been tried from time to time' (Churchill,

1947: 207). All the secret histories, re-imaginings and new possibilities in the world will not solve the deep-seated and intractable problems that human beings face: global warming, over-population, food shortages, financial meltdowns, deadly pandemics and our reliance on diminishing resources like oil. The only solution to these problems is human action; and, while democracy can be an effective way to co-ordinate large-scale human action, this action must be preceded by strong will and relentless determination. In the end, democracy is just another form of government, and it is only as successful as the commitment that humans bring to it.

Democracy and the future

Beyond such concerns, however, there is a central theme here which suggests that democracy itself is a varied and adaptable organism. From the village to the nation, from five continents over five thousand years, from collective enterprises like the Buffalo Hunt to Islamic feminists, democracy can be seen to be at work in many ways, mostly productive ones. From this sheer diversity comes a realization that, by creating a sense of people's 'ownership' over democracy, *The Secret History of Democracy* could help to encourage people's struggles against oppression and towards social solidarity and equality. By encouraging people to engage with their own diverse traditions and indigenous cultures, this book assists them to recover those moments, those practices and customs, those traditions and narratives which emulate the spirit of democracy and are already inherent in their own society. Opening awareness of the breadth of democratic forms gives people the means to deepen, strengthen and develop democratic practice and the opportunity to promulgate democracy more widely.

The diversity of democratic forms is also a timely reminder to those who seek to capture democracy in just one theory. It is easy enough to design rigid criteria by which to measure the democratic quality of this election in comparison to that, this electoral system in comparison to that, this nation in comparison to that. But each democratic moment is the product of its own history of human ingenuity and compromise. The qualitative experience of the power of politics by the people goes well beyond the crudeness of polling data or the awkwardness of making human interaction and achievement fit into academic models. The theoretician is wise to celebrate the difference that democracy brings and to acknowledge the impossibility of measuring people's experiences of democracy and the surprising lengths they will go to in order to fight on its behalf and ensure its continuation.

Another theme that emerges from many of the individual chapters is that cultures and peoples across the globe need to look *inside*, not *outside*. Democracy is not just ideas and institutions; it is also a way in which people relate to each other. At a number of key moments in this secret history – in Confucian philosophy, in Aboriginal ritual, in African clans, in Shia Arab protests – whenever people can put their feuds behind them, the importance of considering the cultural, the emotional and, at times, the spiritual dimension of democracy can be seen. Studies of democracy and of its history have all too often focused on the rational and emphasized the outcomes. However, people's sensibilities and the historical rubric through which they grow and develop are necessary if one is to ensure that the issues that most deeply concern the citizens are brought to the agenda. In the balance between the pragmatic and the personal, there is an opportunity to discern the basis for the common decency and group solidarity that lies at the heart of making democracy work. It is in the complex and varied processes we use to negotiate this terrain that human individuals find their powers and limitations reflected in the responses of others. The alternative is the socio-pathology that refuses to listen, denies negotiation, ignores the needs of fellow humans and ends in violence or despotism.

Finally, the range of democratic methods and moments discussed in this book suggests that old notions of democracy have much that is useful in facilitating new improvements. The work of democracy is far from done, and changing conditions demand new ways to do democracy and new ways to think about its past. There is a pressing need to move beyond the reductive and simplistic historical account that underpins democracy, towards a more inclusive and robust narrative, one that makes room for marginalized movements, histories and stories. There is much scholarly work left to be done if we are to broaden the traditional narrative of democracy and to find alternative visions of rule by the people for the twenty-first century and beyond.

References

Abdalla, M. and Rane, H. (2009). Islam and the Struggle for Democracy. In M. Heazle, M. Griffiths and T. Conley (eds), *Foreign Policy Challenges in the 21st Century* (pp. 164–184). Cheltenham: Edward Elgar.

Abisaab, M. and Abisaab, R. J. (2000). A Century after Qasim Amin: Fictive Kinship and Historical Uses of 'Tahrir al-Mara'. *Al Jadid*, 6(32), 8–11.

Aboriginal and Torres Strait Islander Commission (ATSIC) Act (Cth) (1989). (No. 150). Canberra: Commonwealth of Australia.

Abu-Lughod, L. (1998). The Marriage of Feminism and Islamism in Egypt: Selective Repudiation as a Dynamic of Postcolonial Cultural Politics. In L. Abu-Lughod (ed.), *Remaking Women: Feminism and Modernity in the Middle East* (pp. 243–270). Princeton: Princeton University Press.

Achebe, C. (1990). African Literature as Restoration of Celebration. In K. H. Petersen and A. Rutherford (eds), *Chinua Achebe: A Celebration* (pp. 1–10). Oxford: Heinemann.

Aeschines (2001). *Against Timarchus* (N. R. E. Fisher, trans.). Oxford: Oxford University Press.

Afsaruddin, A. (2006). The 'Islamic State': Genealogy, Facts, and Myths. *Journal of Church and State*, 48(1), 153–173.

Agrawala, V. S. (1963 [1953]). *India as Known to Panini: A Study of the Cultural Material in the Ashatadhyayi* (2nd edn). Varanasi: Prithvi Prakashan.

Ahmed, H. (2009, 21 March). Protests Mark Iraq War's 6th Year. *The Seattle Times*.

Ahmed, L. (1992). *Women and Gender in Islam*. New Haven: Yale University Press.

Ake, C. (1996). Rethinking African Democracy. In L. Diamond and M. F. Plattner (eds) *The Global Resurgence of Democracy*. (pp. 63–75). Baltimore: John Hopkins University Press.

Al-Buti, M. S. R. (2001). *The Jurisprudence of the Prophetic Biography & A Brief History of the Orthodox Caliphate* (N. Roberts, trans.). Damascus: Dar Al-Fikr.

Al-Dhahabi, I. (2001). *Siyar A'lam al-Nubala* (Vol. 3): Al-Risala Foundation.

Al-Din, O. S. and El-Yassari, K. Y. (2005, 19 June). Criminal Violation of Law of Land Warfare Confirmed again: U.S. Officers Forced to Release Women Hostages. *Islam Online*.

Al-Dulaimy, M. and Allam, H. (2005, 30 May). Welcome to Liberated Iraq: Students Non-Violently Protesting U.S. Occupation Raids on Their Campus Get a Quick Response: More Raids. *Global Resistance News*.

Al-Khairalla, M. (2005a, 19 July). Baghdad Hospital Doctors on Strike against Soldiers. *Reuters*.

Al-Khairalla, M. (2005b, 9 April). Iraqis Protest on Anniversary of Saddam's Fall. *Common Dreams*.

Al-Marashi, I. (2007). The Dynamics of Iraq's Media: Ethno-Sectarian Violence, Political Islam, Public Advocacy, and Globalisation. *Cardozo Arts and Entertainment Law Journal*, 25(95), 96–140.

Al-Rahim, A. H. (2005). The Sistani Factor. *Journal of Democracy*, 16(3), 50–53.

226 *References*

Al-Sheikh, B. (2004, 3 April). A Limitless Inferno. *World Press*.

Aldred, C. (1998). *The Egyptians* (3rd edn). London: Thames and Hudson.

Alitto, G. (1979). *The Last Confucian: Liang Shu-ming and the Chinese Dilemma of Modernity*. Berkeley: University of California Press.

Altekar, A. S. (1958 [1949]). *State and Government in Ancient India* (3rd edn). Delhi: Motilal Banarsidass.

Amin, Q. (2000). *The Liberation of Women and The New Woman: Two Documents in the History of Egyptian Feminism* (S. S. Peterson, trans.). Cairo: The American University in Cairo Press.

An-Nawawi, I. (1999). *Riyad-us-Saliheen*. Riyadh: Darussalam.

Anderson, P. (1974). *Passages from Antiquity to Feudalism*. London: New Left Books.

Anti-US Protest Marks Anniversary of Saddam's Overthrow (2005, 9 April). *ABC*.

Arato, A. (2004). Sistani v. Bush: Constitutional Politics in Iraq. *Constellations*, 11(2), 174–192.

Archontidou-Argyri, A. and Kyriakopoulou, T. (eds). (2000). *Chios – Oinopion's Town*. Chios: Ministry of Culture.

Aristotle (1981). *The Politics* (T. A. Sinclair, trans.). London: Penguin Classics.

Aristotle (1984). *The Athenian Constitution* (P. J. Rhodes, trans.). Harmondswoth: Penguin.

Arnold, T. W. (2001). *Preaching of Islam: A History of the Propagation of the Muslim Faith*. India: Adam Publishers & Distributors.

Arrian (1893). *Anabasis Alexandri* (E. J. Chinnock, rans.). London: George Bell and Sons.

Arrian (1970). *The Life of Alexander the Great*. London: Folio Society.

Assaf, S. (2005, 21 May). General Strike against Occupation in Iraqi City of Ramadi. *Socialist Worker Online*.

Atwater, C. (2009 [1829]). Description of Winnebago Government. In D. E. Wilkins (ed.), *Documents of Native American Political Development 1500s to 1933* (pp. 67–69). Oxford: Oxford University Press.

Aubert, M. E. (2001). *The Phoenicians and the West*. Cambridge: Cambridge University Press.

Australian Bureau of Statistics (2008). *Population Characteristics, Aboriginal and Torres Strait Islander Peoples, 2006* (No. 4713.0). Canberra: Australian Government.

Awwad, H. J. a. (2007, 11 June). Iraqi Oil Workers Claim Tactical Victory as Negotiations Resume and Ministry of Oil rebuked. *Naftana*.

Bagge, S. (2001). Law and Justice in Norway in the Middle Ages: A Case Study. In L. Bisgaard, J. Lind, C. S. Jensen and K. V. Jensen (eds), *Medieval Spirituality in Scandinavia and Europe: A Collection of Essays in Honour of Tore Nyberg* (pp. 73–85). Odense: Odense University Press.

Bailkey, N. (1967). Early Mesopotamian Constitutional Development. *The American Historical Review*, 72(4), 1211–1236.

Bakker, P. (1997). *A Language of Our Own: The Genesis of Michif, the Mixed Cree-French Language of the Canadian Métis*. Oxford: Oxford University Press.

Barabankawi, M. (1997). *Al-'Abuab 'al-Muntakhaba: Mishkat 'Al-Masabih*. New Delhi: Maktabat Al-'ilm.

Barkwell, L. J., Acco, A. C. and Rozyk, A. (2007). *The Origins of Métis Customary Law With a Discussion of Métis Legal Traditions*. Winnipeg: Louis Riel Institute.

Barlow, J. P. (1996, 8 February). A Declaration of the Independence of Cyberspace. *Electronic Frontier Foundation*.

Basra Oil Workers out on Strike (2005, 17 July). BBC News.

Bayly, C. A. (2004). *The Birth of the Modern World, 1780–1914: Global Connections and Comparisons*. Malden, MA: Blackwell.

Behrendt, L. (2003). ATSIC Bashing. *Arena*, 67(October–November), 27–29.

Behrendt, L. (2005). The Abolition of ATSIC – Implications for Democracy: Issues Paper. Paper presented at the Democratic Audit of Australia.

Behrendt, L. and Kelly, L. (2008). *Resolving Indigenous Disputes: Land Conflict and Beyond*. Annandale: The Federation Press.

Beinart, W. (2001). *Twentieth Century South Africa*. Oxford: Oxford University Press.

Bernal, M. (1991 [1987]). *Black Athena: The Afroasiatic Roots of Classical Civilisation, Volume I: The Fabrication of Ancient Greece 1785–1985*. London: Vintage.

Bernal, M. (1991). *Black Athena: The Afroasiatic Roots of Classical Civilisation, Volume II: The Archaeological and Documentary Evidence*. London: Free Association.

Bernal, M. (2001 [1990]). Phoenician Politics and Egyptian Justice in Ancient Greece. In M. Bernal (ed), *Black Athena Writes Back: Martin Bernal Responds to his Critics* (pp. 345–370). Duke University Press: Durham.

Bernal, M. (2006). *Black Athena: The Afroasiatic Roots of Classical Civilisation, Volume III: The Linguistic Evidence*. New Brunswick: Rutgers University Press.

Berndt, R. and Berndt, C. (1999). *The World of the First Australians: Aboriginal Traditional Life: Past and Present*. Canberra: Aboriginal Studies Press.

Bewley, A. (2004). *Muslim Women: A Biographical Dictionary*. London: Ta-Ha Publishers.

Bhandarkar, D. R. (1919). *Lectures on the Ancient History of India on the Period from 650 to 325 BCE*. Calcutta: University of Calcutta.

Bianchi, E., Righi, N. and Terzaghi, M. (1997). *The Doge's Palace in Venice*. Milan: Electa.

Bickford-Smith, V. (1995). Black Ethnicities, Communities and Political Expression in Late Victorian Cape Town. *Journal of African History*, 36, 443–465.

Black, A. (1997). Christianity and Republicanism: From St Cyprian to Rousseau. *American Political Science Review*, 91, 647–656.

Bloomfield, L. (ed.). (1943). *Plains Cree Texts*. New York: American Ethnological Society.

Bondi, S. F. (2001). Political and Administrative Organization. In S. Moscati (ed.), *The Phoenicians* (pp. 153–159). London: I. B. Tauris.

Booth, M. (1997). May Her Likes Be Multiplied: 'Famous Women' Biography and Gendered Prescription in Egypt, 1892–1935. *Signs*, 22(4), 827–890.

Booth, W. (2003, May 14). In Najaf, New Mayor is Outsider Viewed with Suspicion. *Washington Post*.

Booth, W. and Chandrasekaran, R. (2003, 28 June). Occupation Forces Halt Elections Throughout Iraq. *Washington Post*.

Bornstein, D. (1993). Giovanni Dominici, the Bianchi, and Venice: Symbolic Action and Interpretive Grids. *The Journal of Medieval and Renaissance Studies*, 23(2), 143–174.

Boulhosa, P. P. (2005). *Icelanders and the Kings of Norway: Mediaeval Sagas and Legal Texts*. Leiden: Brill.

228 *References*

Bouwsma, W. J. (1968). *Venice and the Defense of Republican Liberty: Renaissance Values in the Age of the Counter Reformation*. Berkley: University of California Press.

Brink, J. W. (2008). *Imagining Head-Smashed-In: Aboriginal Buffalo Hunting on the Northern Plains*. Edmonton: Athabaka University Press.

Brownlee, C. P. (1897). *Reminiscences of Kafir Life and Other Papers*. Lovedale: Lovedale Press.

Bryce, J. (1921). *Modern Democracies* (Vol. I). London: Macmillan.

Buber, M. (1967). *Kingship of God*. New York: Harper & Row.

Bundy, C. (1988). *The Rise and Fall of the South African Peasantry*. Cape Town: David Phillip.

Burkert, W. (1992). *The Orientalizing Revolution: Near Eastern Influence on Greek Culture in the Early Archaic Age* (M. E. Pinder and W. Burkert, trans.). Cambridge, MA: Harvard University Press.

Butler, A. (1998). *Democracy and Apartheid: Political Theory, Comparative Politics and the Modern South African State*. London: Macmillan.

Byock, J. (1982). *Feud in the Icelandic Saga*. Berkeley: University of California Press.

Carl, T. (2005, 10 April). Iraqi Protesters Call for U.S. Pullout. *Associated Press*.

Carr, J. (2005, 3 June). Don't Pay Money for the Enemy's Weapons: Iraqi Activists Plan to Boycott US Goods. *Electronic Iraq*.

Carver, M. (ed.). (1995). *Letters of a Victorian Army Officer, Edward Wellesley, Major, 73rd Regiment of Foot, 1840–1854*. Hartnolls: The Army Records Society.

Cassiodorus (1886). *The Letters of Cassiodorus: Variae Epistolae* (T. Hodgkin, trans.). London: Henry Frowde.

Chan, S. (1998). Village Self-Government and Civil Society. In J. Cheng (ed.), *China Review* (pp. 235–258). Hong Kong: Chinese University Press.

Charette, G. (ed.). (1976). *L'Espace de Louis Goulet*. Winnipeg: Éditions Bois-brûlés.

Chege, M. (1996). Between Africa's Extremes. In L. Diamond and M. F. Plattner (eds), *The Global Resurgence of Democracy* (pp. 350–357). Baltimore: The John Hopkins University Press.

Chen, Q. (1997). Confucianism, Democracy and Humanism. In P. Cam, I. S. Cha and M. Tamtha (eds), *Philosophy and Democracy in Asia*. Seoul: Korean National Commission for UNESCO.

Choate, A. C. (1997). *Local Governance in China: An Assessment of Villagers Committees*. Working Paper #1: The Asia Foundation.

Chulov, M. (2008, 22 November). Shias Stage Protests against Iraq-US Pact. *The Guardian*.

Churchill, W. (1947). British Parliament Bill. *Hansard*, 444 (11 November), 206–207.

Cicero, M. T. (1998). *The Republic and The Laws* (N. Rudd, trans.). Oxford: Oxford University Press.

Clark, J. J. (1997). *Oriental Enlightenment: The Encounter between Asian and Western Thought*. New York: Routledge.

Cobley, A. G. (1990). *Class and Consciousness: The Black Petty Bourgeoisie in South Africa, 1924–1950*. New York: Greenwood Press.

Cogan, M. (2003). Achaemenid Inscriptions: Cyrus Cylinder. In W. W. Hallo and K. L. Younger (eds), *The Context of Scripture: Monumental Inscriptions from the Biblical World* (Vol. 2). Leiden: Brill.

Cohen, R. and Westbrook, R. (eds). (2000). *Amarna Diplomacy: The Beginnings of International Relations*. Baltimore: John Hopkins University Press.

Cole, J. (1999). *Colonialism and Revolution in the Middle East: Social and Cultural Origins of Egypt's 'Urabi Movement*. Cairo: American University in Cairo Press.

Cowell, E. B. (ed.). (1895). *The Jataka, or Stories of the Buddha's Former Births*. Oxford: Pali Text Society.

Crais, C. (2002). *The Politics of Evil: Magic, State Power, and the Political Imagination in South Africa*. Cambridge: Cambridge University Press.

Creel, H. G. (1960). *Confucius and the Chinese Way*. New York: Harper.

Culican, W. (1975). Some Phoenician Masks and Other Terracottas. *Berytus Archaeological Studies*, 24, 47–87.

Dahl, R. (1998). *On Democracy*. New Haven: Yale University Press.

Davidson, B. (1969). *A History of East and Central Africa*. New York: Doubleday.

Davies, J. K. (1978). *Democracy and Classical Greece*. Glasgow: Fontana.

Davis, E. (2004, June). Democracy's Prospects in Iraq. *Foreign Policy Research Institute E-Notes*, 1–3.

Davis, E. (2005a). National Assembly Elections: Prelude to Democracy or Instability? *Middle East Policy*, 12(1), 114–119.

Davis, E. (2005b). The New Iraq: The Uses of Historical Memory. *Journal of Democracy*, 16(3), 54–68.

Davis, E. (2007, Spring). The Formation of Political Identities in Ethnically Divided Societies: Implications for a Democratic Transition in Iraq. *Taari*, 3–4.

Davis, U. (1999). *Citizenship and the State: A Comparative Study of Citizenship Legislation in Israel, Jordan, Palestine, Syria and Lebanon*. London: Ithaca.

de Bary, W. T. (1983). *The Liberal Tradition in China*. Hong Kong: Chinese University of Hong Kong Press.

de Bary, W. T. (1993). *Waiting for the Dawn: A Plan for the Prince: A Study and Translation of Huang Tsung-hsi's Ming-I-Tai-Fang Lu*. New York: Columbia University Press.

de Bary, W. T. (1998). *Asian Values and Human Rights: A Confucian Communitarian Perspective*. Cambridge, MA: Harvard University Press.

De Tocqueville, A. (1864 [1835]). *Democracy in America* (H. Reeve, trans., 4 edn, Vol. 1). Cambridge: Sever and Francis.

Democracy's Century: A Survey of Global Political Change in the 20th Century (1999). New York: Freedom House.

Deng, F. M. (2004). Human Rights in the African Context. In K. Wiredu (ed.), *Companion to African Philosophy* (pp. 499–508). Malden: Blackwell.

Derrida, J. (2006 [1993]). *Spectres of Marx: The State of the Debt, the Work of Mourning, and the New International* (P. Kamuf, trans.). New York: Routledge.

Des Forges, R. V. (1993). Democracy in Chinese History. In R. V. Des Forges, L. Ning and Y. B. Wu (eds), *Chinese Democracy and the Crisis of 1989* (pp. 21–52). New York: State University of New York Press.

Desai, G. (2001). *Subject to Colonialism: African Self-Fashioning and the Colonial Library*. Durham: Duke University Press.

Diamond, L., Linz, J. and Lipset, S. M. (1989). Preface. In L. Diamond, J. Linz and S. M. Lipset (eds), *Democracy in Asia* (Vol. 3, pp. ix–xxvii). New Delhi: Vistaar.

Diamond, L. and Plattner, M. (eds). (1996). *The Global Resurgence of Democracy* (2nd edn). Baltimore: Johns Hopkins University Press.

Dodge, D. (1966). *African Politics in Perspective*. Princeton: D. Van Nostrand.

230 *References*

Dozens Rally Demonstrations to Protest Corruption in Muthana (2008, 24 August). *Voices of Iraq.*

Drekmeier, C. (1962). *Kingship and Community in Early India.* Stanford: Stanford University Press.

Drews, R. (1979). Phoenicians, Carthage and the Spartan Eunomia. *American Journal of Philology,* 100(1), 45–58.

Duara, P. (1995). *Rescuing History from the Nation: Questioning Narratives of Modern China.* Chicago: University of Chicago Press.

Duhuk Demo Ends by Presenting Warrant of Protest against Elections Law (2008, 31 July). *Voices of Iraq.*

Dumont, G. (2006). Récit Gabriel Dumont. On *Les Mémoires dictés par Gabriel Dumont et le Récit Gabriel Dumont; Textes établis et annotés par Denis Combet* [Oral transcription]. Saint-Boniface: Éditions du Blé.

Dunn, J. (ed.). (1992). *Democracy: The Unfinished Journey, 508 BCE to CE 1993.* Oxford: Oxford University Press.

Dunn, J. (2006). *Democracy: A History.* New York: Atlantic.

Easton, S. C. (1970). *The Heritage of the Ancient World* (2nd edn). Sydney: Holt, Rinehart & Winston.

El Saadawi, N. (1980). *The Hidden Face of Eve.* London: Zed.

Elman, B. (1989). Imperial Politics and Confucian Societies in Late Imperial China: The Hanlin and Donglin Academies. *Modern China,* 15(4), 379–418.

Elphick, R. (1987). Mission Christianity and Interwar Liberalism. In J. Butler, R. Elphick and D. Welsh (eds), *Democratic Liberalism in South Africa: Its History and Prospect* (pp. 58–79). Middletown: Wesleyan University Press.

Evans, G. (1958). Ancient Mesopotamian Assemblies – An Addendum. *Journal of the American Oriental Society,* 78(2), 114–115.

Fairbank, J. K. and Goldman, M. (2006). *China: A New History.* Cambridge: Belknap.

Fawwaz, Z. (2004 [1891]). Fair and Equal Treatment. In M. Badran and M. Cooke (eds), *Opening the Gates: An Anthology of Arab Feminist Writing* (2nd edn, pp. 220–227). Bloomington: Indiana University Press.

Feldman, N. (2003). *After Jihad.* New York: Farrar, Straus and Giroux.

Fine Day (1926). *Incidents of the Rebellion, as Related by Fine Day.* Battleford: Canadian North-West Historical Society.

Finer, S. E. (1997). *The History of Government.* Oxford: Oxford University Press.

Finley, M. I. (1973). *Democracy Ancient and Modern.* New Brunswick: Rutgers University Press.

Finn, E. (2004, 4 February). Grand Ayatollah Sayyid Ali Husaini Sistani: Why We'd Better Listen to Iraq's Influential Cleric. *Slate.*

Finsen, V. (1873). Om de islandske love i fristastiden. *Aarbøger for nordisk oldkyndighed og historie* (pp. 101–250).

Fitzhardinge, L. F. (1980). *The Spartans.* London: Thames and Hudson.

Fleming, D. E. (2004). *Democracy's Ancient Ancestors: Mari and Early Collective Governance.* Cambridge: Cambridge University Press.

Foote, P. (1977). Some Lines in Lögréttuþáttr: A Comparison and Some Conclusions. In E. G. Pétursson and J. Kristjánsson (eds), *Sjötíu ritgerðir helgaðar Jakobi Benediktssyni 20* (Vol. 1, pp. 198–207). Reykjavík: Stofnun Árna Magnússonar.

Forrest, W. G. (1966). *The Emergence of Greek Democracy, 800–400 BCE.* New York: McGraw-Hill.

References   231

Forrest, W. G. (1980). *A History of Sparta*. London: Duckworth.

Foster, J. E. (2002). Wintering, the Outsider Adult Male and the Ethnogenesis of the Western Plains Métis. In P. Douaud (ed.), *The Western Métis: Profile of a People* (pp. 91–104). Regina: University of Regina Press.

Franchére, G. (1969). *The Journal of Gabriel Franchére*. Toronto: Champlain Society.

Frankfort, H. (1978 [1948]). *Kingship and the Gods: A Study of Ancient Near Eastern Religion as the Integration of Society and Nature*. Chicago: University of Chicago Press.

Franks, C. E. S. (2002). In Search of the Savage Sauvage: An Exploration into North America's Political Cultures. *American Review of Canadian Studies*, Winter, 547–580.

Fukuyama, F. (1989). The End of History? *The National Interest*, 16, 1–18.

Fukuyama, F. (1992). *The End of History and the Last Man*. London: Penguin.

Fung, A. and Wright, E. O. (2003). Thinking about Empowered Participatory Governance. In A. Fung and E. O. Wright (eds), *Deepening Democracy. Institutional Innovations in Empowered Participatory Governance* (Vol. 4, pp. 3–42). London: Verso.

Gandolfo, K. L. (2011). The Liberation of Women, by Qassim Amin. In T. K. Wayne (ed.), *Historical Encyclopedia of Feminist Thought*. Westport: Greenwood.

Gaza: Rescind Religious Dress Code for Girls (2009, 4 September). *Human Rights Watch*.

Gerecht, R. M. (2004, 1 September). Ayatollah Democracy. *The Atlantic Monthly*.

Gettleman, J. (2004, 29 March). G. I.'s Padlock Baghdad Paper Accused of Lies. *The New York Times*.

Ghoshal, U. N. (1966). *The Pre-Maurya and Maurya Period* (Vol. 2). Oxford: Oxford University Press.

Giliomee, H. (1995). The Non-Racial Franchise and Afrikaner and Coloured Identities, 1910–1994. *African Affairs*, 94, 199–225.

Giraud, M. (1945). *Le Métis Canadien*. Paris: Musée National d'Histoire Naturelle.

Glassman, R. M. (1986). *Democracy and Despotism in Primitive Societies: A Neo-Weberian Approach to Political Theory. Volume 1: Primitive Democracy*. Millwood: Associated Faculty.

Goedicke, H. (1975). *The Report of Wenamun*. Baltimore: John Hopkins University Press.

Goffman, D. (2002). *The Ottoman Empire and Early Modern Europe*. Cambridge: Cambridge University Press.

Goldman, M. (1981). *China's Intellectuals: Advise and Dissent*. Cambridge: Harvard University Press.

Goodall, H. (2008). *Invasion to Embassy: Land in Aboriginal Politics in New South Wales, 1770–1972*. Sydney: Sydney University Press.

Goody, J. (1996). *The East in the West*. Cambridge: Cambridge University Press.

Goody, J. (2006). *The Theft of History*. Cambridge: Cambridge University Press.

Gore, R. (2004). Who were the Phoenicians? New Clues from Ancient Bones and Modern Blood. *National Geographic*, 206 (October), 26–49.

Grágás-K (1850–1852). In V. Finsen (ed.), *Grágás: Islændernes lovbog i fristatens tid udgivet efter der kongelige bibliotheks haandskrift*. Copenhagen: Brødrene.

232 References

Gregg, J. (1954 [1844]). *Commerce of the Prairies*. Norman: University of Oklahoma Press.

Grieder, J. (1981). *Intellectuals and the State in Modern China: A Narrative History*. New York: The Free Press.

Gukiina, P. M. (1972). *Uganda: A Case Study in African Political Development*. Notre Dame: University of Notre Dame.

Habermas, J. (1987 [1981]). *The Theory of Communicative Action* (T. McCarthy, trans.). Boston: Beacon.

Habermas, J. (1996). *Between Facts and Norms: Contributions to a Discourse Theory of Law and Democracy*. Cambridge, MA: MIT Press.

Hakim, R. (2008, 3 October). The Largest Assyrian–Chaldean Demonstration in Northern Iraq. *Ankawa*.

Hama-Saeed, M. (2007, 26 March). Media in Iraq at Risk. *Assyrian International News Agency*.

Handwerk, B. (2003, October 24). Can Islam and Democracy Coexist? *National Geographic*.

Hannaford, J., Huggins, J. and Collins, B. (2003). *In the Hands of the Regions: A New ATSIC*. Canberra: Commonwealth of Australia.

Hansen, M. H. (1999 [1991]). *The Athenian Democracy in the Age of Demosthenes: Structure, Principles, and Ideology* (J. A. Crook, trans. 2nd edn). London: Bristol Classical.

Hansen, O. (1985). Hestia Boulaia at Erythrai. *Antiquité Classique*, 54, 274–276.

Hassan, A. (2005, 12 July). The Real Terrorists in This Country Are the Police. *Reuters*.

Hassan, F. (2000, 3–9 February). Women's Destiny, Men's Voices. *Al-Ahram Weekly*.

Hasso, F. (2005). *Resistance, Repression, and Gender Politics in Occupied Palestine and Jordan*. New York: Syracuse University Press.

Hattersley, A. F. (1930). *A Short History of Democracy*. Cambridge: Cambridge University Press.

Hazlitt, W. C. (1966 [1900]). *The Venetian Republic: Its Rise, Its Growth, and Its Fall, CE 409–1797* (4th edn). London: Adam and Charles Black.

Hearne, S. (1958). *Selections from the Journals of Samuel Hearne*. Toronto: McClelland & Stewart.

Hegel, G. W. F. (1952 [1837]). The Philosophy of History. In M. J. Adler (ed.), *Great Books of the Western World: Hegel* (Vol. 46, pp. 153–369). Chicago: Encyclopaedia Britannica.

Heirbaut, D. (2007a). The Oldest Part of the Lois des Pers dou Castel de Lille (1283–1308/14) and the Infancy of Case Law and Law Reporting on the Continent. *The Legal History Review*, 75, 139–152.

Heirbaut, D. (2007b). Who Were the Makers of Customary Law in Medieval Europe? Some Answers Based on Sources about the Spokesmen of Flemish Feudal Courts. *The Legal History Review*, 75, 257–274.

Held, D. (2006). *Models of Democracy* (3rd edn). Stanford: Stanford University Press.

Hendawi, H. (2003, 20 May). Shiites Mount Anti-U.S. Protests. *The Russia Journal*, 5.

Herodotus (1996). *The Histories* (G. Rawlinson, trans.). London: Wordsworth Classics.

Heusler, A. (1911). *Das Strafrecht der Isländersagas*. Leipizig: Duncker & Humblot.

Hind, H. Y. (1860). *Narrative of the Canadian Red River Exploring Expedition of 1857 and of the Assiniboine and Saskatchewan Exploring Expedition of 1858*. London: Longman, Green, Longman, and Roberts.

Hobbes, T. (2002 [1651]). *Leviathan*. Project Gutenberg.

Homer (1950). *The Iliad* (E. V. Rieu, trans.). London: Penguin.

Hornblower, S. (1992). Creation and Development of Democratic Institutions in Ancient Greece. In J. Dunn (ed.), *Democracy: The Unfinished Journey, 508 BCE to CE 1993* (pp. 1–17). Oxford: Oxford University Press.

Houtsma, M. T., Wensinck, A. J., Gibb, H. A. R. and Heffening, W. (eds). (1993). *The First Encyclopaedia of Islam 1913–1936* (Vol. 6). New York: E. J. Brill.

Hsü, I. C. Y. (1975). *The Rise of Modern China*. London: Oxford University Press.

Huang, P. C. C. (1993). 'Public Sphere'/'Civil Society' in China? The Third Realm between State and Society. *Modern China*, 19(2), 216–240.

Hundreds of Kurds Protest in Northern Iraq (2008, 30 July). *Monsters and Critics*.

Hundreds Protest in Baghdad over Kirkuk's Status (2008, 4 August). *Agence France Presse*.

Huntington, S. P. (1984). Will More Countries Become Democratic? *Political Science Quarterly*, 99(2), 193–218.

Huntington, S. P. (1991). *The Third Wave: Democratization in the Late Twentieth Century*. Norman: University of Oklahoma Press.

Hyde, J. K. (1973). *Society and Politics in Medieval Italy: The Evolution of the Civil Life, 1000–1350*. New York: St Martin's Press.

Ibbetson, D. (2007). Custom in Medieval Law. In A. Perreau-Saussine and J. B. Murphy (eds), *Nature of Customary Law: Legal, Historical and Philosophical Perspectives* (pp. 151–175). Cambridge: Cambridge University Press.

Ingvarsson, L. (1970). *Goðorð og goðorðsmenn* (Vol. 1). Egilsstaðir: Útgáfa höfundar.

Ip, H. Y. (1991). Liang Shuming and the Idea of Democracy in Modern China. *Modern China*, 17(4), 469–508.

Iraq Government Orders Arrest of Oil Workers' Leaders (2007, 6 June). *Common Dreams*.

IRAQ: Oil Workers on Strike in Basra (2007, 4 June). *On the Barricades*.

Iraqi Oil Exports Suspended for Few Hours by Strike (2005, 17 July). *Global Resistance News*.

Iraqi Oil Workers Hold 24-Hour Strike – Oil Exports Shut Down (2005, 17 July). *Uruknet*.

Isakhan, B. (2006). Read All About It: The Free Press, the Public Sphere and Democracy in Iraq. *Bulletin of the Royal Institute for Inter-Faith Studies*, 8(1 and 2), 119–153.

Isakhan, B. (2007a). Engaging 'Primitive Democracy': Mideast Roots of Collective Governance. *Middle East Policy*, 14(3), 97–117.

Isakhan, B. (2007b). Media Discourse and Iraq's Democratisation: Reporting the 2005 Constitution in the Australian and Middle Eastern Print Media. *Australian Journalism Review*, 29(1), 97–114.

Isakhan, B. (2008a). 'Oriental Despotism' and the Democratisation of Iraq in *The Australian*. *Transformations*, 16th edition.

Isakhan, B. (2008b). The Post-Saddam Iraqi Media: Reporting the Democratic Developments of 2005. *Global Media Journal*, 7(13).

234   *References*

Isakhan, B. (2009). Manufacturing Consent in Iraq: Interference in the Post-Saddam Media Sector. *International Journal of Contemporary Iraqi Studies*, 3(1), 7–26.

Isakhan, B. (2011). *Democracy in Iraq: History, Culture and Politics*. London: Ashgate.

Isham, J. (1949 [1743]). *James Isham's Observations on Hudson's Bay, and A voyage to Hudson's Bay*. Toronto: Champlain Society.

Jacobsen, T. (1939). An Ancient Mesopotamaian Trial for Homicide. *Analecta Biblica et Orientalia*, 12, 130–150.

Jacobsen, T. (1970 [1943]). Primitive Democracy in Ancient Mesopotamia. In W. L. Moran (ed.), *Toward the Image of Tammuz and Other Essays on Mesopotamian History and Culture* (pp. 157–170). Massachusetts: Harvard University Press.

Jacobsen, T. (1970 [1957]). Early Political Development in Mesopotamia. In W. L. Moran (ed.), *Toward the Image of Tammuz and Other Essays on Mesopotamian History and Culture* (pp. 132–156). Massachusetts: Harvard University Press.

Jacobsen, T. (1977a [1951a]). The Cosmos as a State. In H. Frankfort, H. A. Frankfort, J. A. Wilson, T. Jacobsen and W. A. Irwin (eds), *The Intellectual Adventure of Ancient Man: Essays on Speculative Thought in the Ancient Near East* (pp. 125–184). Chicago: University of Chicago Press.

Jacobsen, T. (1977b [1951b]). The Function of the State. In H. Frankfort, H. A. Frankfort, J. A. Wilson, T. Jacobsen and W. A. Irwin (eds), *The Intellectual Adventure of Ancient Man: Essays on Speculative Thought in the Ancient Near East* (pp. 185–201). Chicago: University of Chicago Press.

Jamail, D. (2004, 19 January). Shiites Unity Challenges U.S. Plan in Iraq. *The New Standard*.

Jasim, A. (2005, 9 April). Massive 'End the Occupation' Protest in Baghdad Dwarfs the 'Saddam Toppled' rally. *China Daily*.

Jayaswal, K. P. (1943 [1911–1913]). *Hindu Polity: A Constitutional History of India in Hindu Times*. Bangalore: Bangalore Printing & Publishing Co.

Jeffery, L. H. (1956). The Courts of Justice in Archaic Chios. *Annual of the British School at Athens*, 51, 157–167.

Johnson, K. (2003). Liberal or Liberation Framework? The Contradictions of ANC Rule in South Africa. *Journal of Contemporary African Studies*, 21(2), 321–340.

Jones, A. H. M. (1969 [1953]). *Athenian Democracy*. Oxford: Basil Blackwell.

Jónsson, A. (1985). *Crymogæa* (H. Pálsson, trans.). Reykjavík: Sögufélag.

Joseph, S. (2000). *Gender and Citizenship in Middle East*. New York: Syracuse University Press.

Josephus, F. (1700). *Against Apion* (W. Whiston, trans.). Project Gutenburg.

Kaggwa, A. (1934 [1905]). *The Customs of the Baganda* (E. Kalibbala, trans.). New York: Columbia University Press.

Kamali, M. H. (2002). *Freedom, Equality and Justice in Islam*. Kuala Lumpur: Ilmiah.

Kandiyoti, D. (1991). Women, Islam and the State. *Middle East Report and Information Project*, 173, 9–14.

Kane, P. (1859). *Wanderings of an Artist among the Indians of North America*. London: Longman, Brown, Green, Longmans & Roberts.

Kang, Y. (1956). *Da Tong Shu*. Beijing: The Classics Publishing House.

Karlsson, G. (1972). Goðar og bændr. *Saga*, 10, 5–57.

Karlsson, G. (1977). Goðar and Höfðingjar in Medieval Iceland. *Saga-Book of the Viking Society*, 19, 358–370.

Karlsson, G. (2002). Aðgreining löggjafarvalds og dómsvalds í íslenska þjóðveldinu. *Gripla*, 13, 7–32.

Kathir, I. (2000). *Tafsir Ibn Kathir (Abridged)* (S. Al-Mubarakpuri, trans., Vol. 1). New York: Darussalam.

Kautilya (1951). *Kautilya's Arthasastra* (R. Shamasastry, trans., 4th edn). Mysore: Mysore Printing and Publishing House.

Keane, J. (2004). *Violence and Democracy*. Cambridge: Cambridge University Press.

Keane, J. (2009). *The Life and Death of Democracy*. New York: Simon and Schuster.

Kenyatta, J. (1962). *Facing Mount Kenya*. New York: Vintage.

Kiwanuka, S. M. S. M. (1972). *A History of Buganda: From the Foundation of the Kingdom to 1900*. New York: Africana.

Kjartansson, H. S. (1989). *Fjöldi goðorða samkvæmt Grágás: erindi flutt á málstefnu Stofnunar Sigurðar Nordals 24.–26. júlí 1988*. Reykjavík: Félag Áhugamanna um Réttarsögu.

Klein, N. (2007). *The Shock Doctrine: The Rise of Disaster Capitalism*. New York: Allen Lane.

Kramer, M. (1993). Islam vs Democracy. *Commentary, January*, 35–42.

Kramer, S. N. (1963). *The Sumerians: Their History, Culture and Character*. Chicago: University of Chicago Press.

Kuhn, P. (2008). Toward the Nineteenth Century. [Supplement]. *Late Imperial China*, 29(1), 1–6.

'Kullavagga' (T. W. Rhys Davids and H. Oldenberg, trans.) (1882). In F. M. Müller (ed.), *Sacred Books of the East* (Vol. 17). Oxford: Oxford University Press.

Kurzman, C. (2008). *Democracy Denied, 1905–1915: Intellectuals and the Fate of Democracy*. Cambridge: Harvard University Press.

Laclau, E. and Mouffe, C. (1985). *Hegemony and Socialist Strategy: Towards a Radical Democratic Politics*. London: Verso.

Laix, R. A. d. (1973). *Probouleusis at Athens: A Study of Political Decision Making*. Berkeley: University of California Press.

Lane, F. C. (1973). *Venice, a Maritime Republic*. Baltimore: John Hopkins University Press.

Lapidus, I. M. (1975). The Separation of State and Religion in the Development of Early Islamic Society. *International Journal of Middle East Studies*, 6(4), 363–385.

Lapidus, I. M. (2002). *A History of Islamic Societies*. Cambridge: Cambridge University Press.

Larsen, J. A. O. (1954). The Judgement of Antiquity on Democracy. *Classical Philology*, 49, 1–14.

Larsen, M. T. (1976). *The Old Assyrian City-State and Its Colonies*. Copenhagen: Akademisk Forlag.

Laudicina, N. (2009). The Rules of Red River: The Council of Assiniboia and Its Impact on the Colony, 1820–1869. *Past Imperfect*, 15, 36–75.

Laws I (1980). In *The Laws of Early Iceland* (A. Dennis, P. Foote and R. Perkins, trans., Vol. 1). Winnipeg: University of Manitoba Press.

Lazreg, M. (1988). Feminism and Difference: The Perils of Writing as a Woman on Women in Algeria. *Feminist Studies*, 14(1), 81–107.

Leick, G. (2001). *Mesopotamia: The Invention of the City*. London: Penguin.

236 *References*

Levenson, J. R. (1968). *Confucian China and its Modern Fate* (Vol. 2). Berkeley: University of California Press.

Lewis, B. (1993). Islam and Liberal Democracy. *The Atlantic, February*, 89–98.

Lincoln, A. (1863, 19 November). *Gettysburg Address*. Vol. IX.

Líndal, S. (1969). Sendiför Úlfljóts. *Skírnir*, 143, 5–26.

Líndal, S. (1993). Law and Legislation in the Icelandic Commonwealth. *Scandinavian Studies in Law*, 37, 53–92.

Lings, M. (1983). *Muhammad: His Life Based on the Earliest Sources*. Vermont: Inner Traditions International.

Lipinski, E. (2004). *Itineraria Phoenicia, Orientalia Lovaniensia* (Vol. 127). Leuven: Peeters Publishers.

Logan, R. K. (2004). *The Alphabet Effect*. Cresskill: Hampton Press.

Lund, N. (1995). Scandinavia c. 700–1066. In R. McKitterick (ed.), *The New Cambridge Medieval History c.700–c.900* (pp. 202–227). Cambridge: Cambridge University Press.

Lynch, A. H., Beringer, J., Kershaw, P., Marshall, A., Mooney, S., Tapper, N., et al. (2007). Using the Paleorecord to Evaluate Climate and Fire Interactions in Australia. *Annual Review of Earth and Planetary Sciences*, 35, 215–239.

MacKenzie, A. (1801). *Voyages from Montreal*. Edinburgh: Noble.

Maddock, K. (1982 [1972]). *The Australian Aborigines: A Portrait of their Society* (2nd edn). Ringwood: Penguin.

'Maha-Parinibbana-Suttanta: Buddhist Suttas' (T. W. Rhys Davids, trans.) (1881). In F. M. Müller (ed.), *Sacred Books of the East* (Vol. 1). Oxford: Oxford University Press.

'Mahavagga' (T. W. Rhys Davids and H. Oldenberg, trans.) (1881). In F. M. Müller (ed.), *Sacred Books of the East* (Vol. 13). Oxford: Oxford University Press.

Maine, H. S. (1974 [1889]). *Village Communities in the East and West*. New York: Arno.

Majid, A. (1998). The Politics of Feminism in Islam. *Signs: Journal of Women in Culture and Society*, 23(2), 321–361.

Majumdar, A. K. (1980). *Concise History of Ancient India* (Vol. 2). New Delhi: Munshiram Manoharlal.

Majumdar, R. C. (1951). *The Age of Imperial Unity* (Vol. 2). Bombay: Bharatiya Vidya Bhavan.

Majumdar, R. C. (1960). *The Classical Accounts of India*. Calcutta: Firma K. L. Mukhopadhyay.

Majumdar, R. C. (1969 [1918]). *Corporate Life in Ancient India* (3rd edn). Calcutta: Firma K. L. Mukhopadhyay.

Mandelbaum, D. G. (1979). *The Plains Cree: An Ethnographic, Historical, and Comparative Study*. Regina: University of Regina Press.

Manglapus, R. S. (2004). Mesopotamia: Earliest Formal Democracy? *Asia Pacific Report*, 66.

Manu (1886). The Laws of Manu (G. Bühler, trans.). In F. M. F. Max Müller (ed.), *Sacred Books of the East* (Vol. 25). Oxford: Oxford University Press.

Markoe, G. (2005). *The Phoenicians*. London: Folio Society.

Marks, S. (1986). *The Ambiguities of Dependence in South Africa: Class, Nationalism and the State in Twentieth Century Natal*. Johannesburg: Ravan Press.

Martin, M. and Snell, D. C. (2005). Democracy and Freedom. In D. C. Snell (ed.), *A Companion to the Ancient Near East* (pp. 397–407). Malden: Blackwell.

Mass protest over Basra insecurity (2008, 9 March). *Al-Jazeera English*.

Maurer, K. (1874). *Island von seiner ersten Entdeckung bis zum Untergange des Freistaats*. Munich: Kaiser.

Maurer, K. (1878). *Udsigt over de nordgermaniske retskilders historie* (E. Hertzberg, trans.). Oslo: Brøgger.

Mazrui, A. A. (1986). *The Africans: A Triple Heritage*. Boston: Little, Brown.

Mbeki, G. (1992). *The Struggle for Liberation in South Africa: A Short History*. Cape Town: David Philip.

Mbeki, T. (1984). The Fatton Thesis: A Rejoinder. *Canadian Journal of African Studies*, 8(3), 609–612.

McCracken, J. (1963). *The Cape Parliament 1854–1910*. Oxford: Clarendon Press.

McGlynn, M. P. (2009). Orality in the Old Icelandic Grágás: Legal Formulae in the Assembly Procedures Section. *Neophilologus*, 93, 521–536.

McLean, J. (1932). *Notes of Twenty-five Year's Service in the Hudson's Bay Territories*. Toronto: Champlain Society.

Meiggs, T. and Lewis, D. (1988). *Greek Historical Inscriptions*. Oxford: Clarendon Press.

MENA Development Report (2004). *Gender and Development in the Middle East and North Africa: Women in the Public Sphere*. Washington: The World Bank.

Mill, J. (1972 [1817]). *The History of British India*. London: Associated.

Miller, I. M. (1990). *Bloodtaking and Peacemaking: Feud, Law, and Society in Saga Iceland*. Chicago: University of Chicago Press.

Miller, J. (1993). The Challenge of Radical Islam. *Foreign Affairs*, 72(3), 43–55.

Milloy, J. S. (1988). *The Plains Cree: Trade, Diplomacy and War, 1790 to 1870*. Winnipeg: University of Manitoba.

Moran, W. L. (ed.). (1992). *The Amarna Letters*. Baltimore: Johns Hopkins University Press.

Morris, S. (1992). *Daidalos and the Origins of Greek Art*. Princeton: Princeton University Press.

Morton, W. L. (1957). *Manitoba: A History*. Toronto: University of Toronto Press.

Mossmann, M. (2002). The Charismatic Pattern: Canada's Riel Rebellion of 1885 as a Millenarian Protest Movement. In P. Douaud (ed.), *The Western Métis: Profile of a People* (pp. 185–202). Regina: University of Regina Press.

Mote, F. W. (1999). *Imperial China, 900–1800*. Cambridge: Harvard University Press.

Muhlberger, S. and Paine, P. (1993). Democracy's Place in World History. *Journal of World History*, 4(1), 23–47.

Muhsin, M. (2008, 18 November). 'When Believing Women Come to You to Take the Oath of Allegiance ... 'An Interview with Dr Aminah Nasir. *Islam Today*.

Muir, E. (1999). The Sources of Civil Society in Italy. *The Journal of Interdisciplinary History*, 29(3), 379–380.

Mullen, E. T. (1980). *The Assembly of the Gods: The Divine Council in Canaanite and Early Hebrew Literature*. Chicago: Scholars.

Mundy, J. H. (1954). *Liberty and Political Power in Toulouse 1050–1230*. New York: Columbia University Press.

Murray, M. J. (1994). *Revolution Deferred: The Painful Birth of Post-Apartheid South Africa*. London: Verso.

Nasr, M. A. (2005, 13 October). Demonstrations Sweep Iraqi Towns. *Free Arab Voice*.

238 *References*

Nattrass, N. and Seekings, J. (2001). Democracy and Distribution in Highly Unequal Economies: The Case of South Africa. *The Journal of Modern African Studies*, 39(3), 471–498.

Nelson, C. (1996). *Doria Shafiq, Egyptian Feminist: A Woman Apart*. Gainesville: University Press of Florida.

Norwich, J. J. (2003). *A History of Venice*. London: Penguin.

Nourredin, N. (2005, 30 October). Sectarian Protest Rocks Key North Iraq Province. *Reuters*.

Ober, J. (1989). *Mass and Elite in Democratic Athens: Rhetoric, Ideology, and the Power of the People*. Princeton: Princeton University Press.

Ober, J. (1994). How to Criticise Democracy in Late Fifth- and Fourth-Century Athens. In J. P. Euben, J. R. Wallach and J. Ober (eds), *Athenian Political Thought and the Reconstruction of American Democracy* (pp. 149–171). Ithaca: Cornell University Press.

Ober, J. (2008). What the Ancient Greeks Can Tell Us about Democracy. *Annual Review of Political Science*, 11, 67–91.

Odendaal, A. (1983). African Political Mobilisation in the Eastern Cape, 1880–1910. Unpublished PhD Cambridge University.

Ono, K. (1989). *Chinese Women in a Century of Revolution, 1850–1950* (J. A. Fogel, trans.). Stanford: Stanford University Press.

Oppenheim, A. L. (1969). Mesopotamia: Land of Many Cities. In I. M. Lapidus (ed.), *Middle Eastern Cities: A Symposium on Ancient Islamic and Contemporary Middle Eastern Urbanism*. Berkeley: University of California Press.

Orwell, G. (1968). *The Collected Essays, Journalism and Letters of George Orwell: In Front of Your Nose 1945–1950* (Vol. 4). New York: Harcourt, Brace & World.

Palestinian Center for Human Rights (2009). *Through Women's Eyes: A PCHR Report on the Gender-Specific Impact and Consequences of Operation Cast Lead*. Gaza: PCHR.

Pateman, C. (1970). *Participation and Democratic Theory*. London: Cambridge University Press.

'Pattimokkha' (T. W. Rhys Davids and H. Oldenberg, trans.) (1885). In F. M. Müller (ed.), *Sacred Books of the East* (Vol. 20). Oxford: Oxford University Press.

Pausanias (1918 [100]). *Description of Greece* (W. H. S. Jones and H. A. Ormerod, trans.). Cambridge: Harvard University Press.

Pearson, L. (1937). Party Politics and Free Speech in Democratic Athens. *Greece and Rome*, 7, 41–50.

Perlman, S. (1963). The Politicians in the Athenian Democracy of the Fourth Century BCE. *Athenaeum*, 41, 327–355.

Perlman, S. (1967). Political Leadership in Athens in the Fouth Century BCE. *Parola del Passato*, 22, 161–176.

Perreau-Saussine, A. and Murphy, J. B. (2007). The Character of Customary Law: An Introduction. In A. Perreau-Saussine and J. B. Murphy (eds), *Nature of Customary Law: Legal, Historical and Philosophical Perspectives* (pp. 1–10). Cambridge: Cambridge University Press.

Perry, E. (2008). Chinese Conceptions of Rights: From Mencius to Mao – and Now. *Perspectives on Politics*, 6(1), 37–50.

Peters, R. (2006, 2 November). Last Gasp in Iraq. *USA Today*.

Petrie, W. M. F. (1898). *Syria and Egypt*. London: Methuen.

Plato (1976). *Protagoras* (C. C. W. Taylor, trans.). Oxford: Clarendon Press.

Polybius (1889). *The Histories of Polybius* (E. Shuckburgh, trans.). London: Macmillan.

Pritchard, D. (2007). How do Democracy and War Affect Each Other? The Case Study of Ancient Athens. *Polis: The Journal of the Society for Greek Political Thought*, 24(2), 328–352.

Protestors in Sulaimaniya Present Warrant of Protest against Election Law (2008, 31 July). *Voices of Iraq*.

Rawls, J. (2001). *Justice as Fairness: A Restatement*. Cambridge: Belknap Press.

Reid, R. (2005). Nationhood, Power and History: Unfinished Business and the Longue Durée in Uganda. *Journal of African History*, 46, 321–325.

Resolutions and Proceedings of the Congress of Delegates from the Various Farmers' Associations (1877). Grahamstown: H. Guest and Son.

Reynolds, H. (1995). *Fate of a Free People: A Radical Re-Examination of the Tasmanian Wars*. Ringwood: Penguin.

Rhys Davids, T. W. R. (1903). *Buddhist India*. London: T. Fisher Unwin.

Rich, E. E. (ed.). (1948). *Hudson's Bay Company, Copy-book of Letters Outward: Begins 29th May, 1680 ends 5 July, 1687*. Toronto: Champlain Society.

Ridolfo, K. (2006, 25 August). Iraq: Security, Political Pressure Affect Media Performance. *Radio Free Europe: Radio Liberty*.

Riel, L. (1985 [1869]). *Les Écrits complets de Louis Riel*, R. Huel (ed.) Edmonton: University of Alberta.

Robinson, E. W. (1997). *The First Democracies*. Stuttgart: Franz Steiner Verlag.

Robinson, P. T. (1986). New Conflicts. In A. A. Mazrui and T. K. Levine (eds), *The Africans: A Reader* (pp. 133–155). New York: Praeger.

Rogers, H. (2007). *The History of Democracy: From the Middle East to Western Civilisation*. Bloomington: AuthorHouse.

Rosen, N. (2004, 8 April). The Shi'ite Voice That Will Be Heard. *Asia Times Online*.

Ross, A. (1856). *The Red River Settlement, its Rise, Progress, and Present State*. London: Smith, Elder & Co.

Ross, R. (1999). *A Concise History of South Africa*. Cambridge: Cambridge University Press.

Rossiter, C. (1961 [1788]). *The Federalist Papers: Alexander Hamilton, James Madison, John Jay*. New York: Mentor.

Roth, M. T. (1997 [1995]). *Law Collections from Mesopotamia and Asia Minor* (2nd edn). Atalanta: Scholars.

Rowse, T. (2001). Democratic Systems are an Alien Thing to Aboriginal Culture. In M. Sawer and G. Zappala (eds), *Speaking for the People: Representation in Australian Politics* (pp. 103–133). Melbourne: Melbourne University Press.

Royal Commission into Aboriginal Deaths in Custody (RCADC) (1991). (National Report No. 1). Canberra: AGPS.

Rufus, Q. C. (2001). *The History of Alexander* (J. Yardley, trans.). London: Penguin.

Ruggiero, G. (1980). *Violence in Early Renaissance Venice*. New Brunswick: Rutgers University Press.

Sadr Supporters Protest Planned US-Iraqi Security Agreement (2008, 30 May). *Voice of America*.

Saggs, H. W. F. (2004). *The Babylonians: A Survey of the Ancient Civilizations of the Tigris-Euphrates Valley* (9th edn). London: Folio.

Said, E. W. (2003 [1978]). *Orientalism*. London: Penguin.

240   *References*

Samman, G. (2004 [1961]). 'Let Us Pray for the Slave Who is Flogged'. In M. Badran and M. Cooke (eds), *Opening the Gates: An Anthology of Arab Feminist Writing* (2nd edn, pp. 138–142). Bloomington: Indiana University Press.

Sandvik, G. and Sigurðsson, J. V. (2004). Laws. In R. McTurk (ed.), *Companion to Old Norse-Icelandic Literature and Culture* (pp. 223–244). Oxford: Blackwell.

Schauer, F. (2007). Pitfalls in the Interpretation of Customary Law. In A. Perreau-Saussine and J. B. Murphy (eds), *Nature of Customary Law: Legal, Historical and Philosophical Perspectives* (pp. 13–34). Cambridge: Cambridge University Press.

Schemeil, Y. (2000). Democracy before Democracy? *International Political Science Review*, 21(2), 99–120.

Schrecker, J. (2004). *The Chinese Revolution in Historical Perspective* (2nd edn). Westport: Praeger.

Schubert, G. (2002). Village Elections in the PRC: A Trojan Horse of Democracy? In C. Derichs and T. Heberer (eds), *Political Discourses on Reform and Democratisation in Light of New Processes of Regional Community-Building* (pp. 1–35). Duisberg, Germany: Institute for East Asian Studies/East Asian Politics.

Schultz, J. P. (1981). *Judaism and the Gentile Faiths: Comparative Studies in Religion*. London: Associated University Press.

Schumpeter, J. (1947 [1942]). *Capitalism, Socialism, and Democracy*. New York: Harper and Brothers.

Schwartzenberg, J. E. (ed.). (1978). *A Historical Atlas of South Asia*. Chicago: University of Chicago Press.

Scott, J. (2004). What Were Commonwealth Principles? *The Historical Journal*, 47, 591–613.

Sen, A. (1999). Democracy as a Universal Value. *Journal of Democracy*, 10(3), 3–17.

Sen, A. (2003). Democracy and Its Global Roots: Why Democratisation Is Not the Same as Westernisation. *The New Republic*, 229(14), 28–35.

Sen, B. (1974). *Studies in the Buddhist Jatakas: Tradition and Polity*. Calcutta: Saraswat Library.

Shafiq, D. (2004 [1952]). Islam and the Constitutional Rights of Woman. In M. Badran and M. Cooke (eds), *Opening the Gates: An Anthology of Arab Feminist Writing* (2nd edn, pp. 352–357). Bloomington: Indiana University Press.

Sharma, J. P. (1968). *Republics in Ancient India, c. 1500 BCE.–500 BCE.* Leiden: E. J. Brill.

Sharma, R. S. (1991 [1959]). *Aspects of Political Ideas and Institutions in Ancient India* (3rd edn). Delhi: Motilal Banarsidass.

Siddiqi, M. Z. (1961). *Hadith Literature: Its Origin, Development, Special Features & Criticism*. Calcutta: Calcutta University Press.

Siggins, M. (2005). *Bitter Embrace: White Society's Assault on the Woodland Cree*. Toronto: McLelland & Steward.

Sigurðsson, J. V. (1995). The Icelandic Aristocracy after the Fall of the Free State. *Scandinavian Journal of History*, 20, 153–166.

Sigurðsson, J. V. (1999). *Chieftains and Power in the Icelandic Commonwealth*. Odense: Odense University Press.

Sigurðsson, J. V. (2007). Changing Layers of Jurisdiction and the Reshaping of Icelandic Society c. 1220–1350. In J. Pan-Montojo and F. Pedersen (eds), *Communities in European History: Representations, Jurisdictions, Conflicts* (pp. 173–187). Pisa: Pisa University Press.

Sigurðsson, J. V., Pedersen, F. and Berge, A. (2008). Making and Using the Law in the North, c. 900–1350. In G. Lottes, E. Medijainen and J. V. Sigurðsson (eds), *Making, Using and Resisting the Law in European History* (pp. 37–64). Pisa: Pisa University Press.

Simpson, A. W. B. (1987). *Legal Theory and Legal History*. London: Hambledon.

Sjöholm, E. (1990). Sweden's Medieval Laws: European Legal Tradition – Political Change. *Scandinavian Journal of History*, 15, 65–87.

Snell, D. C. (2001). *Flight and Freedom in the Ancient Near East*. Leiden: Brill.

Solmsen, F. (1975). *Intellectual Experiments of the Greek Enlightenment*. Princeton: Princeton University Press.

South African Native Affairs Commission 1903–1905 (1904) (Vol. 2). Cape Town: Cape Times Limited.

Southwold, M. (1964). Leadership, Authority and the Village Community. In L. A. Fallers (ed.), *The King's Men: Leadership and Status in Buganda on the Eve of Independence* (pp. 211–255). London: Oxford University Press.

Spence, J. (1999). *The Search for Modern China* (2nd edn). New York: W. W. Norton.

Sprenger, H. (1987). The Métis Nation: Buffalo Hunting versus Agriculture in the Red River Settlement, 1810–1870. In B. A. Cox (ed.), *Native People, Native Lands: Canadian Indians, Inuit and Metis* (pp. 120–135). Ottawa: Carlton University Press.

St-Onge, N. (2004). *Saint-Laurent, Manitoba: Evolving Métis Identitites, 1850–1914*. Regina: University of Regina Press.

Stanley, G. F. G. (1936). The Half-Breed 'Rising'. *Canadian Historical Review*, 17(4), 399–412.

Stanley, G. F. G. (1960). *The Birth of Western Canada*. Toronto: University of Toronto.

Stein, B. (1985). Politics, Peasants and the Deconstruction of Feudalism in Medieval India. *Journal of Peasant Studies*, 12, 54–86.

Stein, O. (1893). Megasthenes (2). In A. von Pauly and G. Wissowa (eds), *Real-Encyclopädie der classischen Altertumswissenschaft* (Vol. 15). Stuttgart: J. B. Metzlerscher Verlag et al.

Stewart, W. (ed.). (1934). *Documents Relating to the North West Company*. Toronto: Champlain Society.

Svavarsson, S. H. (2003). Greatness Revived: The Latin Dissemination of the Icelandic Past. In E. Keßler and H. C. Kuhn (eds), *Germania Latina, Latinitas Teutonica: Politik, Wissenschaft, Humanistische Kultur vom Späten Mittelalter bis in Unsere Zeit* (pp. 553–562). München: W. Fink.

Switzer, L. (1993). *Power and Resistance in an African Society: The Ciskei Xhosa and the Making of South Africa*. Madison: University of Wisconsin Press.

Taché, A. (1885). *La Situation au Nord-Ouest*. Québec: J. O. Filteau.

Tatz, C. (1962). *Shadow and Substance in South Africa: A Study in Land and Franchise Policies Affecting Africans, 1910–1960*. Pietermaritzburg: University of Natal Press.

Tawfeeq, M., Wald, J. and Sterling, J. (2008, 25 March). Peaceful Iraq Protests Spark Clashes; 50 Reported Dead. CNN.

Teffo, J. (2002). Monarchy and Democracy: Towards a Cultural Renaissance. *Journal on African Philosophy*, 1(1), 1–17.

242   References

Teffo, J. (2004). Democracy, Kingship, and Consensus: A South African Perspective. In K. Wiredu (ed.), *A Companion to African Philosophy* (pp. 443–449). Malden: Blackwell.

Thompson, D. (1916). *David Thompson's Narrative of His Explorations in Western America, 1784–1812*. Toronto: Champlain Society.

Thompson, R. (1988). Statecraft and Self-Government: Competing Visions of Community and State in Late Imperial China. *Modern China*, 14(2), 188–221.

Þórðardóttir, S. A. (2005). *Keynote Address*. Paper presented at the Fouth International Women and Democracy Conference, St Petersburg, Russia.

Thucydides (1972). *History of the Peloponnesian War* (R. Warner, trans.). Harmondsworth: Penguin.

Toussaint, I. (2005). *Louis Riel – Journaux de guerre et de prison; Présentation, notes et chronologie métisse 1604–2006*. Paris: Éditions Alain Stanké.

Traynor, I. (2009, 30 January). Iceland to Be Fast-Tracked into the EU. *The Guardian*.

Trémaudan, A.-H. d. (1936). *Histoire de la nation métisse dans l'Ouest canadien*. Saint-Boniface: Éditions des Plaines.

Tyrrell, J. B. (ed.). (1934). *Journals of Samuel Hearne and Philip Turnor*. Toronto: Champlain Society.

Van den Boorn, G. P. F. (1988). *The Duties of the Vizir: Civil Administration in the Early New Kingdom*. London: Kegan Paul.

Vésteinsson, O. (2007). A Divided Society: Peasants and the Aristocracy in Medieval Iceland. *Medieval and Viking Scandinavia*, 3, 117–139.

von Hayek, F. (1979). *Legislation and Liberty: The Political Order of a Free People*. London: Henley.

Wagle, N. K. (1966). *Society at the Time of the Buddha*. Bombay: Popular Prakashan.

Wakeman, F. (1972). The Price of Autonomy: Intellectuals in Ming and Ch'ing Politics. *Daedalus*, 101(2), 35–70.

Walker, J. (2005, 8 March). Behind the Cedars: Nonviolent Protest in the Middle East. *Reason Online*.

Walther, W. (1993). *Women in Islam* (C. S. V. Salt, trans.). Princeton: Markus Weiner.

Wang, X. (2003). *Mutual Empowerment of State and Peasantry: Village Self-Government in China*. New York: Nova Science.

West, M. L. (1997). *The East Face of Helicon: West Asiatic Elements in Greek Poetry and Myth*. Oxford: Clarendon Press.

Williams, N. (1987). *Two Worlds: Managing Indigenous Dispute Resolution in a Contemporary Aboriginal Community*. Canberra: Australian Institute of Aboriginal Studies.

Wilson, J. A. (1945). The Assembly of a Phoenician City. *Journal of Near Eastern Studies*, 4(4), 245.

Wolf, C. U. (1947). Traces of Primitive Democracy in Ancient Israel. *Journal of Near Eastern Studies*, 6(2), 98–108.

Woodcock, G. (1975). *Gabriel Dumont, The Métis Chief and His Lost World*. Edmonton: Hurtig.

Wooton, D. (2006). The True Origins of Republicanism, or *de vera respublica*. In M. Albertone (ed.), *Il repubblicanesimo moderno: L'idea di Repubblica nella riflessione storica di Franco Venturi* (pp. 271–304). Naples: Bibliopolis.

Wormald, P. (1977). Lex Scripta and Verbum Regis: Legislation and Germanic Kingship, from Euric to Cnut. In P. H. Sawyer and I. N. Wood (eds), *Early Medieval Kingship* (pp. 105–138). Leeds: University of Leeds.

Wormald, P. (2001). *The Making of English Law: Legislation and its Limits*. Oxford: Blackwell.

Xenophon (1897). *The Apology of Socrates* (H. G. Dakyns, trans.). London: Macmillan.

Xenophon (1986). *The Persian Expedition* (R. Warner, trans.). Middlesex: Penguin.

Yang, G. (2005). *Is There an Environmental Movement in China? Beware of the 'River of Anger'*. Asia Programme Special Report No. 124, Washington: Woodrow Wilson International Center.

Yaphe, J. S. (2008). After the Surge: Next Steps in Iraq. *Strategic Forum*, 230, 1–6.

Zalewski, M. (2000). *Feminism after Postmodernism: Theorising Through Practice*. London: Routledge.

Zeidan, J. T. (1995). *Arab Women Novelists: The Formative Years and Beyond*. New York: State University of New York Press.

Zittrain, J. (2008). *The Future of the Internet, and How to Stop It*. New Haven: Caravan.

Index

Abbasid Dynasty, 90
Aboriginal Australians, 3–4, 14, 148–61, 224
Aboriginal and Torres Strait Islander Commission (ATSIC), 149, 157–61
accountability, 43, 124, 178, 206, 208, 215, 218
administration, 13, 19, 23, 31, 67, 83, 85–6, 89, 93, 124–5, 127–30, 132, 133, 135, 140–1, 164, 199, 203, 220
Aegean, 42, 44–5
Africa, 3, 10, 11, 14, 36, 46, 80, 123–35, 162–74, 177, 218, 224
African National Congress, 162–6, 170, 174
agenda, 22, 70, 118, 159, 162, 182, 187–90, 224
agriculture, 25, 43, 146, 187
Akkad, 25, 30
Alexander the Great, 5, 41, 51
alphabet, 35, 37, 42, 46
Al-Sadr, Moqtada, 196–8, 202–3
Al-Sistani, Ali, 194–6, 203
Alþingi, 93, 96, 98, 103–4
Amarna, 38–9
ambassador, 41, 51, 115
America, *see* Latin America, Native America, United States of America
Amin, Qassim, 178–82, 184, 190
anarchy, 33, 109, 138
anti-Semitism, 10
apartheid, 14, 162–6, 173–4
Arab, 80, 82, 85, 185–8, 192–9, 224
Arengo, Venetian, 108–16
Argos, 45
arguments, 3, 29, 31, 44, 96–8, 179
aristocracy, 5, 22, 58, 64, 92–3, 105, 113–14, 116–19, 142
Aristotle, 9, 19–20, 28, 33, 41, 44, 46
army, 41, 86, 89, 107, 167, 191
Arnhem Land, 149, 153

Ashur, 23
Asia, 8, 10, 80, 205, 219
assassination, 109, 111–14, 203
assembly, 5, 7, 9, 13–14, 21, 23–33, 36–43, 46–7, 50, 53–4, 60, 80, 90, 93, 96, 98–104, 106–9, 112–13, 116, 119, 127, 140, 153, 157, 170, 193–5, 205, 208, 211, 215–18, 220
Assyria, 23–4, 28–31, 40, 42, 45, 199–200
Athens, 5–6, 11, 13, 19–33, 35–6, 43, 46–8, 52, 57, 118, 147
Atlantic Ocean, 36
Attica, 9, 23, 30
Australia, 14, 148–61, 205, 207
authoritarian, 12, 15, 44, 61, 68, 70, 90, 145, 152
autocracy, 6, 9, 42, 44, 46, 58, 61, 79, 105, 111–12, 115, 220
autonomy, 14, 37, 58, 67, 69, 71, 74, 102, 111, 130, 131, 141, 199

Ba'ath Party, 192, 201, 203
Babylon, 25–6, 29–31, 40, 42
Baganda, 3, 14, 123, 129–35
Baghdad, 192–7, 199, 202
Bantu, 125, 129
barbarian, 67, 105–6, 108
battle, 30, 46, 82, 86, 137, 154, 221
Beijing, 72–4
Bernal, Martin, 10, 35, 38, 39
boule, 22, 43
Brahman, 50, 53, 56
bribe, 43, 117
Britain, 7–9, 36, 50, 55, 129, 136, 148–9, 152, 162, 165–8, 171–2, 180–1
Buddha, 50–1, 53–5, 57, 59
Buganda, 128–34
bureaucracy, 24, 26–7, 50, 56, 62, 64–7, 116, 219
Byblos, 36, 38–40, 42

244

Index 245

caliphate, 83–4, 86–90
campaign, 41, 66, 117–19, 178–9, 181, 186–90, 193, 195–7, 200–1, 213, 215, 219–20, *see also* political campaign
Canaanites, 37
Canada, 3, 14, 136–7, 142, 144–6
candidate, 25, 53, 114, 115, 139, 171–2, 193
Cape Colony, 3, 14, 162–74
caravan, 24, 37
Carthage, 36, 40–1, 45–7
Cassiodorus, 107
caste system, 49–50, 52, *see also varna*
Chaldeans, 21, 199–200
Chartists, 8
checks and balances, 41, 106–7, 112–13, 128, 130, 211
China, 3, 11, 13, 60–75, 221
Chios, 43–4
Christian, 52, 79, 83–4, 91, 112, 115, 118, 193, 197–9, 202, 222
church, 29, 83, 109, 111, 143
Churchill, Winston, 222
Cicero, 5, 93
citizen, 2, 5, 7, 13–14, 22–31, 33, 36–9, 41, 43, 47–8, 52, 57, 60–1, 80, 83, 87, 105–6, 108, 110, 113, 115–19, 173, 178–9, 185, 188–9, 193, 200, 202–11, 213–15, 217, 220–1, 224
city-state, 3, 5, 12–13, 21, 23, 27, 32, 35, 38–9, 42–7, 49, 113, 222
civic virtue, 3, 6, 9, 54
civil law, 26, 33, 46, 144
civil service, 64, 65, 172
civil society, 15, 20, 61, 117, 192, 204–5, 207–8, 210, 214, 218
clan, 5, 13, 50, 52, 56, 109, 125, 127–34, 143, 148, 151, 153–4, 186, 224
class, 7–8, 31, 40, 43, 50, 52, 56, 70, 72, 81–2, 117–18, 147, 165–6, 172–3, 181–2, 187
Cleisthenes, 5, 12, 22–3, 35, 43, 47
Coalition of the Willing, 191, 193–4, 196–7
coinage, 43, 47, 55
Cold War, 1, 8, 219

collective, 3, 11–12, 14, 23, 29, 46, 71, 74, 87, 118, 142, 149, 221, 222–3
colony, 3, 9–10, 14, 124–9, 143, 145, 149, 155, 163–74, 179–81, 220–1
commoners, 5, 23, 31, 75, 82, 106, 117–18
commonwealth, 41, 92–3, 158
communal, 55, 63, 75, 88, 113, 124, 151–2, 169
communication, 2, 22, 85, 205, 207, 209, 211–17
communitarian, 61, 63, 68, 71–2, 100, 102
community, 3, 5, 12–14, 21, 23, 26, 29, 41–2, 49, 51, 55, 59, 64, 71–2, 74, 81, 83, 85–8, 102, 103–4, 116, 118, 125, 139–40, 145, 148–61, 166, 168, 169, 171–4, 189, 209, 213, 215, 218
complexity, 1–3, 5–6, 9–11, 13, 15, 21, 24–8, 32–3, 37, 49, 51, 54, 100, 112–16, 123, 145, 148–9, 165, 191–2, 194, 205–6, 215, 217, 221, 224
compromises, 61, 163, 216, 223
concord, 54–5
confederation, 54, 137, 141–2, 145
conflict resolution, 127, 149, 151–2
Confucianism, 10, 13, 61–74, 224
consensus, 2, 14, 20, 23, 31, 74, 81, 124–8, 130–3, 135, 141–2, 148, 151–3, 161, 217
consent, 11, 24–5, 83, 127, 133, 142
conspiracy, 105, 109, 111, 116
Constantinople, 106, 109, 115
constitution, 1, 5–7, 33, 35, 38–41, 44, 46–7, 56, 68, 71–2, 74, 83–5, 88, 92–3, 106–7, 110, 112–17, 125, 132, 145, 162, 166–7, 183–7, 194–5, 198, 206, 218
consultation, 12, 14, 26, 38, 81, 85–6, 88, 90, 128, 133, 135, 148–9, 155–7, 160–1, 218, 222
cooperation, 24, 63, 71–2, 74, 83, 92, 108, 119, 127, 141, 155–6, 158, 161
corruption, 5–6, 29, 65–6, 72, 117, 181, 191–2, 200–1, 208, 211, 214, 218, 220–1

246 *Index*

council, 5, 13, 22–4, 26–7, 37–40,
  42–3, 46, 93, 95, 105–6, 112–17,
  124, 126–8, 133, 138–42, 144,
  153, 157–60, 170–1, 194–5, 200,
  218, 220
Council of Ten, 105, 116
courts of law, 22–3, 25–7, 31, 72, 81,
  89, 93–4, 96–101, 103, 112, 114,
  134–5, 153, 179, 218
covenant, 37
Cree Nation, 136, 140, 142, 145
criminal, 25–6, 117, 134, 160, 218
cult, 44, 64, 117
custom, 67, 94, 98, 101, 103, 143, 155,
  157, 213, 223
Cyrus the Great, 30, 32

da Gama, Vasco, 36
Dahl, Robert, 6
Damascus, 37
Dark Ages, 3, 13–14, 42, 81, 105, 108,
  220
datong, 63–4, 75, *see also* harmony
death penalty, 25
debt, 25, 29
decision-making, 2, 12–14, 28, 31, 36,
  46, 53, 88, 106, 112, 125, 129,
  135, 142, 149, 151–3, 155, 161,
  211
deliberation, 3, 23–4, 38–9, 42, 52,
  117, 148–9, 156, 191–2, 202–3,
  207, 209, 215, 218
democratization, 9, 73–4, 124, 164,
  166, 192, 194, 218, 219
demokratia, 1, 5, 22, 36, 47
demonstration, 133, 193–4, 197–9,
  203, 219
demos, 5, 33, 43
despotism, 6, 9–10, 12, 24, 29, 58, 61,
  65, 67, 118, 128, 130, 133, 192,
  221–2, 224
de Tocqueville, Alexis, 7, 164, 210
dictatorship, 8, 148, 200
dignity, 85, 129
disenfranchisement, 163, 165, 169
dispute resolution, 149, 151–2, 154–6,
  161, 220
dissent, 53, 66, 70, 141
diversity, 9, 11, 150, 208, 223

Doge, Venetian, 105, 109–17
Donglin Academy, 66–7, 69
Dunn, John, 6, 35, 80
Dutch, 166–7

Eastern Europe, 8, 219
Ebla, 27
education, 20, 22, 31, 61, 63–6, 74–5,
  106, 156, 158–9, 164, 167–8, 172,
  174, 179–80, 187, 189
egalitarian, 4–5, 11, 14, 20, 27–9, 32,
  37, 56–7, 63; 87, 89, 103, 105–7,
  116, 138, 141, 147, 149, 151–2,
  182, 186–7, 189, 203
Egypt, 21, 26, 37–8, 39–40, 42, 45, 58,
  84, 179–82, 184, 187
elders, 23–4, 26–8, 31, 38, 40–1, 46,
  54–5, 89, 126–8, 139, 150–1,
  153–4, 157, 193, 215
election, 1, 3, 8, 22, 27, 30, 40–1, 46,
  60, 72, 81, 87–8, 90, 110, 112–15,
  117, 119, 139, 142, 151, 159–60,
  162–4, 167–73, 171, 184, 192–5,
  199, 203, 205–6, 208–9, 211, 217,
  223
elite, 1–2, 5, 19–20, 22–3, 29, 31–3, 40,
  60–1, 63, 65, 69–70, 72, 119, 143,
  146, 164–5, 173, 182, 219–20
emancipation, 2, 179–82, 185–7, 190
emperor, 50, 51, 61, 63, 65, 108
empire, 23, 32, 105, 111, 205
  African, 128
  Assyrian, 31
  Austro-Hungarian, 8
  Babylonian, 25, 30–1
  Byzantine (Eastern), 106–9, 111,
    114–15
  Hittite, 38
  Holy Roman (Western), 110–11, 113
  Islamic, 3
  Persian, 20, 30
  Roman, 6, 106–7
  Venetian, 115
empower, 12, 72, 74, 110, 116, 132,
  142, 144, 178, 185, 207–9, 215
enfranchise, 52, 162, 170, 172, 207
English, 1, 7, 14, 92–3, 136–7, 143,
  145, 217
enlightenment, 43, 64, 70, 75

Epic of Gilgamesh, 21, 32
equal, 2, 5, 7, 25–30, 36, 41, 47, 51,
    57, 63, 75, 80, 81–5, 87, 89, 91,
    103, 105–7, 118, 130–1, 134, 137,
    146, 163, 166, 168, 172, 178–80,
    182, 183–90, 209, 213, 215, 221–3
Erythrae, 44
ethnic, 123–8, 135–6, 146, 162, 166–7,
    191, 199–200, 213
Eualeyai Nation, 149–50
eunomia, 46
Euro-centric, 10, 11, 16, 32, 148
Europe, 6–11, 14, 16, 32, 50, 52, 58,
    64, 70, 79, 81, 92–3, 105, 108,
    112–13, 118, 129, 131, 136,
    141–3, 146, 149–50, 157, 165,
    170–1, 181–2, 188, 205, 207, 210,
    219–20
exclusion, 4, 9, 22, 30, 56, 164, 166,
    174
executive, 23, 46, 56–7, 100, 114, 158

factions, 110–11, 115–17, 191–2, 203,
    220–1
fairness, 9, 65, 81, 131, 134, 179,
    182–3, 194–5, 201, 203
Far East, 36
farm, 63, 99–100, 102, 125, 127, 130,
    137–8, 146, 168, 187
fascism, 2, 8
fatwa, 194, 195
Fawwaz, Zainab, 179, 182–4, 190
feminism, 3, 15, 177–89, 223
fengjian, 62–4, 70–3
feudal, 7, 62, 70, 105–6, 111–12, 118,
    220
Finley, Moses, 4, 22
flexibility, 102, 141
folk, 61, 143, 146, 173
foreign policy, 27, 33, 40, 46, 219
France, 6–8, 136–7, 143, 145, 166,
    179–80
franchise, 8, 14, 52, 163–74, 209
freedom, 6, 12, 22–3, 28–31, 33, 36,
    49, 51, 54, 99–102, 105–6,
    110–11, 113, 125, 131, 134–6,
    139, 143, 146, 152, 164, 166–7,
    172, 178, 180, 185–8, 190, 194–5,
    202–3, 206, 210, 219

free speech, 2–3, 5, 13, 28–30, 42, 81,
    84–6, 90, 117–18, 152, 181,
    214, 222
Fukuyama, Francis, 8, 204
fundamentalism, 10, 189–90, 222

gana, 51–3, 56–7, *see also* republic
Gaza, 189–90
gender, 30–1, 82, 126, 128, 130, 148,
    166, 177–9, 182–3, 186–90
Germany, 8, 166, 169, 180, 218, 222
glass, 37
global, 1, 4, 8–11, 14, 80, 125, 135,
    146–7, 190, 207, 210, 212,
    217–19, 223–4
goðar, 96, 98–100, 103–4
Goody, Jack, 12, 38
Grágás, 93–104
grassroots, 58, 71–4, 149, 160–1, 203,
    208, 220
Greece, 1, 3–6, 9, 12–13, 19–20, 22,
    23, 26, 31–3, 35–6, 38, 40–52, 55,
    57, 105, 107, 209, 212
guild, 41, 51–2, 58

Habermas, Jurgen, 2, 93
Hadith, 82, 84–6, 89–90
Hammurabi Code, 25–6, 31–3
Han Dynasty, 61, 63, 66–7
happiness, 30, 56, 68, 146, 181
harmony, 61, 63–4, 74, *see also datong*
Hebrew, 39, 83
hegemony, 9, 70, 131, 194, 203
hereditary, 56, 62, 64, 110–11, 127,
    133, 152
Herodotus, 9, 20, 36, 41–2, 45
hierarchy, 4, 24, 49, 56–7, 75, 81, 95,
    105, 124, 128–30, 132–3, 149, 215
historiography, 10, 58, 165
Hornblower, Simon, 35, 46
Hudson's Bay Company, 136–7,
    143–4
humanism, 63, 118
humanity, 56, 79, 187
hunger, 29, 143
hunt, 12, 14, 127, 136–47, 150–1, 156,
    214, 223
Huntington, Samuel, 8, 10, 204

248 *Index*

Iceland, 3, 14, 92–104, 220–1
imperial, 36, 50, 61–73, 107, 109
imperialism, 80, 143, 221
inclusion, 2, 4–5, 9, 14–15, 123, 126,
    148, 152, 161, 166–7, 172, 174,
    190–1, 196, 199–200, 224
incumbent, 27–8, 183
independence, 1, 7, 55–6, 100, 106–7,
    113, 136, 186, 197, 213
independent, 28, 37, 51, 70, 81, 89,
    95, 98, 100, 108, 111, 113, 115,
    136–7, 167, 180, 186, 201–3, 205,
    211, 218
India, 11, 13, 49–59, 174, 218, 221
indigenous, 3, 14, 50, 70, 73, 121,
    123, 125, 129, 135, 148–61, 163,
    194, 202, 223
individual, 10, 26, 30, 84–5, 109, 116,
    125–6, 128, 130–1, 135, 141–2,
    151–2, 154, 160, 164, 167, 169,
    171–2, 178, 220–1, 224
Indus Valley, 3, 13
internet, 212–13, 216–17
Iran, 8, 58, 190, 203
Iraq, 3, 8, 15, 34, 191–203, 220–1
isegoria, 5, 28–9, *see also* free speech
Islam, 3, 10, 14–15, 79–91, 177–90,
    195–6, 200, 202, 220, 223
Israel, 24, 29, 37, 42, 189, 196
Istanbul, 37, 43
Italy, 8, 45, 57, 106–8, 113

Jacobsen, Thorkild, 21, 23, 26–7, 31
Japan, 8, 70, 205
Jerusalem, 83, 112
Jews, 20, 83–4, 118
Josephus, Flavius, 20–1, 35, 40
journalism, 10, 212, 214
judge, 23, 26, 29, 33, 37, 40, 43, 66,
    84, 89, 94, 96–100, 103, 111–12,
    179, 182, 211, *see also* suffete
jury, 53, 135, 166
justice, 2, 22, 25, 28, 30, 32, 63, 81, 83,
    85, 131, 144, 154, 160, 200, 215

Kammillaroi Nation, 149
Keane, John, 12, 15, 21, 70, 80
kin, 13, 51, 125, 127, 131, 152, 154,
    156, 182

king, 6, 24–30, 33, 37–43, 46, 50–4,
    57, 59, 64, 68, 90, 92–5, 100–1,
    107–8, 112, 114, 125, 127–9,
    131–4, 152, 222
Kurds, 193, 198–9, 202

labor, 31, 36, 125–7, 130, 172
Lagash Dynasty, 29
land, 23, 25–6, 29, 30, 62–3, 72, 75,
    99, 101, 106–7, 125, 130, 134,
    144, 148, 150–6, 160, 169, 172
Latin America, 8, 80, 219
law, 14, 22, 25–8, 31–3, 36–7, 43, 46,
    54, 59, 65–8, 71, 75, 79, 82–5,
    88–9, 92–103, 106, 117, 124,
    134–9, 144–8, 150–4, 156–7, 163,
    166–8, 170, 172, 179, 183,
    187–91, 195, 199, 210, 212, *see
    also* rule of law, shari'a law
Lawspeaker, 93, 96, 98
leader, 13, 21, 23–4, 27, 37, 42, 57, 72,
    83, 85–9, 104, 109–12, 123,
    127–8, 131–3, 135, 137–8, 141,
    151–2, 166, 173–4, 193, 196, 200,
    202, 212, 220
Lebanon, 8, 36, 179, 182, 184, 222
legal, 14, 24, 32, 68, 81, 86, 93–104,
    136, 148–54, 160–1, 170–1, 177,
    180, 183, 186, 189, 209–11, 216
legal codes, 25, 26
legislation, 22, 82, 95–6, 112, 115,
    156, 158, 160, 165, 167–9, 211
legitimacy, 7, 10, 53, 62–3, 74–5, 85,
    87–90, 92, 148, 202, 209
Levant, 33, 37–8, 115
Liang Qichao, 61, 71
liberal, 8, 9, 28, 61, 69, 79, 163–7,
    169–70, 172–4, 204, 221–2
liberation, 165, 181, 184, 200
liberty, 7, 20, 28–9, 49, 87, 188
lineage, 25, 126, 129, 131–2, 186
local, 11, 28, 38–9, 50, 58, 61, 65–7,
    71–3, 96, 109, 124, 138, 156,
    159–60, 162, 167, 169, 171,
    193–4, 200, 207, 209, 217–18
Løgrétta, 93–4, 96–8, 100, 103
Lombard League, 113, 114
Lombards, 106, 108–9
Lycurgus, 46

Index 249

magistrates, 23, 27, 40, 43, 72, 106–7, 109, 144, 171
Magna Carta, 1, 6
Maha–Parinibbana–Suttanta, 53–5
Mahdi Army, 196–7, 203
majority, 1, 3, 5, 20, 22, 24–5, 30–1, 53, 59, 87–8, 96, 136, 140, 148, 152, 164, 169–70, 174, 193, 195, 198, 206, 213
Manchu Dynasty, 60, 67, 70, 72
mandate, 22, 24, 62, 63, 90, 144, 158
Mandela, Nelson, 162, 174
Mao Zedong, 73, 75
market, 136, 167, 172, 197–8, 200, 210, 214–15
marriage, 25, 143, 152, 153, 180, 182, 184, 186–7, 189
Marx, Karl, 38, 180
masks, 46, 216, 222
mass, 20, 33, 73, 88–9, 193, 199–200, 203, 212, 214, 220
mathematics, 43, 183
matrilineal, 150
mayor, 26, 194
media, 1, 191–3, 199, 203, 205, 211–14, 216–17
medieval, 3, 11, 14, 52, 83, 92–4, 102, 217, 220
Medina, 86–8, 824
Mediterranean Sea, 13, 35–7, 45, 220
Mencius, 62–3, 75
merchant, 24, 28, 31, 37, 40, 105, 117
Mesopotamia, 3, 21, 27, 29, 33, 215, 221–2
Métis, 3, 14, 136–47
Middle East, 8, 13, 15, 19, 21–3, 25, 29, 31–4, 80, 177–9, 183–4, 186, 188, 190–1, 203
military, 30–1, 58, 82, 84–6, 108, 111, 140–1, 194, 196, 203, 213
Ming Dynasty, 66–7, 69, 75
mining, 43, 155, 168
monarchy, 7, 24, 37–41, 49–51, 56–8, 60–2, 68–9, 72, 87–90, 92, 105, 126
monitory democracy, 15, 204–18, 221
Montesquieu, Charles, 68, 75
moral, 5, 50, 62–4, 66, 71, 73, 112, 181, 185, 189, 201

Moses, 24, 37, 39
Mounted Police, 144–5
movement
    environment, 73–4
    feminist, 177–8, 184, 186
    freedom of, 85, 100
    political, 8–9, 15, 56, 60, 66, 68–74, 79, 137, 145, 165, 179, 180, 192, 197, 200–3, 219, 224
Mu'awiya, Caliph, 83, 90
Muhammad, Prophet, 81–91, 185–6
municipal, 23, 39, 110, 166
Muslim, 79–80, 82–4, 86–91, 118, 183, 186, 188, 192–3, 196–7
myth, 21, 42, 46, 51, 109, 150, 174

nanotechnology, 210
Napoleon, 7, 105
narrative, 1, 9–11, 15, 20, 61, 70, 101, 163, 165, 174, 223–4
nation, 7–8, 60–1, 72, 109, 123, 129, 135, 148–9, 157, 160, 163, 177, 179, 181, 187–9, 192–8, 200–1, 203, 209, 219, 223
nationalism, 50, 57, 70, 179–82, 187, 197
nation-states, 123, 129, 135
Native America, 11, 14, 136–47
negotiation, 29, 73, 95, 101, 137, 149, 152–3, 160, 178, 216, 224
nepotism, 65, 112, 116, 200–1
news, 1, 8, 192, 214, 216
newspaper, 162, 173, 179, 183, 212
Norway, 92–5, 100–2

Ober, Josiah, 19, 33
oligarchy, 5, 13, 19, 22, 37, 40–2, 44, 46, 50, 100, 102, 104–6, 114–15, 118, 220, 222
olive oil, 37, 107
oppression, 16, 20, 29–30, 101, 109, 181, 186, 221, 223
ordinary people, 31, 98, 200, 209
Orientalism, 10, 58, 191–2, 203
origins of democracy, 4, 13, 32–3, 35
Orwell, George, 123

palace, 23, 29, 31, 134
Palestine, 8, 189–90

250 *Index*

Pali Canon, 50–1, 53, 55
papyrus, 35, 212
parish, 132–3, 135
parliament, 1, 6–7, 9, 14, 50, 54, 72, 92–4, 157, 168–71, 174, 198–9, 201, 205–8, 216, 218
participation, 1, 2, 5, 29, 31, 33, 36–7, 39, 41, 52–3, 73–4, 81–4, 87, 88–9, 91, 93, 99–100, 102, 110, 116, 124–5, 128–9, 132, 135, 148, 152, 155, 158, 161, 166, 178, 183, 186, 189, 203, 205–8, 210, 215, 217, 222
parties, 60, 69–70, 74, 96–7, 100, 135, 138, 142, 144–5, 155, 157, 159, 163, 192–3, 205–8, 212, 216
patrilineal, 130, 133–4, 150
Pausanias, 44–5
people, the, 2, 5–6, 9, 16, 22–4, 27–30, 36–44, 47, 62–5, 68, 71, 73, 80, 86–9, 106–16, 127, 129, 133, 164, 194–5, 198, 200–3, 206, 209, 218, 220–4
Pericles, 20, 25, 33–4
Persia, 9, 40, 45
petitions, 149, 207, 218
philosophy, 11, 29, 42, 55, 61, 64, 67, 83, 150, 183, 224
Phoenicia, 3, 4, 13, 21, 35–48, 222
Plato, 19, 30–1, 34
pluralism, 11, 79, 216
polis, 5, 6, 35, 49, 52
political campaign, 117, 119, 178–9, 193, 195, *see also* campaign
political institutions, 37, 47, 137, 145, 147, 211
poor, 29, 31, 100, 107, 162, 165, 182, 201, 213
popular government, 6–7, 13, 36, 43, 47–9, 110, 114, 220
population, 7–8, 23, 31, 65, 75, 108, 132, 157, 159, 168, 189, 194, 198–9, 217, 223
poverty, 141, 143, 145, 189–90
power, 3–6, 9, 14–15, 22–7, 29, 33, 37–8, 40–3, 46, 48, 52–3, 57, 60–1, 65, 67–8, 71–3, 84, 92, 98–102, 104–8, 110–19, 125–7, 132–3, 141–2, 145, 148, 151–4, 157,

160–2, 170, 172, 188, 195, 198–216, 218, 220, 223
priest, 23–4, 39–40, 50, 81, 118
primitive democracy, 11, 13, 19, 21, 33, 36
property, 14, 25, 29, 63, 81, 85, 98, 100, 127, 135, 141, 162, 166–7, 172, 186–7, 210
protest, 8, 15, 22, 62, 144, 174, 193–203, 224
proto-democracy, 3, 13, 36
public opinion, 90, 151

Qin Dynasty, 67, 71
Qing Dynasty, 67–9, 72
Quran, 81–9, 186

race, 10, 14, 20, 32, 56, 81–2, 136, 143, 148, 163–74, 213, 220
radio, 193, 212
raja, 52–3, 57–9
Rashidun, 81, 83–4, 86–8, 90–1
rebel, 7, 39, 62–4, 67, 70, 109, 144–5
referendum, 157, 193, 195, 198
reform, 8, 12, 23, 35, 43, 47, 57, 60, 62–4, 66–9, 70, 72, 111–12, 160, 165, 167, 179–80, 182, 188, 190, 203
Reform Act of 1832 (UK), 8, 167
religion, 13, 24, 30, 37, 39, 46, 49, 50, 59, 79, 81–7, 89, 91, 103, 110, 116, 126, 136–7, 141–2, 145, 150–1, 154–5, 177–8, 181, 183–7, 190–6, 199–200, 202–3, 213, 218
Renaissance, 14, 105–6, 113, 119, 163
representation, 1, 2, 5, 14–15, 60, 67, 80, 91, 101, 106, 108, 114, 124, 126, 128–9, 131, 149, 157, 160–1, 164–5, 167, 170–2, 178, 194–5, 200, 206, 208–10, 213, 220
representative democracy, 7, 9, 149, 158, 161, 204–12, 215, 218
repression, 61, 188
Republic
  Chinese, 60, 72
  Congo, 127, 222
  Indian, 11, 13, 49–59
  Roman, 1, 5–6, 13–14

Second French, 8
Venetian, 14, 105–19
republic, 38, 40, 92, 93, 129, 139, 196
Revolution
American, 7
Chinese, 60, 72
French, 1, 11, 64
revolution, 8, 19, 32, 62–4, 69, 162, 166, 170, 213
rhetoric, 24, 187, 191, 196
Rhodes, Cecil, 42, 169
Rialto, 106, 110, 113
Riel, Louis, 137, 140, 145
righteous, 55, 62
rights, 2, 7, 22, 25, 27, 29–31, 41, 73–4, 81, 83–5, 88–9, 94–5, 101, 107–8, 113, 135, 137, 142, 152, 155, 159–60, 164, 166, 172–4, 177–88, 190, 200–2, 210
Robinson, Eric, 35–6, 43–6
Rome, 1, 5, 6, 11, 13–14, 37, 40–1, 50, 79, 91, 102, 105–9, 111, 113
rule of law, 3, 25, 28, 60, 81, 91, 191

sacred, 21, 30, 39, 152, 156, 210
Saddam Hussein, 3, 15, 191, 193–4, 196–7, 199–200, 203, 222
saga, 93, 99, 101, 102, 104
Said, Edward, 10, 203
Samman, Ghada, 179, 184–6
sangha, 51, 53–5, 57, 59
Saracens, 111, 115
Sarpi, Paolo, 118
Saskatchewan, 142–3
satire, 53, 90
secular, 55, 186, 193, 195
segregation, 165, 187
self-government, 6, 14, 50–1, 61, 70–5, 101, 113, 139, 147, 200, 205
self-rule, 51, 129, 136
senate, 5, 40–1, 107, 112, 114–15, 157
Serenissima, 105, 116
settlers, 101–2, 137, 145, 165–8, 172
Shaarawi, Huda, 179, 182
Shafiq, Doria, 177, 179, 182, 187, 190
shari'a law, 81, 89, 180, 182
Shia, 193–8, 203, 224
Sicily, 45, 46
Sidon, 36–7, 39, 41–2

slavery, 5, 7, 20, 25, 30–1, 36, 38, 52, 82, 84, 101, 123, 167, 179, 184, 221
social justice, 25, 30, 81, 200
socio-economic, 31, 113, 159, 161, 177–8, 187–8
Socrates, 29, 34, 36
Solomon, 37
Solon, 43
Song Dynasty, 66, 68, 71, 72
sorcery, 152, 154
South Africa, 3, 14, 128, 162–74, 218
sovereign, 1, 14, 36, 39, 47, 51–3, 57–8, 62, 89, 91, 106, 108, 110–11, 113–16, 119, 127–8, 148, 182, 218
Sparta, 5, 22, 46–7
speech, 3, 20, 22–3, 25, 28–30, 85, 90, 105, 117–18, 141
sphinx, 44
Stalinism, 8
standard history of democracy, 1, 4–13, 15, 219, 221
street-lighting, 113
suffete, 40–1, *see also* judge
suffrage, 7–8, 147, 178–9, 184–6, 209
Sumer, 24–5, 30
Sumerian, 24
Sunni, 80, 193, 195, 197–9

television, 193, 212, 217
temple, 23–4, 29, 37, 41, 44
terra nullius, 148
Thales of Miletus, 42–3
throne, 25, 29, 69, 133
Thucydides, 19–20, 25, 34
tolerance, 30, 116–18, 196, 219–20
totalitarian, 8, 67, 105
tribe, 11, 13, 43, 81–3, 89–90, 106, 136, 141, 144, 149–51, 153, 160, 171, 193, 220
tribunes, 5, 106–11, 119
tyranny, 10, 12, 16, 20, 36, 43, 89–90, 101, 115, 219, 221, 222
Tyre, 36, 40–2, 44–5, 47

Uganda, 3, 14, 123, 129, 135
Umayyad Dynasty, 81, 83, 89
umma, 81, 85, 86, 91

252 *Index*

unanimous, 41, 53, 86, 96
underground, 61, 150
United States of America, 1, 7, 9, 32, 64, 138, 144, 147, 162–4, 180, 191–203, 205, 207, 213, 219
utopia, 20, 64, 141, 147, 213–14

varna, 50, 56, *see also* caste system
veil, 79, 180–1, 183, 188
vendettas, 108, 111, 117
Venice, 3, 14, 105–19, 220
veto, 24, 107
village, 11, 43, 50–1, 73–5, 124, 127, 132–5, 143, 223
violence, 9, 25, 36, 61, 70, 117, 145, 154, 156, 159, 166, 191–3, 196, 199, 203, 224
viral, 214, 216
voice, 28, 65, 124–6, 128, 130–5, 146–7, 151, 157–8, 160, 203, 206, 221
Voltaire, 64
voluntary, 141, 145, 159, 193
vote, 3, 7, 13, 22, 24, 27–8, 31–2, 36, 53–4, 59, 96, 139–42, 152, 159, 164–74, 184–5, 194–5, 207, 209–10, 217

war and peace, 5, 21–2
Warring States period, 61–2, 67
wealth, 7–8, 20, 22–4, 31, 37, 40, 43, 52, 60, 84, 107–8, 113, 117, 141, 143, 173, 179, 213
welfare, 5, 30, 55, 63, 81, 86, 126, 196
Wenamun, 39
West, 1, 3, 8–12, 16, 32, 43, 49, 60–1, 65, 71–3, 79–80, 84–5, 91, 109, 111, 123–5, 128, 146, 149, 151–2, 154–5, 158, 161–2, 178–80, 183, 185, 188–92, 202, 204, 207, 219
will of the people, 1–2, 4, 12, 22, 39, 119
wine, 37, 44, 107
Wolf, C. Umhau, 24–5, 29, 37
women, 8, 15, 31, 36, 42, 81, 84, 86–8, 92, 126–7, 136, 141, 147, 153–4, 170, 177–90, 194, 200–1, 209, 220–1

Xenophon, 9, 19, 34

Yolngu Nation, 149, 153, 155

Zakarbaal, 39–40

Manufactured by Amazon.ca
Acheson, AB